My Family
And Other Strangers

JEREMY HARDY

My Family

And Other Strangers

ADVENTURES

in Family History

EBURY
PRESS

1 3 5 7 9 10 8 6 4 2

First published in 2010 by Ebury Press, an imprint
of Ebury Publishing
A Random House Group company

Copyright © Jeremy Hardy 2010

Jeremy Hardy has asserted his right to be identified as the author of this
work in accordance with the Copyright, Designs and Patents Act 1988

The Random House Group Limited Reg. No. 954009

Addresses for companies within the Random House Group can
be found at www.randomhouse.co.uk

A CIP catalogue record for this book is available from
the British Library

The Random House Group Limited supports The Forest Stewardship
Council (FSC), the leading international forest certification
organisation. All our titles that are printed on Greenpeace approved
FSC certified paper carry the FSC logo.
Our paper procurement policy can be found at
www.rbooks.co.uk/environment

Mixed Sources
Product group from well-managed
forests and other controlled sources
www.fsc.org Cert no. TT-COC-2139
© 1996 Forest Stewardship Council
FSC

Printed in the UK by CPI Mackays, Chatham, ME5 8TD

ISBN 9780091927509

To buy books by your favourite authors and register for offers visit
www.rbooks.co.uk

To everyone I love

Contents

GREAT-GREAT-GRANDPARENTS

Charles Hardy   Jane   Henry Aylott   Sarah Bell   Henry Hewett   Charlotte Maria Watford   James Hammond   Clara

GREAT-GRANDPARENTS

Alfred Hardy   Ann Aylott   Albert M Hewett   Clara E Hammond

GRANDPARENTS

Lionel Hardy   Audrey Hewett

PARENTS

Donald Hardy

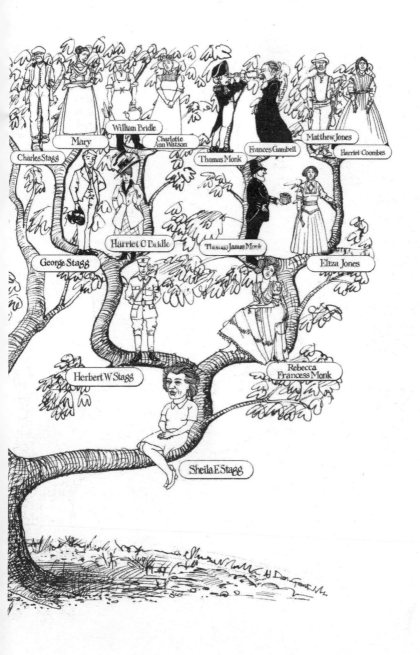

INTRODUCTION

I Know Who I Am – That's Not the Point

December 2007

I am Jeremy James Hardy. That much I know. My parents are Donald and Sheila and my siblings are Susan, Serena, Joy and Simon. I am the youngest. I am loath to tell you more because once you have my date of birth and my mother's maiden name, you can ring my mobile phone service provider and pretend to be me. Where such an act of identity fraud might get you, I don't know, but it is hardly surprising there is so much of it about. If you asked me to come up with something that only I could possibly know, I might select something more discreet than when I was born and who my mum is. If such facts were not now so readily available, I would not be embarking on a quest to learn more about my ancestors. We have the Internet now. I would not be happy to bugger about in country churches for two years in my search for forebears who were not as ethnically and culturally uninteresting as I am.

From what I know, my heritage is not what you might call 'diverse'. But maybe that is in itself a bit interesting. I am the whitest, most Anglo Saxon Protestant I know. Perhaps that will be the story, but I have to say, I'm hoping it won't be. This can't be all there is, surely. I have always thought I should be Jewish, but as far as I know, I am not. I am, along with Barry Cryer, one of Britain's most unlikely gentiles. I don't know why I'm not Jewish. I should be. I did apply, but I passed the medical.

I'm not even Catholic. I've always thought I'd like to be something more exotic than C of E. I can't even say I'm lapsed. You don't *lose* your faith when you are Church of England – you just can't remember where you left it. I believe my great-grandfather converted to Catholicism, but also that my grandfather converted back. I know that my dad used to be High Anglican, which seems to involve being a Protestant but with all the camp and theatre of being a Catholic – a case of wanting to have your sacrament and eat it.

I also know that my mother's mother, Rebecca Stagg *née* Monk, got involved in some sort of sect called Moral Rearmament in the thirties. She became a pacifist in the twenties, a noble stance except that she maintained it into the forties, which smacks of not paying attention. During the First World War, when pacifism had credibility, she served as whatever was the acronym for a woman army volunteer at that time, which is how she met my grandfather, Herbert Stagg. My mother was always puzzled by her mother's inability to cope with the installation of a telephone in the 1960s. Grandma always answered the phone as though its ringing was quite the most baffling event that had ever occurred, and yet in the First World War she was a wireless operator.

She was somewhat other-worldly, Rebecca. She seemed antiquated even for her age. She said things like 'Hark' and 'It's five-and-twenty past the hour.' Everything gave her indigestion. She had me peel grapes for her because of her dentures, and she got the skin off a tomato by sticking it on a fork and holding it over a gas hob. Lunch was a poached chicken breast. She was finicky and methodical, always carrying out her routine in exactly the same way. It took her about half an hour to prepare and drink her glass of Fybogel, making sure that every particle went into the glass, and none remained on the side when she drank it. And she painted her feet with iodine every day, so they were bright yellow. They were sore and deformed from wearing uncomfortable shoes. She was worried my fringe would wear away my eyebrows and once greased my hair back with lanolin. Mum went mental, as she did when her mother lent me a book about Christian martyrs being tortured by the Romans.

Rebecca's husband Herbert, my grandpa, was a hero in the Great War. He volunteered as a nurse in the Royal Army Medical Corps in 1914, and he was in the Battle of the Somme. His ambulance driver was killed by a shell and he had to set up a field hospital in a barn. Well, I think that's the truth. It's possible that he escaped military service on the grounds of split ends and spent the war in Catterick. I doubt it, but we'll see.

Oh, and apparently he was a mason – is that interesting? And if he was, why don't I get off my parking tickets? It's hard to imagine him having been a mason; I guess it came with a job. He was a gentle and charming man and very proper; I can't imagine him up to anything dodgy. He used to help my mum a lot when he was well enough. He would always ask me what I wanted for my tea, which was always peanut butter sandwiches, because that's all I ate; but Mum says he was a really good cook and made wonderful cakes, always with butter, never marge. When he was bedridden, he got Meals on Wheels, but never liked it so I usually ate it.

I suppose I would like to find out more about my grand-parents because I knew them when I was too young to grasp that they were interesting people. They were my grandparents, source of treats. I've always been fascinated by the term 'Nanny State', because when I was a boy, Nanny was your dad's mum, and not only did she let you do whatever you wanted, she fuelled you with Quality Street and Tizer to ensure that you would.

My nanny Audrey and my grandad, Lionel, my dad's parents, were lovely. They bickered adoringly for the whole of their life together, and were only ever apart when the other was in hospital. They seemed to me to be very respectable. I once overheard Nan use the word 'sods' to describe local kids who banged on their back door and ran away. I memorised the word and repeated it in front of them and my parents on Christmas Day, to my grandparents' great mortification. I was very proud of the new word and found it applicable in any situation, despite gleaning that it referred to a man engaging in 'unnatural intercourse with another man or an animal'.

Nan smoked fags, something that was strongly disapproved of in my family. Grandad smoked a pipe or Cigarillos. He liked mint humbugs and kept tropical fish and a budgie. He had white hair with a side parting and I never saw him without a tie. Nan had tightly curled hair and made crinkle-cut chips, which were the best. They had a posh front room that they hardly ever used. Nan had a display cabinet full of ornaments, including one of those test tubes filled with layers of differently coloured sand from the Isle of Wight. They were both jolly. Grandad told funny stories and was able to flatten his nose to his face because he'd lost the bone in it boxing. It was therefore hard to tell what his nose really looked like, though it was big. Nan's was pronounced but quite straight. I gather that both their fathers had large, hooked noses ('aquiline'), so my dad never stood a chance. I also know that Nan's family were Hewetts, and her mother's maiden name was Clara Hammond, and that Clara spoke in the old rural Surrey accent that no longer exists. I can't remember the first name of her father or that of Grandad's, but I know Grandad's mother was Annie Aylott.

Nan and Grandad were both amateur musicians. Nan played the violin, apparently quite badly, but I'm not about to make an issue of that because the words 'played the violin' are sufficient to assure me that music is in my blood. Indeed, Grandad was by my father's account an excellent pianist. In fact, he could do all sorts of things. In the army, he was a marksman, a boxer and a footballer. I don't know whether he played football with the Germans on that Christmas morning when the guns fell silent, but if he did, I bet he won. I am strangely proud that he could do everything I can't do. He was even numerate. Professionally he was a clerk, working in the accounts department of the Royal Aircraft Establishment at Farnborough. (Notice how I avoided the exact word 'accountant'.) Apparently, he could have gone far but lacked ambition, and he and Nanny lived in the same rented end-of terrace house until my parents took them in during their last years.

Most families have legends, and the exciting thing about the Hardy line, which will involve some investigation and which I am looking forward to researching, is that it leads back to an unwed mother, Lionel's great-grandmother, I think. So my name should not be Hardy and we don't know who the father of my great-great-grandfather was. Apparently, my great-great-great-grandmother never revealed who had sired the baby – indeed, she might not have known – but the thing that has always slightly fascinated the family is that, despite being disgraced and a mere servant on a large estate, she was given a cottage and kept on – grounds for suspicion that the rascally young heir to the estate (assuming there was one) was the father of the bastard. I picture him leaping from a foaming stallion to ask for water from the young fair maid as to the well she did go. She winched the pail up from the well and blushed as the young buck poured gushing water straight from it into his open mouth and down his shirt, sticking the ruffled front to his hardened chest. He ensnared her in his web of passion and from that day, many times a-calling did he go and they would lay atop the haywain, until such time as she was great with child and then, as summer waned so did his passion, and he cast her aside. I reckon.

So, did his father, the old Squire, take pity on the wronged girl, or was she bought off to avoid any challenge to the inheritance? Either way, I reckon the Hardys are due a big slice of a country estate, and I'm not above demanding a bit of exhumation and DNA testing to get it.

Oddly enough, we also seem to have been robbed of our rightful inheritance on my mother's side. Mum's parents Rebecca and Herbert, lived across the road from us with my mum's sister, Joan. Grandpa was quite deaf, and more and more infirm in the last seven or eight years of his life, which was most of the time when I knew him. When I was very young, he came across the road every weekday morning to help my mum. Like Lionel, he always wore a tie and had white hair with a side-parting. He also wore a hearing aid. I don't remember him talking about the Great War.

My grandma, Rebecca, knew Paul Robeson briefly in the twenties. That, I think is extremely interesting, except that I never meet anyone under forty who knows who Paul Robeson was. If you fall into that category, he was a very famous African–American actor, singer, orator and activist, who spent long periods in this country. If I remember the story correctly, before my mother was born, the family was staying in a boarding house in Portsmouth. Paul Robeson stayed there for a few days when he was on a concert tour. My grandmother would play the piano and they would sing together, while Robeson bounced my aunt Joan on his knee. I am also told that when he returned to England in the thirties, he said in a radio interview that he would like to meet up with the family he had met in Portsmouth, but that my grandfather was against the idea. This story is by far the most interesting part of my family history that I have heard so far; although, in truth, whenever I have regaled people with it, the best response I have elicited was a kindly nod.

I did once go to a book signing when Paul Robeson Junior was launching a biography of his father. I mentioned the story as I submitted several copies for signing. 'That would have been in 1923,' he confirmed, before pausing for me to get out of line. In fairness, I was eclipsed by a number of very old East End communists and radical actors who had actually known the great man, so 'my aunt sat on his knee' can't have held that much interest for him. I suppose it was unrealistic to hope he might say, 'You're Rebecca's grandson? So it's all true. And there's me thinking it was just one of Dad's stories.' In any event, a quick rummage through the first tenth of the book found Robeson in Portsmouth in 1923, and I'm pretty sure my aunt remembered the knee, so I don't think it was just another of Rebecca's stories.

Rebecca, who called herself Frances, her second name, although she was known to all her relatives as Becky, was a great one for stories. I was excited as a young boy to learn that her grandfather was from Wales. I don't know why the thought of being one sixteenth Welsh sent me running back across the road to tell my mother the wonderful news. Perhaps there was a serialisation of *How Green Was My Valley* on the telly. He was also a miner, my grandmother said. But I think her announcement was before the big pit strikes of the seventies when I was enchanted by the idea of blackened, lilting colliers from the Valleys tunefully bringing down the Heath administration in alliance with their earthy and jocular Yorkshire comrades. I was not only a precocious radical; I also felt culturally non-existent from an early age. The idea that my bloodlines might not run solely to the bottom right-hand corner of England was hugely important to me.

It was Grandma herself who admitted to me years later that her grandfather might not have been Welsh or a miner. His name was Jones, which led her to believe he was Welsh, and extrapolate from that that he was a pitman, mining being the only skill of the Welsh, save for singing, for which they didn't get paid until the 1950s. Grandma herself, I'm told, had a beautiful voice, and never made any money from it. The family wonders whether Paul Robeson might have made her famous had Grandpa not thwarted their reunion. Maybe she'd have had a hit with 'Bread of Heaven', and Welsh cousins would have poured out of the woodwork to claim her as a granddaughter of the Valleys. I don't know.

Indeed, I don't know much about Mum's side at all. I know we proudly walked around as kids announcing to people that we were descended from Sir Christopher Wren. I would write it under our name in visitors' books in historic buildings, as soon as I was old enough to spell 'descendants'. That was at a time when schoolchildren learnt random unconnected facts, such as that Sir Christopher Wren built St Paul's Cathedral, a building we knew from London Weekend Television. I was taken to St Paul's as a lad. We went right to the top, I think you can't get up there now. It involved a rickety ladder, and a man grasping my wrist to haul me up to a platform to see the view. But I couldn't see over the parapet.

Anyway, I'm guessing the Wren thing mightn't be true, mainly because Grandma had such flights of fancy that I now discount much of what she told me. The Jones thing was a strangely proletarian tangent on her part; generally she would upscale. As far as I know, her mother was a midwife who grew up in a servant family on the Duke of Norfolk's estate at Arundel. According to great-aunts, she was a big, jolly lady who would come in from a day's birthing and send the kids to the pub with an empty jug to be filled with beer. However, Grandma always made her sound like Celia Johnson playing Florence Nightingale. I don't know if Celia Johnson ever played Florence Nightingale, by the way, but I can imagine.

I believe that Rebecca's father was a policeman. According to her, he was a Royal protection officer, in fact the Prince of Wales's personal bodyguard, in fact more of a confidant than an employee, a friend really, or brother. Whether he did actually have anything to do with the prince – the prince being, I guess, the future Edward VII – I don't know. Come with me on this whirlwind rollercoaster ride of discovery to find out how much of a fibber my grandmother was.

Which brings me to the family's stolen land in Kent. This story was the inspiration for a short story I wrote for Radio 4, in which a man investigates such a family legend. And, in turn, having written it, I started to think I should actually start to do what the man in the story did, and explore my family history.

There are no details of the land because Rebecca's father, after spending years in Chancery trying to recover his lost birthright, threw all the papers on the fire, so that no son of his would waste his life in vain pursuit of justice. I'm convinced there's something to it because it's preposterous enough to be true.

So, I might have to get contact details for various second, third and fourth cousins on my mother's side. I have no first cousins. Both my parents had one sister each, and neither Joan nor my aunt Muriel had children. Rebecca had twelve siblings, nine of whom survived childhood, so my mum has many cousins, but I'm very short of family on my dad's side. Grandad had one brother, who died in police custody. I'm ashamed to say that I once invoked his memory to explain writing newspaper columns about people killed by the police. The fact was, my great-uncle had fallen off a bar stool and hit his head. Found reeling outside the pub, the police locked him up overnight. In the morning, he was dead from a brain haemorrhage.

Now, that would merit demands for an investigation today, but it's possible he was often found drunk and incapable and routinely put in the cells overnight. I suppose I would like to know more about it, because it obviously affected Grandad. But I am disappointed in myself for appropriating the tragedy. Apart from anything else, it was unnecessary. Were not my writings the more credible for having no personal axe to grind? Why did I succumb to the temptation of writing myself into the story? Audrey, my dad's mother, also lost a sibling, a sister who was hit by a train when they were children. Their father was a signalman and they lived by the railway. She must have been playing on the tracks. I never really spoke to Nan about it. I don't know why I mention it. I suppose I just feel like I should acknowledge my great-aunt. Now I think about it, I'd like to find out her name.

I have to say that, other than finding out the truth behind Rebecca's stories, I'm not sure what I think I'll really *learn* by finding out more about my forebears. I'm not convinced that finding out about our ancestors tells us very much about ourselves, although, always having been firmly assured of the primacy of Nurture over Nature, I am dismayed by each new discovery that points out the role genetic factors play in determining human characteristics. Then again, a genetic scientist described the combining of Nature with Nurture as being like making a cake – once it's baked, all the ingredients have been mixed and changed and can't be separated. That analogy doesn't work with fruitcake, because you can still pick the bits out, but I think the point still stands.

True, there are all those stories about twins separated at birth then reunited to discover that their lives have followed similar paths, but the ones who are completely unalike don't get much press. And, in terms of personality, genetic traits are combined with environmental ones from the moment we are born. It is impossible to have a personality immune from human contact – unless perhaps that's what causes estate agents. As for those people who spend their lives trying to prove genetic racial differences, what interests me is not their findings, but rather what they are hoping to find and why. There are, regrettably, a handful of academics in British universities who attempt to show that black people are less intelligent than white people. They announce their theory as though it were something entirely new that they stumbled upon innocently one day in the lab, when they knocked a flask of sperm over *The Times* crossword. They act as though they had approached their research with an open mind and have no axe to grind whatsoever. But I doubt they would publicise their findings if they were drawn to the inescapable conclusion that black men are naturally bookish and sexually under-confident, or that the French were superior to us. The superiority of the Germans, however, is, I'm sure, something they take for granted.

In fact, I've never seen convincing evidence of profound differences among the races. I'm not even convinced that anyone has yet devised an accurate way of measuring innate intelligence. I know some people are very good at solving puzzles. I also know they have difficulty in forming relationships. The intellect is a complex thing and involves far more than proficiency at sudoku. There have been hundreds of years of scientific research into the human brain and so far all that's been established is that it's a big spongy thing that lives in your head.

On the other hand, quite a lot is known about the neck downwards. More and more medical conditions have been found to involve a genetic link. And we obviously inherit physical characteristics and mannerisms. Something like a 'sense of rhythm' is much more a physical than a mental thing. Nonetheless, there is no proof of the legend that black people have a naturally good sense of rhythm. What is undoubtedly true is that white people have an unnaturally bad sense of rhythm.

Anyhow, as we trace my ancestors, we will see if there are coincidences that suggest inherited traits that go beyond a big nose and irritable bowel syndrome. I am a bit of a medical disaster. I thought I was a hypochondriac but then I found out that that was psychosomatic and I'm actually sick. But will I learn that performing is in my blood? Was one of my great-grandparents a seal? And will I seize on things in the way that credulous people do when they read horoscopes: 'Wow, that's amazing; I *do* feel unappreciated at work.'

You see, if I find out I have a Jewish ancestor, I'm bound to start using my shoulders more. If I find I'm part Huguenot, I'll start pulling threads out of towels and weaving them together. I'll think that what I've discovered *explains* things. I already know that my fear of Surrey results from the child-hood trauma of living there. But will I find that aspects of my personality have resonances in earlier generations? Is there anyone back there who's anything like me? Has anyone ever made a living in the way that I do? Even though I seriously doubt the existence of a comedy gene, it would be nice to find *somebody*. I don't know why it would be nice. Maybe I'll find out. I've hardly yet begun.

My brother-in-law Richard has done some of our family history, which is extremely decent of him. Perhaps it takes an incomer to observe a family as a phenomenon. Before even thinking about researching my own family, I'd already urged my partner, Katie, to find out if she's really related to Charlie

Chaplin as her family claims, if she's really descended from circus people and whether there really is Romany ancestry in the family. Already her ancestry sounds more interesting than mine. I even bought her a DNA testing kit from America so she can find out how black she is. Apparently, most British people are more black than we think. I already know her grandfather was Welsh so she's beaten me on that score before I've even got started. The test showed quite a bit of South Asian ancestry, which would confirm the Romany thing, as they came from India originally.

I have a special interest in that ethnicity because my daughter is adopted, which means my definition of 'family' isn't quite as genetically orientated as some people's. My daughter Betty is not of the same race as me. By birth she is a Romanian Gypsy. In Romania she would not be considered white. The Gypsies, or Romanies, or Roma, left Rajasthan in Northern India a thousand years ago and have been the most consistently oppressed ethnic group in Europe. Betty's ancestors in the nineteenth century would have been kept as slaves. In the 1940s, hundreds of thousands of her people died in Nazi concentration and extermination camps. Members of her family would have been deported and murdered. She went to Ukraine to stay with a friend's family last year. I didn't tell her that that's where much of the killing of Romanian Gypsies took place. Across Europe, racial attacks and murder are still being inflicted on Roma by the extreme Right. And people think I'm being 'too PC' when I flinch on hearing 'gypsy' or 'pikey' used as terms of abuse.

My idea of family is not dominated by blood ties. Families are fragile things and I think it is social pressure and emotional attachments that keep them together. In my culture the family has become a weak and unstable unit. It's much stronger in Muslim, Hindu and Jewish culture, perhaps because those cultures don't have Christmas. The family isn't under anything like the same pressure.

I'm curious about my racial origins, but I don't think they're vitally important. Fascinating maybe, but not crucial. I could do the DNA test myself. I did ask the lady in America whether it could detect Jewish ancestry. She said, 'Oh no, we can't tell people's religion.' I've never understood why some people define Jewishness purely as a faith. I don't know any Jews who are religious. Come to that, I don't know any Catholics who are religious. In any case, I'll try to get myself one of those mouth-scraping kits from America. Perhaps Paul Robeson romanced Rebecca one steamy night in that Portsmouth flophouse in 1923, while Joan slept soundly and Grandpa was at a lodge meeting. Mum was born in 1924. This could be good.

In the meantime, I'll see what Richard has got. I know he recently had to dust off his research because there was some dispute with the American wing of the family, the Dowlings. Brian Dowling is the grandson of Esther, Rebecca's sister. He has, it seems, done extensive research into our shared Monk family history and has challenged some of Richard's findings. Mind you, the Americans are still in bad odour with me since a family reunion about 18 years ago. What outraged me was that the Americans of my generation didn't remember the Hardys at all. Diana, my mum's first cousin, who'd moved there in the late fifties, knew who we were, but the kids didn't. I was really upset. They'd stayed with us once but they had no recollection. *We* all remembered it. It was an event for us, to have our American cousins come and stay in our little bungalow. We knew the Dutch cousins, the Santings, and we liked them, but they came over all the time. They could even play cricket, being half English. We obviously knew some of the Sussex cousins, and we liked them, especially the Tourles, even though Roger broke my Adam Adamant sword when we were fencing and has never replaced it.

But we didn't know the Americans very well and their visit stuck vividly in all our minds. I remember it very clearly because there was always a shortage of bathwater in our house, and it was thought appropriate that I should be bathed standing back-to-back with Alan, who was my age, about six. Our respective mothers, happy cousins reunited, sponged us down using the inch of tepid water in the bottom of the bath, while we stood with our buttocks facing each other's. It's not a happy memory but I'm able to be amused by it forty-odd years later. So I thought it would be a suitable gambit with which to approach Alan at this family reunion. I greeted him with, 'Hello, we once had a bath together.' He looked somewhat uncomfortable, as I suppose he had every right to.

So my instinct is to support Richard's research against theirs. Damn them Yankees. They obviously know nothing about the family. I say this even though at this point I have no idea what the dispute is about. I think it's time to talk to Richard.

CHAPTER 1

Initial Soundings

Having ended the Introduction with such a flourish (for me, a flourish) I must confess that I haven't yet spoken to Richard. Well, I have, but only to say Merry Christmas. I saw various family members over the festive season but my plan to use the opportunity to pick brains foundered rather. I started to feel like a grubby reporter chasing after a story, using my loved ones for personal gain, even when I was asking things that were really just for my interest, such as the name of my great-aunt who was killed by a train. It was Hilda. Dad remembers his grandmother talking about 'My Hilda'. After the accident, the railway company moved my great-grandfather from Betchworth in Surrey to North Camp in Hampshire. The driver of the train knew the family well and was never able to drive again.

But despite the fact that I was feeling very self-conscious with my family, I received unexpected inspiration. I'd made a conscious decision not to interview my parents, because it was Christmas, but, for some reason, we got onto the subject of how they met and fell in love. It only occurs to me now that this story is crucial to my existence. When they were telling it, frankly I was overwhelmed. I should know it already. Why

I've never asked is beyond me. I knew that they had met on a rambling holiday. Until now, that idea has mostly amused me. How English, I thought. How like us. I have always secretly liked us, the English, despite colonial shame. We are people who take cuttings from things. And anything we can't take a cutting from, we put a brave a face on.

Anyhow, rather than being titillated by quaintness, I was reminded that my mum and dad are people, people who had a life together for many years before I bawled my way into it. I have asked them things about their young lives before and been interested to find out – mostly about the war. But this was more vital. And perhaps I've never heard them talk about each other in that way before.

Dad was a great one for exploring the country. He was a keen cyclist and motorcyclist. By the late forties, having explored much of England and Wales on two wheels, Dad got into walking and became some sort of team leader with the Co-operative Holidays Association, the CHA, also known as the Catch a Husband Association.

Mum and her sister Joan, both single, decided to take one of the holidays in the Lake District in 1951. Dad got on well with them, especially with Mum. He took lots of pictures. He always took lots of pictures, indeed most of my childhood was spent standing very still. After the holiday, some weeks went by before he wrote to Mum, enclosing copies of the photos with the letter. Mum had been about to give up on him but wrote back to ask whether he was going to the up-coming reunion in London. He quickly bought a ticket and went along. Soon after, he took her to the theatre. And imme-diately after that, he wrote to propose.

The next morning he received a telegram worded 'Yes –

ignore letter.' The letter arrived the next day, saying that Mum would like to keep seeing him but she wasn't ready to marry him. Dad read it and ignored it.

They arranged to meet in London so that she could bring him to her parents' house to get formal approval. Her parents were not keen to encourage their daughters to entertain young men. They both had good jobs; Joan worked in insurance and Mum was a secretary for the leader of a trade union, the Association of Broadcasting Staff. They were aged 31 and 27, and both lived at home. Their parents Rebecca and Herbert had assumed that that's how things would stay. They didn't begrudge them happiness but they liked being part of a team of four people and didn't want it to change.

Dad travelled from Farnborough, Mum from Richmond. They arranged to meet under the clock at Waterloo Station. Mum was late. She had been about to set off when she realised her mother had bought no food, so she had to do a hurried shop. Mum finally got to Waterloo and made her way from the platform towards the clock.

My dad is a great talker. He will talk for hours about engineering, physics, cheese, wine, airports and people I have never met but am supposed to know. And he knows more about Hampshire than any man alive. But when he said, 'I saw this slim, beautiful figure walking towards me' I started to cry. Because he was talking about my mum. And because she would have had a hat on and there would have been steam everywhere and train whistles and Rachmaninov playing in the background and it would have been in black and white. But mostly because he was talking about Mum.

*

Anyway, at Mum and Dad's house, the courtship story completed, Sue, my eldest sister, produced a book of old photographs which I pored over with Katie and my daughter, Betty. I suppose I might need copies of some of them for the book. It's normal to have some old photos in the middle, isn't it?

But as I say, I wasn't really thinking so much about this project. I was slightly on the back foot, because, before going to see Mum and Dad, I had popped in to see my sister Serena, who counselled that I risk upsetting people by writing a book about the family. This leaves me in a fix, since the things that will be most interesting to strangers is the stuff most likely to cause embarrassment to the family.

Despite worrying me with this caution, Serena also sprang on me the fact that she had Uncle Mattie's medals for me. Rebecca, Mum's mum, had always promised me that I would inherit her brother's medals from the Great War. My elder brother Simon would get Grandpa's. And the girls, being girls, would get none. I had long since given up on any medals, but Aunt Joan had been holding them for us. It was exactly two years since her death when I went round to Serena's. Maybe that's what reminded Serena, who had taken guardianship of them, to pass them on to me.

I have them with me on my desk. There are five medals in a small cardboard box, the lid of which has a stamp and a partly visible address in Portsmouth where Grandma and her family lived. Only one is inscribed with his name: Lance Corporal MW Monk KRRCo (King's Royal Rifle Corps). It is dated 1914–15.

There are two prize medals. Googling the Empire Day Challenge Cup medal, I find a site with a picture of the medal, with identical details to Mattie's. I am slightly excited by this; I feel I am investigating; even though this is basically how young children do their homework. The website confirms that the medal was presented by Lt Col RW Schumacher of the Witwatersrand Rifles, as the inscription reads. The other shooting medal is the Henry Whiteread Cup, dated 1913, so it seems that Mattie was a professional soldier before the war.

I have to say I take no pride in his pre-war service. One can argue that troops defended the country in the First World War, and there is no question that the defeat of Hitler in the Second World War was absolutely imperative, but in general I'd say the British Army is not a good thing. I learnt that at a young age, growing up in the Aldershot area. In the sixties and seventies, we were thinking of calling in the IRA as a peacekeeping force.

Nevertheless, people had different ideas a hundred years ago and clearly Uncle Mattie was a good shot, and Grandma adored him. Two of his medals must be posthumous because they appear to have been awarded at the end of the war. One has the King on the back and is dated 1914–1918. On the front is a naked man on a horse – fair enough, it was wartime. The other has a winged figure on the front and on the back the words 'The Great War for Civilisation 1914–1919'. Clearly, there were differing ideas about when the war ended, but I google these exact words on the off chance something might come up and find out it's worth £7.27 on eBay. Some mercenary bastard doesn't care about his great-uncle's bravery. Then I find a BBC website that shows both these medals. The first is the British War Medal and the second is the Victory Medal. The winged figure is

Victory. The naked horseman is St George. I also see a medal like the one with Matthew's name on. It is the 1914–1915 Star. Apparently, this trio of medals is known as 'Pip, Squeak and Wilfred', characters that appeared in a *Daily Mirror* cartoon after the war.

All of these medals were given out to all those who served, except the Star which wasn't given to those whose service began after 1914; they got something else. Rather than be disappointed that there is not a medal bearing the inscription, 'To Mattie Monk – Simply the Best, from your pal King George VI and all the gang at The Empire', I feel that there is something special in the fact that the medals are not unique, that everyone got one. It is completely arguable that the Great War was a war fought for selfish reasons and perhaps was the climax of our centuries-old imperial adventure, but it was also one of the few times when this country genuinely feared invasion, when young British men went abroad to protect their own families.

Of course, it also involved an unseemly grab for more Empire from the losers, Britain racing to beat the French to the Northern oilfields of Mesopotamia. New Labour's bellicose progressive flag-wavers will say, 'Yeah, yeah, we know all that, but things are different now', just as then Britain's leaders assured the public that oil played no part in our foreign policy. At the same time as we were seizing the lands that we turned into Iraq, we were devising an interesting future for our new protectorate in Palestine, and simultaneously trying to pacify Ireland, where we hit upon the solution of partition in 1921, thereby securing a peaceful resolution to the conflict only 86 years later. Partition went so well that it was later done to India and of course Palestine. Find a long-running blood-soaked territorial dispute anywhere in the world, and there's a familiar red postbox not very far away.

I digress. I am still looking at Mattie's medals. Also in the box are rosary beads, which were found on his body. Seemingly, most of the army chaplains were Catholics. I don't know whether he carried these beads with him or whether they were put on his body by a priest administering the last rites. But they seem to me to be intimately connected with the end of his life, and through them I feel some physical connection to a soldier, a relation of mine, who fought and died in the First World War. I think this is important, not because I am trying to write myself into that story in some vain, solipsistic way, but rather because of some notion – a notion which a brighter man might expand into something substantial – that we are all connected to everything.

Apparently, some physicists argue that Time is curved. I suppose this means that the past is in some way still present. I have tried to read scientific articles about Space Time and got nowhere. I am, in fact, convinced that Physics is all made up. Dad was an applied physicist, meaning that he was an engineer who actually did Physics rather than just speculating about it. He designed satellites and I suppose he must understand physical theory, but he's never been able to explain anything physics-related to me. Even when I was doing O-Level, I didn't bother to ask him because I could never make head nor tail of anything he told me, despite getting a B which means I can't have been completely useless.

Dad wasn't a woolly academic; he got into space stuff by accident. He started in weapons research at RAE in Farnborough after leaving school at 15. He applied to serve in the RAF without telling his bosses but was rejected because of his eyesight. So he went back to weapons research, trying to invent a way of destroying U-boats from the air. He would test his bombs in Staines reservoir and off the Dorset Coast. One idea involved firing missiles vertically downward from the underside of aeroplane wings. I think there's a very good reason why you've never heard of the invention.

But his experiments saved his life. He had become fed up with hiding in the cupboard under the stairs all night during air raids and had decided to take his chances trying to sleep in bed. One day he came back from Dorset to find the road had been hit. He was relieved to find his parents and sister were alive but one bomb had landed in the field at the bottom of the garden and part of the shell casing had gone through the roof and was sticking into his bed. I also remember my Nan pointing to the wall that separated the front room from the back room: 'That came down in the war. I wouldn't have had it put back if I'd known how fashionable it would be to knock through.'

After the war, Dad did his National Service in the Navy. He wanted to be a photographer but they had enough of them so they made him do radar. After that, he went back to RAE and worked on missiles until deciding, it being peace-time, to do something more constructive. I suppose there wasn't a well-worn path into the British space programme because we didn't really have a space programme. Dad was one of the pioneers of it. You might not have heard of it but it was a big thing in my family. He is very well known in the field of what is known as Remote Sensing, and designed this country's weather and communication satellites.

In any event, having learnt on the job, one might have expected him to have a layman's knack for explanation, but when he talked to me about physics I always found him incomprehensible. Then again, I have occasionally met old schoolfriends of mine who ended up working for him at RAE and they describe him as a great communicator, so perhaps it's me. Perhaps it's my lurking and crippling doubt that Physics is a real science. Chemistry seems to be pretty much nailed down, and Biology gains ground all the time. But physics seems to be mired in idle rumination. They think a Big Bang started the universe but they don't really know. If there was an almighty explosion, what exploded? There was nothing. Time hadn't started. And what was the catalyst for the explosion? And given that it was all a very long time ago, isn't it time we drew a line under it and moved on? Even if there *was* an explosion, no one was hurt, no damage was done and no one was responsible. Or were they? And if there was a God who caused the explosion, surely he must have been demolishing some pre-existing universe that was in danger of collapse. Or was God the first terrorist? Or was it an insurance job?

Time marches on, curved or not. In fact, quite some time passed between my writing the words 'insurance job' and the words 'Time marches on'. Weeks, actually. I could have got away with it but I wanted to be honest with you. I have been distracted. But I haven't been doing nothing. I have been to see Mum and Dad again, and also collected the findings of Richard, my brother-in-law. Mum has told me a little bit about her childhood in Malta, where she lived between the ages of two and eight. Her father had a job with NAAFI and Malta was at that time a British colony and naval base. He signed a six-year contract and took the family from Portsmouth to a new colonial lifestyle in the Mediterranean. They had a maid called Stella and later there was a governess for my mother, who did not attend school. Joan went to a convent but Mum had no formal education until they returned to Portsmouth.

Mum has always been a woman of conscience, and was aware even as a very young girl that the Maltese were discriminated against. She only got to socialise with Maltese children at the family's holiday home, which as she remembers was in a place called Ramla. Dad went to Malta a while back and the only place he could find called Ramla is on Gozo, the second island, where Katie's aunt has a holiday flat. We've decided to spend Easter there so I can get a sense of what it might have been like for Mum living there as a child. Conversely, we are not going to spend a week in Portsmouth, trying to get a sense of what the rest of her childhood was like.

It was bad timing to return in 1932. The Depression was biting hard and Grandpa could not find work. The family went from a blessed Imperial existence to serious hardship and she had to start school for the first time aged eight. Grandpa's search for work eventually took the family to leafy Richmond, when he was able to use his RAMC background to get an admin job in a military hospital. Life might then have been quite cushy had Hitler not invaded Poland.

Mum was 15 when the war started, and started work in an office. By the age of 18 she was also an ARP warden. I've never been able to understand how risk-averse my mum is. She hated conkers, pea shooters and anything that could have someone's eye out. In fact, more or less anything could have someone's eye out: skipping, swinging on your chair, talking with your mouth full. I think there must have been something deficient in the diet in 1920s Portsmouth and people were born with very weak eye sockets, so that if you burped a baby over-zealously, there was a risk its eye would pop out over your shoulder. I understand that Mum grew up in a time of danger and that she wanted us all to be safe, but I sometimes wonder how she got through the war at all. How did she function as an ARP warden, venturing out during the Blitz in a tin hat, looking for fires, injured people, unexploded bombs and possible German paratroopers? She could cope with all that, but if a Jerry had crept up on her with a snowball, she'd have panicked because there could be some grit in that and that can have someone's eye out.

I asked my brother, Simon, who was also visiting Mum when I went on Mother's Day, to bring Grandpa's WWI medals so that we could compare them with Mattie's. He arrived with a box containing Pip, Squeak and Wilfred, all with the ribbons intact and all polished and in excellent condition. But there were no additional ones, and no one could remember the story about Herbert's heroism. Mum confirmed that he never spoke much about the war, and that it clearly caused him distress. He was an emotional man and his deafness was thought to have been brought on and exacerbated by strain. I hesitate to use the word stress because my generation has trivialised it so much.

I increasingly admire my grandparents' generation. They were stoics. Their philosophy was 'Mustn't grumble'. Of course, they did grumble, but not in proportion to what they went through in their lives: two world wars involving terrible carnage and the loss of family and friends; the Great Depression; hands twisted out of shape by arthritis. They didn't have the luxury of allergies. Things they ate simply didn't agree with them. They liked cucumber but it didn't like them. They knew there was nothing special about them; they were just unpopular among certain vegetables. Today, an adverse reaction to cucumber would be enough to warrant a whole chunk of *Woman's Hour* and funding for your own theatre company.

There was no post-traumatic stress counselling for war veterans, but then I suppose there were the Legion and the Working Men's Clubs. Herbert enjoyed family occasions when Lionel was present because then they could talk about the trenches, the two being the only people there with that experience. I suppose it's a shame our family was too big. Five kids in a small house meant that at some point it was decided that we couldn't have all the grandparents on Christmas Day, so Mum's parents came one day and Dad's the next, when the whole meal would be replicated using leftovers – and this was before microwaves. The trick was to reheat the meat in the gravy.

I haven't yet probed Dad about his father's experience in the trenches. I'm still unsure how he feels about this book, but he did advise that I should 'get on the programme'. I thought he meant rehab until I realised he was referring to the television programme in which all the research is done for you and you just have to say 'Gosh' to affect surprise that an ancestor's name was written down somewhere. I was flattered by Dad's confidence in my celebrity status but I had to tell him that if I have not appeared on a television programme, it's not because I haven't got round to calling them to arrange it. This is not to say that I would have wanted to do the programme. I would probably not be asked and, if I were, it would be because people in TV imagine that a comedian is necessarily someone that people have heard of. And I would hate to be on a programme called *Who Do You Think You Are?* when most viewers would be thinking, 'Who is he?'

I'm not saying I'm not at all famous. I'm famous to people who know who I am. I'm in that infuriating category described by Mark Steel as 'slightly successful'.

Let me give you an example of the status of semi-success. I once made a live video, which was recorded at the Theatre Royal, Stratford, in East London. On the day of the recording, a car was sent for me, a black taxi driven by an old East End Jewish cabbie. The conversation went as follows:

'It's Jeremy, isn't it?'

'That's right.'

'Sorry, I don't know the name.'

'That's OK.'

'I hope you're not offended.'

'No.'

'Only sometimes people get offended.'

'It's fine, honestly.'

'They say, "Don't you know who I am?" and I say, "I'm a cab driver. All day I'm in a cab. I get home, I have my dinner, I sit down in front of the telly and I'm asleep before I find out who anyone is." You might be the biggest star in the West End, Jeremy. The fact that I don't know who you are means nothing. You might be top of the bill at the Palladium and meet the Queen, I still won't have heard of you, so I hope you're not offended.'

'No.'

'Because a lot of people are.'

'I'm not, really.'

'Good. Because I wouldn't want you to be offended.'

'No.'

'Good. Only...how you going to sell tickets for a show when no one knows who you are?'

Anyhow, the point is, I haven't been asked to appear on *Who Do You Think You Are?* so I don't have to worry about viewers wondering who I think I am. No, actually, the point is that there's no one to do my research for me so it's just as well Richard has got the ball rolling. I feel I am cheating by borrowing his research, but I am also honouring it because it was a Trojan effort and not one that any of the Hardys were prepared to make. And I'm going to have to start from scratch anyway because I need to find out how one does this stuff today.

CHAPTER 2

Herbert of Croydon

Susan, if you have forgotten already, is my eldest sister, and Richard is my brother-in-law. He started to do both their family trees about 25 years ago, before this stuff was online. I didn't ask to see his research at the time, I just thought it was nice of him. It never occurred to me that he was doing it for his daughters, Hattie and Laura. In fact, that only clicked when I went round the other day. Laura was there with her daughter Aiysha, my great-niece. Now that I am a great-uncle, I have a slight sense that my great-uncles and -aunts were significantly related to me, and that I should perhaps know more about some of them. I would hate my great-niece one day to write, 'I think my nanna had two brothers and one of them might have been a comic. His name was Jemima.'

Rick's work is not complete but is extensive and he has lent me two folders with lots of stuff in them. The criticism from Brian the American cousin was that Grandma's maternal grandmother is recorded by Rick as being one Eliza Sharp. That is what Grandma had told Richard. It turns out that there was an Eliza Sharp in the area at around that time but that she was not Becky's grandmother.

According to Brian, our great-great-grandmother was Harriet Coombs, and Richard now thinks he's right, so the rift with America is over.

Twenty-five years ago, Richard had to spend hours and hours in the national Archives at Kew, looking at census returns, before he could even start tracking down certificates of births, deaths and marriages. I feel I am cheating, but I have a quick rummage through his work to find surnames. I know already that on Dad's side there are Hewetts, Aylotts and Hammonds. On Mum's side, I know the names Stagg, Monk and Jones. I pull out a certificate at random and see the name Harriet Briole. French? Tragic though it might seem to you, I get very excited at the first vaguely exotic sighting of my research. I google the name. A French actress called Vera Briole comes up. I google images to see if she looks like me but there are no pictures.

I go back to the certificates and realise that the name was Bridle. How many genealogical forays have been sent awry because of clumsy penmanship? I thought they all wrote beautifully in the nineteenth century – those who could write at all. This entry looks like it was made by a child with a fat biro. Oh, it's a transcription of an original, rather than a photocopy, and was filled in using a fat biro. I google 'Harriet Bridle' in the hope that the gods are toying with me and that there is a prize; that she was Rasputin's bodyguard or something. But I find only the author of a book called *Woody Bay*, about an inlet in North Devon. It costs £9.95 and weighs 350 grams. At a rough calculation, that's about 30 grams per pound. Is that good for a book? I don't know. I still don't do metric.

The document I found is the marriage certificate of

Harriet and George Stagg, who I'm guessing, are the parents of Herbert Stagg, my grandfather. Another forage through the certificates reveals that this is indeed the case, and that Grandpa was born on 6 December 1889 at 26 St John's Grove in Croydon.

As I've already said, I am hoping to find ancestors from some interesting places. It might surprise you but I am quite excited to learn that one of my bloodlines runs to Croydon.

For those who don't know, Croydon is a south London suburb on the A23. It used to be a town in Surrey but now it is sprawl. It's on the Brighton road, also the main route between London and Gatwick, making Croydon one of those places that's on the way to other places, a town that, like puberty, nobody enjoys but everybody has to go through at some time. But it happens to be down the road from me. Streatham is not far at all from Croydon. About three miles. On a good day, I can drive there in under four hours. And that's my plan: have a shufti through the A–Z, jump in the car, head down to St John's Grove and see if the house is still there. If it is, I'll knock on the door. When the people answer, which of course they will because they always do on telly, I'll show them the birth certificate, say that Herbert was my grandfather and ask if there's any chance I could go in and try to imagine what it must have been like 120 years ago. Take pictures even. Find the smallest bedroom because the cot would have gone in there.

As you can see, I did not mentally prepare myself for the fact that the house might no longer be there. When, I look in the A–Z and find that the street itself is no longer there, I feel completely cheated. I go online to check and it definitely isn't there. I can't even find a record of it ever existing and the maps of the period I can find are too indistinct for me to pick it out. But there is a St John's Road, a St John the Baptist Church and a St John the Baptist Memorial Garden, which I find in the parks section. The garden used to be the graveyard but in 1957 road alterations necessitated the moving of a war memorial, so plans for the new garden were drawn up. It's looking likely St John's Grove was demolished but I'm hoping it was renamed.

I've emailed the people at the Croydon Online website to ask for their help. They also have a section called Genealogy, so surely that's worth a look. Clicking on 'Parish Registers', I find out they are held in the Surrey History Centre. There's a Surrey history centre? It's in Woking, further than Croydon but not far, half an hour from Clapham Junction.

There is also a section called 'The Diverse Cultures of Surrey'. I click on the link; I have to see this. There was no diversity in Surrey when I was growing up. Methodists were hunted for sport up until the 1960s. It turns out that the oldest and largest ethic minority are the Gypsies, which I suppose is true of the whole country. I also find the story of John Springfield, a cobbler from Zanzibar who became 'Guildford's first black man' in the 1870s. In Mytchett, we didn't get ours until the 1980s. Actually, I am told that when I was very young, I saw a black man when out with my mum, and thought he was made of chocolate. I find that very unlikely. It seems much more probable to me that I saw a man made of chocolate than a black man in Mytchett in the early sixties.

John Springfield's story is very interesting: the son of a chief, he was abducted by Portuguese pirates at the age of nine, then abandoned, and then rescued by Dr Livingstone.

He served as a valet to the captain of the HMS *Victoria* until the age of 20, when he went to America to campaign against slavery. According to Surrey County Council he then 'went to America to preach anti-slavery but America was unreceptive so he decided to try England.' That would have been in 1867 when America had just endured a four-year civil war in which the issue of slavery had featured prominently, so 'unreceptive' seems a bit of a generalisation. Anyway, America's loss was Surrey's gain. John came to Croydon and married a local girl in 1870. He might have bought the wedding ring from my great-grandfather George Stagg, who I note was a watchmaker and jeweller. From Croydon, he moved to Guildford, and now I come to think of it, I think some of my dad's ancestors came from there as well.

Well, this is a promising start and I'm not as pessimistic about my ancestry as I was. But I am about to make a journey even more exciting than the ones I shall make to Croydon or Woking. I'm going abroad.

CHAPTER 3

Proper Overseas-Type Research

It's March 2008. Katie and I are due a holiday and there is just one week when I can fit one in. I don't structure work very well. Even if there isn't very much in the diary, there never seems to be a fortnight when there isn't something I have to do. I'm now on most of the *News Quiz* shows on Radio Four. It's a few weeks before the next series starts, but I have live dates in the meantime. I've got a few stand-up shows and a dozen dates of the *I'm Sorry I Haven't a Clue* tour. There are six of us in the show and finding dates when everyone is available presents the producer, Jon Naismith, with a challenge. Actually, I think we present him with a number of challenges, but everyone involved has great respect for him.

ISIHAC has been a hugely popular radio show for 36 years. I listened to it as a boy, and am now a semi-regular guest. In 2007, we started touring it as a live theatre show. It's very much like a radio recording but the audience seems to be more than happy with it. It's quite clear that a special love is reserved for Humphrey Lyttleton, our chairman and still a revered jazz trumpeter. He is also loved by everyone in the show.

Humph is older than both my parents. Not put together – I mean each of them. Increasingly we all wonder how long he will be with us. I have lost a number of friends, but I've never had a friend who has achieved such longevity. He might see out a century but I still feel that time with him is precious. And although he is nearly 87, I still think that for him to go now would be cruelly early. This is on my mind because he faces a very serious heart operation in a few weeks' time.

Humph is a national treasure, but more than that to those who know him. He is an English gentleman in the best possible way and has the twinkliest eyes I have ever seen. He also has proper genealogy. He is descended from the Humphrey Lyttleton who was hanged (but not drawn or quartered, Humph assures us) for his part in the Gunpowder Plot. There is another ancestor who died childless, or rather, appeared to be dead and was in her coffin awaiting burial when a robber prised open the lid and attempted to sever a finger that bore a valuable ring. She revived, let out a shriek of pain and the robber fled. She survived and went on to have a child, from whom Humph is descended.

I am sure that I will find no such story indicating any precariousness in my bloodlines. Nothing as interesting as that would happen in my ancestry. There is probably a dull inevitability about my appearing on the earth, an unbreakable chain of events that no circumstance could have sabotaged. Maybe some forebear once had a migraine and didn't really feel like it, but a dreary sense of duty will have prevailed.

I'm not a great traveller. Whenever people travel the world seeking enlightenment, they find amazing, happy people with simple lives and want to be like them, never comprehending that the distinctive thing about these beautiful people and their stress-free lives is that they don't travel. But I am going to Malta to research my family history, so I feel less agitated about it than I would normally. And, because Katie's cousin has a house on Gozo, one of the Maltese islands, we have free accommodation on offer. Malta has also become one of those places opened up by 'no frills' airlines. This is a bad thing for a number of reasons and I tend to suspect that one of the frills is safety; but it saves us a lot of money. So we take a chance with Planes R Us and arrive at Malta International Airport the Tuesday before Easter.

I suppose I might have felt something special on first setting foot upon Maltese soil, but Mum arrived on a P & O liner in the harbour at Valetta, and we're at an airport taking a taxi to the Gozo ferry up the other end of the island. The country of Malta comprises of three islands, Malta, Gozo and Comino. Comino has only a handful of residents and its only features are a hotel and a postcard staple, the Blue Lagoon – a bit of light-blue sea. Gozo is a small island but very distinctive and Gozitans are quite clear that they are both Maltese and Gozitan. Everything we have read indicates that Gozo is a much nicer place, and since the Staggs spent their holidays there, by holidaying there myself, I am much closer to their experience than if I stayed on the main island. That's what I reckon anyway.

The guidebooks say that Gozo is a perfect place to unwind after the heady whirlwind that is Malta, although I suspect that Malta is not so much vibrant as merely over-burdened with tourists. The drive from the airport to the ferry tends to confirm this. There is ugly development every-where. Hotels and apartments are being thrown-up faster than duty-free Malibu and look much like tourism developments in Italy, Spain or Greece. But the residential buildings remind me more of housing in the West Bank. Indeed, I start to get the sense that Malta is a bit like lots of places but not quite like anywhere. The first settlers were Sicilians. Then the Phoenicians arrived in 800 BC and after that it was colonised by one power after another, ending up with us between 1800 and 1964.

The bus fleet is made up of bright yellow and orange buses, many of them Leyland and Bedford coaches from the fifties, sixties and seventies. There are red phone boxes and pillar boxes, signs are in English and they drive on the left, as everyone should. Instead of feeling colonial shame or disappointment that it's not exotic enough, I find it quite comforting, like you do when you go to an English seaside resort that's still got some 1950s' tat. Katie's cousin Jan has told us we've got to try the mushy pea pie on the ferry, and we do. It's like a mushy pea pie. I notice from the available drinks in the cafeteria that pale ale is still popular here, and resolve to have one before the week is over.

The cab driver to the ferry port is sullen and a bit rude, which is disappointing, but helps hasten us to Gozo, which will be friendlier, being smaller. The guidebook assures us that all the Maltese are friendly. But guidebooks and tourists always say that people are friendly everywhere. Wherever in the world the British go, we note that people are very friendly, and yet we haven't worked out that there's a pattern to this: it is entirely normal for human beings to be friendly everywhere in the world apart from Britain. And the unfriendliness of the cabbie on Malta is probably a relic of British rule.

But, sure enough, Mario who picks us up on the Gozitan side and is supplying a hire car, is friendly, confirming that we've made the right choice of island on which to stay. Indeed, he assures us that everybody else on Gozo is friendly too.

It is a titchy island and we're in Xhara in no time, having passed the island's only traffic light and various bollards and stop signs that must all have been imported from England. We arrive at night and head straight out to eat.

At this point, I realise quite how far I have wandered into travel writing, and I'm not sure how appropriate it is. I have already been personal and negative about a taxi driver, a man who is a living breathing human who might have been having a bad day. It's unlikely, but just about possible, that he will somehow learn he has been criticised in a book. And I have dismissed him as though he were a person of no value.

I quite enjoy travel writers but I dislike that aspect of it: the fact that people become subjects and characters the moment the writer's dealings with them have finished. It's probably easier for the writer to do this if he is one of those people who believe that the world exists as a backdrop for them, and that all the other people in it exist for their entertainment. You can identify a person like that because he or she enters a room talking, as though it comes to life the moment they set foot in it, or as though everyone was sitting silently, nervously fidgeting and waiting for the arrival of the holder of the key to conversation. Many people who love to travel seem to be like that. They speak of 'discovering' places, rather like the explorers and adventurers of old who would proclaim a place's discovery, to the surprise of the existing population.

The modern world traveller tends to revile tourists, as though they are not tourists themselves. They want to 'get off the tourist trail', by which they mean extend it. 'We found this wonderful little place completely off the beaten track, not in any guidebook. A fantastic village, it only appears once every two hundred years. Lovely people, tiny, no bigger than your thumb, poor but unhappy. And they didn't have a restaurant as such but we were invited into someone's home and they fed us this amazing meal and poured us their own home-made wine, and spoke no English, but luckily we have this innate ability to communicate with all the peoples of the world, and we exchanged stories and danced with them and ate hallucinogenic insects and had sex with them and stayed there for ten years and nearly missed our flight. And it all came to ten pounds a head.'

You can tell I am not well travelled, so I like to think the worst of people who are. I like to ascribe my fear of travel to humility. In truth, there is a bit of that. I can happily stare at the awesome magnitude of nature without thinking it would be fun to ride a quad-bike over it. I am particularly impressed by the sea and think a good deal of humility is in order when in its presence. When I look at a calm sea, I am confused as to why anyone feels it necessary to tear around it on a jet ski, and when I can look at a rough sea, I visualise it smashing jet skis to bits. I like Gozo already, it has a reputation for being quiet.

Wednesday is our first full day here and it's a horrible day. So much so that we decide to investigate the spa facilities at the luxurious Kempinski hotel, which is how we end up in San Laurenz. Before finding the Kempinski, we think we'd better do a shop since we're staying in self-catering accommodation. I always head for the supermarkets in other countries to see what they've got and how different they are. That's probably why I've never gone trekking in the Himalayas: there would be no opportunity to find out what their brands of biscuits are and say, 'Oh look, they spell "mayonnaise" slightly differently.' And in my defence, I do see some evidence of the historic link to Britain. It's hard to tell with globalisation, tourism and increased British immigration, but I do find that the white sliced bread is called 'British plain' and it's not only holidaymakers who are avidly piling it into their trolleys.

Plus we have to go to the supermarket to buy water. The Maltese islands are dry – though damp – and the mains water is desalinated, a process whereby seawater is flavoured with bleach to make it more palatable. Grandma always boiled tap water and stored it in empty milk bottles, a habit she had developed in her colonial heyday here.

Victoria, where the supermarket is, has lots of beautiful old buildings. Significantly, they would have been here when Mum was, so I picture her being led through the narrow streets by her much taller sister, her parents looking grand, Rebecca with a parasol and Herbert in his Panama hat or pith helmet. This might not seem dramatic to you but it's my mum we're talking about.

Having dropped off the groceries, we go to find the Kempinksi. The spa staff are nice and we book to come back for a swim on Thursday, despite the fact that it seems to be the kind of place where holidaymakers sit around an indoor pool all day and you wonder why they bothered to come. Our excuse is that the weather is filthy and we're not going to be able to go in the sea. And on the positive side, the hotel has brought us to the west of the island, where we find Dwejra and the Azure Window. You can see the Azure Window on the front of guidebooks. I doubt its Maltese name translates as 'Azure Window'; it's probably something more similar to 'Durdle Door', the similar phenomenon in Dorset. I think the tourist board has been at the names of things in the Maltese islands. The view through the hole is definitely not azure today. The sea is steely grey. But it is a magnificent coastline and quite weird; and, as a grim day darkens, the menacing eeriness is a reminder that humankind invented soft furnishings for a reason.

So we head off to get some dinner in San Laurenz, where preparations for Easter are in full swing. Like the rest of the island, the town is in the grip of festive Catholic morbidity. Mum remembers there being big Easter processions 80 years ago, but if you're picturing something like *Easter Parade* with Fred Astaire and Judy Garland, you're on the wrong track. Bonnets don't feature prominently. Except ones with thorns.

The church here, like the one in Xhara, has illuminated crosses on it. There are more crosses on lampposts. In the windows of people's homes are burning candles and figurines of Christ, carrying his cross, being on his cross and generally having a bad time because of our sins. Especially nasty are the paintings, big close ups of his bloodied face. I don't see the kids enjoying an Easter egg hunt at the weekend. A game of Pin the Saviour on the Crucifix seems more likely.

There are churches *everywhere* on Gozo, and most seem

to have been adorned with lights. Xhara and Victoria are having the big processions on Friday and Sunday; some other places are having dos on other nights to avoid clashing. And as we finish our dinner in San Laurenz and leave the restaurant, which faces the church, we find a procession is under way right in front of us. It looks like a dress rehearsal because no one's watching, but it goes on for a good two hours and there's a portable PA, candles lit along the whole route and police keeping streets clear. A life-size model of Jesus carrying his cross is brought out of the church and borne aloft through the town. The cross isn't to scale because, if it were, it wouldn't fit through the door. There are various clergy and congregants and relief Jesus-holders, who carry poles to rest the platform on when the procession halts for bits of the service. But the star turn are the *penitenti*, barefoot men wearing robes and hoods, who look a bit like the Ku Klux Klan. They are chained together at the ankles and the sound of the dragging metal would sound mournful and poignant but it's too much like sleigh bells.

They would look threatening if watchstraps weren't showing and if one of them didn't stand with his hand on his hip while waiting for the procession to move on. It's a cold March night and they're barefoot so they must be freezing. I don't really know what to make of all this. I am secure in my atheism and yet feel no impulse to deride or belittle what I am witnessing. There is nothing phoney going on. No one is pretending to faint or speak in tongues. It's all routine, ritual. There's no pretence that anything magical is happening. They're doing what they always do and there's nothing appealing about it. There's no beautiful or uplifting music, nothing seductive at all. It looks like it's a pain in the arse to participate in and that makes me admire people for it. You'd need to be devoted. Either that or this is such a repressively Catholic country that they have no choice, but there are clearly people indoors watching telly, and the restaurant, is open, so I don't get that impression.

Churches are the dominant buildings in every town and each one is extremely ornate and luxurious. One could find it offensive, an extravagant display of the wealth of organised religion in a world stricken by want and hunger. But it is also an expression of the devotion of worshippers. Not only is the church the centre of the community, like in *The Archers*, but here the church is a place where nothing is too much, where no expense is spared when it comes to praising God. It's a bit like having a great big telly in small council flat. The people seem to be saying, 'We might be tiny little town on a tiny little island but we've got a big, fuck-off church and we're going to pray in it.'

The next day, we can use the Kempinski spa all day, but we're not that shallow, so, before going there for our swim, my feeble work-out and Katie's Ayurvedic massage, we go to explore one of the most important archaeological sites in the world. It happens that walking distance from the house is the Ggantija temple, billed as the 'oldest free-standing building in the world', despite being propped up at one end by girders. I don't know the meaning of the term 'free-standing' in this context. Perhaps there are some older back-to-backs in Machu Pichu, but the main thing is that this building is between five and six thousand years old, that people are arriving on coaches from the main island to see it and that it's in our very village. And Mum must surely remember this place.

Friday, the weather turns nice. Cold and windy but very sunny. So we set off to check out Ramla, where we think Mum spent her summers. It's no distance from Xhara, but then nowhere is on Gozo. There's not much in the way of beaches so this stretch of red sand is very popular, and there's a café and toilets. It's very pleasant but there's no view so distinctive that I'm confident of a photo jogging Mum's memory. There's a white statue of the Virgin right on the beach, and I make Katie photograph it because it's the sort of thing that could stick in a child's mind. Then I see it was built in the 1950s. There's farmland all around. The guidebook says there's a Roman temple but it's overgrown and hidden by bamboo. Also it mentions the cave, which is supposed to be the place to where Odysseus was lured by Calypso. However, the guidebook is quite dismissive of it and since this particular guidebook would describe a corpse-filled ditch as an enchanting waterway, if it says that something's not quite all it's cracked up to be, it must be utterly dreadful. Which is fine, because my main aim is to moon about getting a sense of the place and looking for cottages Mum might have stayed in. There are a number of ruined ones near the beach, and no way of telling if one of them was the place. But Mum remembers children nearby, so perhaps it was at the top of the hill, where there are a few houses. It's quite hard to tell how old buildings here are anyway, because it's clear that stones are usually recycled when a place is demolished. I'm not really sure what I'm expecting to find here at Ramla, but I guess the landscape must look pretty much as it did 80 years ago, and Mum remembers summers spent happily here, with the bonus of being able to play with Maltese kids, so it means something to me.

Being on Gozo, is the first time I've really thought about her being a little girl. And it's easier to picture her, here in a place that must have looked much as it does now, than it will be if I make a similar pilgrimage to Portsmouth.

As it's Good Friday we've decided we should see the procession in Xhara, but we're torn because it's a beautiful evening, heading for a fantastic sunset, and Dwejra, at the west end of the island, would have been the perfect place to watch the sun disappear into the sea – although there's always that risk of it going a bit rubbish at the end because of clouds on the horizon. I don't think it did go a bit rubbish, because peering over our shoulders while perched on the steps of a memorial in the town square, what we can see of the western sky looks worthy of a classical music album cover. The sun will be setting at exactly the time the show starts in a few moments.

Clearly it's going to be a spectacular cavalcade, the town is rammed. People must have come from all over the island. Rows of seats have been put out on two sides of the square, and people seem to have tickets. At the far end of the square is the church, and at this end, the procession will pass out into back streets and follow some circuitous route around the whole town. Just to the left of the church entrance is the town band, all seated and in uniform. In front of us, an elderly man on a platform is preparing to video the show. He appears to be the official, professional videographer for the event, but his equipment suggests that the people using their phones will get better footage. Nonetheless, excitement is building and as the sound system speakers whine into life, the parade begins.

Of course, we can't understand the commentary, but the parade is self-explanatory and goes on for ever. We get the whole background to the crucifixion, going back into the Old Testament, and each section of the procession is introduced by a child in biblical-style robes, carrying a sign that tells us where we're up to. The children are cute and look proud and nervous, like kids in a nativity play. But there also dozens, maybe hundreds, of costumed adults involved, some with natural beards, some with false ones. Many hold their arms still in gestures signifying things. It's getting cold now and they're going to get very stiff. The Roman army uniforms are quite impressive and there are real horses. I'm glad that the Romans are picking up their share of the blame for the events about to unfold because otherwise I'd be getting worried by the Scribes and Pharisees section, which seems to go on for ever, and involve people dressed as random Jews, perhaps suggesting Mel Gibson's view of attachable blame.

After a few minutes, it occurs to me that I'm not enjoying this. The quiet respect I felt the other night in San Laurenz has gone. This isn't worship, it's pageantry; and it's all pointing one way: to death. Jesus is not going to get out of this. Angels will not slide down the side of the church on ropes hurling stun grenades into the Roman phalanx. God will not gallop up on a white colt, brandishing a Winchester with which he skilfully shoots through the nails to free his boy, who drops nimbly and unharmed to his feet and leaps up behind him onto the horse with the words, 'Thanks Paw,

I thought for a minute there thou hadst forsaken me.' No, he's going to die. All the fourteen sculptures representing the Stations of the Cross, will be carried from the church one by one, each one showing Christ's window of escape gradually but ineluctably closing.

I've never liked Easter. I'm all right about death, but I think the Christian emphasis on it is unhealthy. I dislike the cult of martyrdom. Perhaps it is because I spring from the Anglican tradition. Anglican guilt is different from the Roman Catholic variety. Catholic guilt is famous, funny and gets tons of books commissioned. Anglican guilt is more insidious. Anglicans are not ashamed of their thoughts or their reproductive organs. Anglicans are ashamed of the crucifixion, because they know it would happen again. They can blame Scribes and Pharisees, Pontius Pilate and the base populism of Barabas. But they know it was their own fault. It was humanity's fault and humanity is even less ready for a Messiah now than it was then. In fact, he might have come back already and been detained without charge, or sectioned and medicated.

In any event, Anglicans don't quite share the Catholic love of Easter. Catholics seem to revel in martyrdom, Jesus frozen in time, eternally quoted and never able to clarify anything or correct misinterpretation. Captured, pinned down, set in stone – then risen and yet strangely silent, save for the odd exhortation to sleeping nuns. Catholics love the crucifixion with a passion. Anglicans, not so much. Because a man's death diminished us all, and he hadn't done anything wrong. At least, he hadn't done the thing he was accused of.

I've always hated that great Easter hit, 'There is a Green

Hill Far Away'. As a boy in assembly, I would dissolve into tears when the piano struck up the tune, or attempted to, groaning and clanking and praying for a blind man to fix it. My sister Joy, too, would cry. The two of us, separated by two years and two rows of little, splintered seats would glance at one another for reassurance before water poured down our reddened cheeks. No one else knew, because people don't see what they're not looking for. No one was looking to catch anyone crying because no one expected it. No one else felt it. No one else was pitched into sudden grief by that awful, despairing tune. The other kids were probably normal kids, hearts full of the certainty of coming chocolate. For them, the crucifixion was palatable, delicious even, covered with thick, thick Cadbury goodness. They didn't ask the agonising theological question: if there is an Easter Bunny, how did he let this happen? Only Joy and I, faces hot with distress and embarrassment, wept silently into our hymn books, rehearsing the words 'hayfever' in case of discovery.

You see, I don't celebrate the fact that the Redeemer died to save us from our sins. I think it would be better if he had lived longer, just as it would have been better if Martin Luther King and Malcolm X had lived longer. They'd have got more done and continued their leftward journeys. The dead do not become more powerful, like Obi Wan Kenobi. If that were the case, they wouldn't have been killed.

On the positive side, invoking martyrs is a way of keeping them alive. The problem is that anybody can invoke them and there's nothing they can do about it. I would like Jesus to weave through the crowd, grab the mike and say,

'What's everyone so solemn about? I rose didn't I?' I'd like him to interrupt Holy Communion, and shout, 'Body of Christ? This is the body of Christ – do I look like a fucking Pringle?'

Sunday would probably be a better day to watch the procession, because it will have a happy ending. And we've missed the sunset now, and that would have said much more about God than this grim carnival. We bail out before the end, with the chains of the hood people echoing through the streets around us.

We have a day off before the resurrection and have booked a boat trip to the third Island, Comino. When we arrive at the harbour in search of our boat, we immediately run into some people with leaflets who tell us the trip is cancelled because the sea's too rough, but that we can book to go tomorrow. The price is a lot cheaper than we were quoted so it all seems a little odd. As we drive back up the hill, the phone rings and Katie recognises the number as that of the captain of the boat we're booked to go on. This is all cocked-up now. We've paid a deposit to go tomorrow with people who are obviously business rivals of the bloke we're supposed to be going with today. We try not answering, then decide we can't leave him waiting around so tell him what the others told us and that we've driven off and are now several miles away. The trouble is, you can't get several miles away on Gozo. In fact, he says, 'I think I can still see you. Is it you in a white hire car from Mario?' Katie pauses and says, 'No' in the determined but unconvincing manner of a nine-year-old who's been caught out. 'Look, we don't want to hold you up, so it's best you go without us,' she says assertively and wraps up the conversation with polite regret, and we both feel ashamed and embarrassed. He even knows Mario's Cars. Everyone knows everyone here. He might ring Mario and mention our names. He might kill his competitor, and then we won't even be able to go tomorrow. Somehow, we will be punished.

But the rest of the day goes well. We have a bit of a drive around and find Ta' Cenc, which has a beautiful limestone pavement like the Burren in Ireland, all covered in pretty flowers that we wouldn't see if we came here in summer. It is also the roof of magnificent cliffs. And there's supposed to be a dolmen but apparently it's fallen over. If there is a punishment it is that the beautiful, sympathetically designed hotel there has spa facilities including a heated outdoor pool and we could have gone there on Thursday, but somehow the fact that it's so very different from the Kempinski is heartening, and we hear that tomorrow will be sunny, so perhaps we won't really meet our come-uppance.

Of course we do. Sunday is indeed a beautiful day. This is all much better, we think. The Blue Lagoon will be blue. Yesterday, it would have been beige. The sea looks gorgeous today. *Looks* gorgeous. We're running late, so we climb quickly into a very small boat. Well, it seems small to me. I don't know how many feet it is. Are boats measured in feet? Anyway, it's small, just big enough for about ten people to drown comfortably. In fact, there are only two other couples, so we're not cramped. Not cramped, just in mortal danger. Harbours being sheltered, we can't really see what kind of mood the Mediterranean is in. It is in a rage. Neptune is pissed-off about something, while Calypso and her siren mates are on outlying rocks screaming, 'Die you bastards!'

I can't tell you the height of the waves. I've read about 40-foot waves but waves don't stay up long enough, neither does the sea stay still enough to guess, let alone measure, the height of a wave. All I know is that it's quite likely that I am about to become an interesting story for one of my descendants researching his family tree. Katie assures me she can save me. She is a very strong swimmer. She'll swim anything at any time. That's why I've never taken her to the west of Ireland. She'd ask, 'How far's America?' and be off. But she won't be able to save me. My luck doesn't work that way.

I have been very lucky in my life, but I'm mishap-prone. I grew up without deprivation or trauma in a warm and funny family. I've never done a day's work and yet I've been very comfortable. I've been very lucky. But if I were to laugh in the face of danger, danger would smash mine in. If I went hang-gliding, I'd land in quicksand, fall down a mine-shaft or crash into the side of an iceberg. Falling out of this fucking stupid boat and drowning while researching an extremely tangential part of my family history is exactly the kind of thing that would happen to me. I'll do exactly whatever it is you're not supposed to do when you fall in water. Katie will search for a while, get irritated and give up. And BBC Radio news will ring someone I don't like for a quote.

But Fortune smiles upon us, or at least rolls her eyes and sighs, 'Go on, then, live.' We chug into the Blue Lagoon, which is blue, and moor up. Katie, who grew up by the river and knows about boat stuff, asks the skipper, 'Will you get back all right?' He replies, 'Hopefully', not looking hopeful. I thought he'd laugh and say, 'You English!' thinking us the most frightful, pasty-faced milksops; but he casts me a look that says, 'You have no idea how close to death you have just been.'

And we have to do it all on the way back unless we charter a helicopter to rescue us. We have a choice of two, four, or six hours on the island. I very much want the return journey over with, and decide that two hours is ample, which it is, because Comino is tiny and quite dull. It's beautiful, but I'm really not in the mood. I want the return journey to be over with.

So we have a bit of a walk, Katie has a bit of swim and I go in up to my waist and it's time to go. We hope the sea has calmed. It hasn't; it's worse than before. I'm trying not to cry. The leaflet people who duped us out of yesterday's excursion are bastards. People will have to campaign for them to be held accountable for my death. Oh Christ, I don't even want a public inquiry, just let me live and I'll never complain about anything again.

Oh, we're back. That will become a humorous holiday anecdote.

We explore more bits of Gozo during the afternoon, and then have to decide whether we want to go to Dwejra for the sunset or back to Xhara for tonight's procession. It's been very sunny and we didn't like Friday's procession so we settle on a rocky seat by the sea to the left of the Azure Window and watch as the sun disappears into clouds on the horizon. Nothing like a sunset happens and we've missed the procession with a happy ending. We've done things the wrong way round. We head back into Xhara and see people clearing up and the risen Christ looking all happy on the stage in front of the church flanked by some dishevelled curtains hanging from a wooden doorframe. I'm guessing that they were pulled open to reveal him by way of a finale and he got a round of applause, and that if I'd seen it I wouldn't have felt so negative about popery. And it was a shit sunset. See how unlucky am I?

Nonetheless, Monday dawns, Jesus is safely on his Father's right hand, and we're off on the ferry to the main island to go to Valetta where Mum lived. It's our last whole day and we planned to get up at six to make the most of the day, but we roll up at the harbour at about noon, and make it to Valetta at lunchtime.

Driving into the city in which my mother spent her early years, I am gripped by two thoughts: 'Where will we park?' and 'Where will we eat?' Surprisingly, there are lots of free parking spaces in the centre, so we pull up on what an old engraved sign on the wall tells us was once 'Old Bakery Street'. The guidebook only deals in the old colonial English names for things, and it turns out that one of its recommended restaurants is right behind us. Given that we are not here to eat, I don't know why we don't grab a sandwich. There is even a Marks and Spencer; we could see if their sandwiches are the same. Instead, we slavishly follow the guidebook and go to an 'authentic' place. It is rather unprepossessing, but I think that's a good sign. We go in and there's no menu – only what they have that day. I think that's an extremely good sign. I hate choice. It just makes me upset because I'm bound to order something I don't want and then look longingly at the plates of everyone else in the restaurant wishing I was having what they're having. It's not so much the disappointment as the fact that it's my mistake, my fault, because it was my choice. I wish there were restaurants where they just gave you your tea on your lap in front of the telly, at half past six.

Anyway, we order starters, and we're only in town for a few hours, so that's cutting our noses off to spite our faces, but the starter is a meze and it's delicious. In fact, all the starters here have been delicious but followed by disappointing main courses, so just having a starter would have been a good bet, and an hour or so after we sit down comes the main course, a slightly revolting dish of tuna in plain wrong sauce. It's so horrible that we don't want it, but because we're too full to eat it anyway after our meze, we have it wrapped to go, as though we might find a use for it later.

Finally we start to explore Valetta. It's actually very nice, although a bit decrepit. I expected it all to be ugly and modern because it was heavily bombed in the war, but most of the buildings look at least a century old. Mum can remember that she lived in Floriana, which is only a ten-minute walk from the centre, but I want to see the harbour first because it was there that her father worked and what colonial Malta was all about. The Grand Harbour is indeed grand. It's huge and there are lots of old ware-houses; trying to work out where the NAAFI stores were without help will be impossible. I haven't planned this at all. I would probably benefit from the help of a naval historian.

There are what look to be Royal Navy buildings on the other side of the harbour. Indeed, something called HMS *Argyle* is moored up on this side, and there are servicemen in Middle East camouflage fatigues on it. I would approach to ask what they're doing here but there's a sign saying something about a high level of terrorist alert and they might shoot me. There are cruise ships coming and going too, and what look like functioning dockyards over the water. It hasn't been completely taken over by marina development. It's quite possible Grandpa's old office hasn't yet been converted into a warehouse apartment. And even if it is, the building is probably still there. Somewhere.

I am proposing to follow one of the recommended walking tours, which leads through Floriana from the city gate. Floriana is Valetta's only suburb and it's right next to it. The whole of Valetta is barely one square mile. One of the things Mum remembers is a large church, which I think must be the church of St Publius. She told me there was an earthquake one day, and the family ran out of their flat to take refuge in the grounds of the church. Police told them to move along because there was a danger of the ground giving way. We arrive at St Publius. There are strange round stones in front of the church. Mum thought the police were telling them get off the 'gravestones' for fear the graves would open up. Looking in the guidebook, I see the strange round flat stones in front of the church are the caps of *grainstores*. Given that Mum left when she was eight, the fact that she remembers the misheard word is remarkable in itself.

I am about to lead us off on the tour, when Katie says, 'Hang on, if your mum's family ran from their flat to the nearest open space, it must have been one of those flats over there.' I am immediately annoyed because my whole schedule has been thrown out by a bout of logic. There are a handful of streets around the main drag, Triq Sant Anna.

The other streets in Floriana are all near to gardens that would have been close enough to run to. So she must have lived on one of these streets. The flats all appear to be Victorian. It would have looked much as it does now. And it was almost certainly here. Some of the shops on the main street still have old frontages, notably the dispensary, where Grandma, I'm sure, whiled away many an hour, being as they termed it then, 'delicate'. Katie takes some photos, and we hope they might jog Mum's memory. Then we have a stroll around the botanical gardens, which she remembers strolling in on a Sunday.

It's getting cold and I've lost interest in the walking tour, having come as close as I'm likely to get to connecting with my mum's past. I am quite emotional. This wouldn't be exciting enough for television and it's just as well I'm not doing it for that purpose. I can imagine the pained look of the person whose job it would be to tell me that this was not what they were hoping for and that we're really going to have to rethink this whole segment of the programme. And I can see me insisting that we film this because it's about my mum, and them saying they understand that completely but wouldn't she prefer to see her brother's grave in France and maybe we could actually film her watching the footage and ideally crying.

One last thing to do is to go for a coffee in Café Cordina, which is old and famous for its ice creams. Mum remembers a café that was famous for its ice-creams, and the décor is such that no one could forget it, so Katie takes photos, I picture Mum sitting here eating ice cream and then we set off for the ferry.

We get lost, miss the boat and have to wait an hour. The

weather has turned stormy. The ferry, of the standard roll-on-roll-over type, was lurching a little on the way over, but going back it's worse. I'd like a day to pass without my nearly drowning. I don't know if a large car ferry can buck and toss, but that seems to me to be what this boat is doing, and my stomach is churning. Being sick in the boat yesterday was the least of my fears, and we were washed down by the sea every few seconds anyway, but here and now, I'm seriously considering the possibility of producing something akin to the sauce the tuna came in. Best to think of something else.

We find a table to hold onto in the cafeteria, and are joined by a very nice lady, who assures us that, although this is a Force 8 gale, the ferry will not sink and that it's often like this. She is also very proud of Gozo in a nice way. I'm not big on pride. It is, after all, one of the Seven Dwarves of the Apocalypse. But when people take a pride in their home that's nothing to do with triumphalist notions of greatness, it can be very endearing. It's the difference between confidence and arrogance. And she knows loads about her island. Much more than British people know about our island. She tells us that there are a large number of endemic species both of flora and fauna and that, although there is not a great diversity among vertebrates, there is a great variety of invertebrates. How many British people on a ferry would even know the difference? I only know because I have a back problem. And I'm sitting smiling and nodding at this charming and knowledgeable lady, thinking, 'Pray God, don't let me throw up in her face.'

We don't die, for the second time in two days, and we

make the short drive back to Xhara to sleep and get ready for our departure.

On our last day, we have a final drive around. We find San Blas, a popular beach reputed to be similar to Ramla. But the sea has washed all the sand away and it looks nothing like its pictures. Mario's wife comes to take the hire car away and Mario drives us back to the ferry to Malta, where we only got back from late last night.

There is not much to buy at the airport. Café Cordina has its own brand, and there's a traditional non-perishable cake that Mum's taste buds might recall. I finally have my pale ale, which is okay, and we board the plane. There's a movie but we balk at paying three pounds for earphones, and you can get the gist of it without them. Katie's mum picks us up from Gatwick and we get home about bedtime. Disappointingly, there is no mountain of post and hardly any voicemail. I always look forward to being annoyed at what a backlog I have to deal with, another justification for never going away.

I have been denied email access, so first thing in the morning, I'm online. I'm feeling quite fired-up about the successes of my quest. My big failure was that I didn't find where Grandpa worked, and it occurs to me only now that it's the sort of thing I ought to have researched before leaving. Still, it would be good to find out now in case we go back. But I doubt it will be easy to find out because NAAFI aren't in Valetta any more, this was 80 years ago and unless something remarkable occurred there, it's unlikely that there'll be an address. So I google 'NAAFI stores Valetta'. And I learn that the NAAFI was housed in St James Cavalier, once a fortification, now the arts centre where Katie stopped to use the toilet when we were looking for the start of the walking tour. So I have, after all, stood outside the place where my grandfather worked from 1926 to 1932, while my girlfriend peed in it.

CHAPTER 4

What About All This Christopher Wren Stuff, Then?

I decide to get down to exploring one of the family legends. Are we or are we not descended from Sir Christopher Wren? With some horror, I find that I might be able to uncover the truth within about five minutes. Where's the drama in that? I type 'Sir Christopher Wren descendants' into a search engine and find a site that has a whole family tree. But then I see it's only got 'male line descendants'. This means that only the offspring of every male descendant is listed. I don't know why the author of this quite impressive piece of work thinks that it's worth going to all that trouble and then leaving out the children of the daughters of each generation. I know why Prince Harry, the youngest of the Queen's grandchildren, has a greater legal claim to the throne than his aunt. It is to preserve dynastic power in the hands of men. And if we are to have a royal family at all, it seems right that it should be completely unjust and antiquated. The whole of idea of monarchy is based on such an appalling principle that its internal agenda might as well be as batty as they can make it.

I am not opposed to nepotism. It seems to me that, if we are so selfish and self-aggrandising as to spill children onto the surface of this wretched orb, then we have a responsibility to make them as happy as possible. I am not one of those who think we should avoid giving them a cushy start. If I could buy a house for my daughter, I would. If I could give her a trust fund, I would. True, she would not know what it is to struggle, but why would I want her to have to struggle? I know people say that the tribulations of their lives have made them better people, but that's how they console themselves. If I'd never had back pain, I'd never have discovered the joy of Nurofen, but clearly I'd be happier without either. The Nietzschean idea that what doesn't destroy us makes us stronger is romantic, self-flagellating, proto-fascist bollocks. People can only take so much. If you damage us, we are damaged. The abused do not necessarily become the abuser; to suggest they always do is a great insult to those who don't. But there is a marked human propensity for the shat-upon to shit on others. Suffering might toughen us, but history shows us that, when the going gets tough, the tough massacre the people in the next village.

Moreover you can teach a child that she is lucky to have comfort and security without plunging her into pain and peril to reinforce the point. Worry is a miserable, debilitating and disabling feeling. And the world is a much more worrying place than it was when I was growing up. If I can pull strings for my daughter, I will. She can always change her name to disguise the fact. If she does develop an interest in comedy, which she hasn't, it shouldn't be surprising given that she's grown up in the midst of it. And children of the famous may get a head start but they still have to prove themselves; they need talent of their own. Liza Tarbuck, for example, is a funny, talented and very appealing person in her own right. One wonders where she gets it from.

Where were we? Oh yes, googling Sir Christopher Wren and wondering why anyone would ignore female line descendants. I suppose that, if your name is Wren you'll only be interested in the men. I don't have that luxury with the name Hardy because of the bastardy. And why would I only be interested in Hardys? But I suspect that the emphasis on Sir Christopher's male line is not because only people with the name Wren want to find out if they related to him but rather that *all* people called Wren want to find out if they are. A surprising number of people ask me if I am related to Oliver Hardy and/or Thomas. Most people mean the poet and novelist, but I've also been asked if the other Thomas Hardy, in whose arms died Horatio Nelson, is any relation. I have as yet no evidence to the contrary but if we were related I'm sure I would have been told by now.

Sir Christopher Wren married twice. His second wife, Jane Fitzwilliam had two children, Jane and William, who had no children. But his first wife, Faith Coghill, had two sons, Gilbert and Christopher. Christopher junior married twice. His second wife, Constance Middleton-Burgoyne had one son, Stephen, who never married. But Christopher junior's first wife, Mary Husard, had another Christopher who married Mary Bartlett, who bore him seven children. Suddenly the search looks more hopeful.

Of the seven, four married. Christopher married Martha Roberts, Thomas married Margaret Hay. Henrietta and Sarah also married but their kids won't be on this family tree so I'll save them up and carry on down the male lines.

Thomas and Margaret seem to have had no children but Christopher and Martha had three. The first, Martha, and second, Christopher David, appear to have died as infants. Another, Christopher survived and married four times. This wasn't because of divorce; three of his wives died. Christ, what miserable times. It seems that herbal medicine has its limitations. Three of the wives each gave him a daughter. So now the website departs from its patriarchal principle and follows the line of the only daughter to marry, Theodosia, who marries Chandos Wren-Hoskyns and has one daughter, Catherine, who marries Charles Pigott but dies childless in 1911. At the bottom of the page is the solemn announcement, 'Catherine Wren Hoskyns was the last known direct descendant from the line of Sir Christopher Wren', despite the fact that the male line actually ended with her grandfather in 1828. Perhaps when the last man dies you're allowed to carry on with the best available woman. In any case, this brings me to several years after Grandma's birth with not a Monk in sight. So let's have a go at some of the female lines.

Two of Sir Christopher's great-granddaughters, Henrietta and Sarah, seem to have married. Googling Sarah and her husband James West, I find a website that tells me that they had a son, James, who married Anne Roberts in 1808 and 'had issue'. It doesn't go any further but possibly brings me close enough to the present to see whether the issue was one of my ancestors. I post the following on the message board: 'There is a family myth/legend that we are descended from Sir Christopher Wren. I have exhausted male line descendants. My only remaining leads are his great-granddaughters Henrietta Wren (1739–1805) who married Clement Newman in 1771, and Sarah Wren

(1751–1836) who married James West in 1774, had a son James, who married Anne Roberts and "had issue". I can't get any further with those two lines of inquiry. Does anyone have any ideas?' I'm glad that at least I can offer specific dates – people whose hobby is ancestry seem to research solely by posting up messages that read, 'My grandmother was born somewhere. Does anybody know who she was? Her name was Gran, or maybe Nana, and I think she was born in this country or abroad. My dad thinks she might have been French but doesn't know because she ran away before he was born and his father died in childbirth or might have been Charles I. Can anyone help me?'

I'm a little worried about sending my email address into cyberspace. My gut tells me that I've entered a world populated by neo-fascists and sex offenders. I long for the clean fresh air of the National Archives.

At some point I shall work backwards through my ancestry to find anyone called West or Newman but it's not looking hopeful that the story is true. But what the hell? Statistically, I must be descended from someone famous. I should have thought everyone is. I'm rather hoping for Sitting Bull or Mary Magdalene.

But it occurs to me, whether or not I'm descended from anyone famous, what difference does it make? It's not an achievement of mine. I have never designed a cathedral, still less led the Sioux nation to victory, or been the first person to chat with the risen Christ. I have done very little. In fact, when Sir Christopher designed St Paul's, he was about the age I am now, and I'm not even close to designing anything. I can't even plan my own kitchen on the squared paper they give you in Ikea.

But then I come full circle and decide it would be quite nice to point to St Paul's and say, '*We* made that.' So I am holding on to the dream, but the search goes on hold for now.

CHAPTER 5

Some Time Later

Not long after we got back from Gozo, I went into a panic. I realised that I had written very little stand-up material in the past year and was going to have to come up with a new live show. I go back to the same towns every two years, and, if the show evolves as it should, it's pretty much new by the time I return. But looking at my notebooks I could see that very little had changed. I was going to do 30 or 40 dates in the autumn, and most of them I'd played in 2006 or 2007. I needed to write a whole new show from scratch. The family history research had to be pushed to one side.

And we were still touring *Clue*. Humph nearly made it to the end of the tour. He only missed one gig. He'd tried to postpone his operation until we'd finished but was taken into hospital suddenly after a check-up and had to miss the last show in Bournemouth. Various people had been on stand-by in case he had to pull out of the tour; Fred MacAulay cancelled a family holiday so he could dep in Edinburgh if necessary. But Humph held on and got through nearly all of the dates.

Our greatest triumph was the Hammersmith Apollo. Three and a half thousand people on their feet for Humph, many of them in tears. And he played his trumpet solo of 'We'll Meet Again' perfectly. It was the show's finale. Lately, he'd been struggling with it, but it was absolutely perfect that night. Thankfully, the sound was recorded. I listen to it sometimes. Years ago, I wouldn't have expected to come to love a Vera Lynn classic, but Humph's solo from that night in Hammersmith means an awful lot to me because I was there with him and I'm so proud of that, and because I loved him and he died not long after.

The Bournemouth show without him was horrible. We were still hoping that Humph would pull through, but the operation the previous morning had not gone well and there were complications. Rob Brydon depped and did very well in difficult circumstances. But Humph was in hospital and, as it turned out, he was dying. That was Tuesday. He went on the Friday. Friends were told he had a few hours left and that we could visit if we liked. I nearly went up to see him. Barry Cryer did, and the band were all there. But I'd visited a few days before the op and he was radiant. I still have that picture in my mind. I spoke to Susan, his partner, and said I'd like to remember him like that, and she thought I might be wise not to come up. I was very uncertain then, but now I think it was the right decision. I was present when Linda Smith died, as I'd planned to be. It was right that I was there, but I'd rather that last image of her was not so vivid in my mind.

There was a lot to do after Humph's passing. I wrote tributes in the *Independent on Sunday* and in the *Guardian*, and gave interviews for tributes on radio and television. I also spoke at his funeral. After the funeral, we went back to his house. It was the first time many of us had been there. It might have felt like an honour but instead it felt like an intrusion. He hadn't invited us, after all.

I've kept in touch with Susan, and the band; and occasionally see members of Humph's family. I've done two gigs with the band, because they sometimes have guest hosts to introduce numbers and do some chat in between. It's weird to dep for Humph. I haven't tried doing much of my own material so far, mostly just pub gags, which seems appropriate because I'm only there to fill in. They're a great band, musically and personally, and Humph always looked after them although, increasingly, they looked after him. He loved them and they loved him, so I have a bond with them.

It's now the middle of January and I'm only just getting back into researching my family history with some difficulty. The *News Quiz* has started up again and that can take up any amount of time. I can read any newspaper, watch or listen to any news broadcast, and it's work. I'm going to have to limit my *News Quiz* preparations to one day a week. But, in poring over the lighter stories, this week, I did find out that the 1911 Census is now online. The hook used in most coverage seems to be that David Beckham had humble ancestors. Why this is remarkable, I don't know. I don't think anyone imagined he had royal blood. He's not that dim.

I register with the 1911 census website and go straight for the Hardys. Knowing that my grandad Lionel was from Hitchin in Hertfordshire, I type that in. This is good, it seems censuses give names, ages, places of birth and occupations.

Lionel is at school, aged 11. His brother's name was Douglas, which I didn't know, but that's my dad's middle name. His dad, Alfred Hardy, was an engineers' pattern maker, which I knew. His mum, Annie, was a telephone operator, of whom there can't have been many in those days. Alfred is from Basingstoke; Annie is a local girl. And they had a servant! I presume she lived in if she's included in the household. She's only 16 and her name was Ruby Saunders. Pattern making and working in an Edwardian call centre must have been lucrative occupations. Douglas is still only seven and appears not to go to school. Annie's working so I suppose childcare is a large part of Ruby's duties. I find myself wanting to find out about Ruby. For some reason I want to know that my great-grandparents treated her all right.

It's also interesting to me because, of all my grandparents, my mum's mum Becky seemed to be the most posh, and yet I've been discovering that her antecedents were not very grand at all. Lionel and Audrey were always much more down-to-earth than Rebecca and Herbert. Lionel and Andrey lived in a small, rented terraced house for the most of their marriage. They didn't get a bathroom or inside toilet until the sixties; I remember it going in. And yet Grandad's family had a servant. Perhaps Ruby's parents were family friends and they died, so employing her was a kindness. This may sound silly but I'm slightly ashamed; I feel a very tiny bit of what I imagine people feel when they find out their ancestors were slave-owners. Becky and Herbert's servants in Malta are more understandable – it went with the job – but a servant in Hitchin is a little weird. But, then, people today have cleaners and childminders, they just don't call them servants. And, even if Ruby was soundly beaten, it's not me doing it, but my great-grand-parent. I'm not worried, so get off my case and stop looking at me.

The only other information available is the address so I google 3 Tilehouse Street to see if it's still there. Blow me, it is. This makes me want to go all the way to Hitchin to see where Grandad lived. But why? He might have only lived there for six months. Why did I have no interest in this when Grandad was alive? It's now the Pentangle Design Centre. Nothing will be the same. A design company's not going to move into a building and not change anything. It's probably a computer simulation now.

I decide to look up my other grandparents, see where they lived. Nan takes some finding, but finally here she is. The census gives her age as eight, which is about right. Marjorie's two and Hilda's not there so I'm guessing she had already died. The family are living in Mytchett Road, Frimley Green. They moved from Betchworth, where Nan was born, after the accident. I google Jesmond Cottages but nothing comes up. I used to get my hair cut in Frimley Green. It might even have been in the same place. The row of buildings the barber's shop was in looked like converted cottages, except that he'd had the shop designed with a Wild West theme to appeal to young lads. I seem to recall that he even dressed as a cowboy, but that might be a dream. In any event, I think his behaviour would arouse suspicions today.

Nan's dad, Albert Hewett, is from Crondall, in Hampshire; her mum, Clara, from Guildford in Surrey. So far, Hitchin is as exotic as I get. I suppose I should try to find Herbert and Rebecca, Mum's parents.

Becky is living with her mum, Eliza, who is still listed as married, but her dad isn't there. Perhaps he's in a nursing home. Eliza is from Arundel, which I knew. Her 31-year-old brother, Harry, is still registered as living at home, but he's in the navy so he's probably mostly away. Eva, my great-aunt, is 19 and in service. She goes on to become a bootlegger in New York so I'm very interested in her. Esther, Grandma's younger sister, is 12 and at school. There is a month-old 'Nurse Child' called Frederick Hill. What's a nurse child, and who is he? Rebecca is 14 and not doing anything. She was, as I've mentioned, delicate. People aren't delicate anymore. They have intolerances and deficit disorders. 'Delicate' is a wonderfully unspecific condition, from the time when people were 'sickly', 'highly strung' or 'fragile'.

Herbert is 21, a clerk and living with an old lady called Charlotte Bridle (not Brioche) who must be his maternal grandmother. She's 70 and was born in Borough, near London Bridge. I am pleased that I have a forebear from the capital. Plus it gives me an excuse to go to Borough Market. I've always wanted to go there. It says she is the mother of the head of household, who is called Henry Flower. Herbert and Henry Stagg – brothers, I guess – are down as Flower's nephews. That can't be right; Flower must actually be Charlotte's son-in-law. His wife, Ellen, must be her daughter, and the boys' aunt. It took me quite a long time to work that out, confused as I was by Charlotte being down as Flower's mother. The fact that census-takers made such elementary mistakes even in the days before computers makes me realise the fragility of this whole method of research. Combined with scratchy writing and identical names, I'd say it means most people's family trees are probably bollocks.

Nonetheless, this all seems way too easy. With care and cross-checking, you can get a long way without ever standing up. I thought finding your ancestors meant you had to dig up the remains of tsars and put hair follicles into little ziplock plastic bags using tweezers, but it's now all online. The day can't be far away when the police can solve crime using Google Felony.

I decide to go on the site Richard uses and to borrow his password. In the early eighties, Richard went to records offices and corresponded with people all over the world. I haven't asked him whether he is at all bitter about the hours he spent in those days, when he could just have waited a few years. I imagine he must feel a bit like Milton's daughters would have felt if he had just finished dictating *Paradise Lost* to them and then been given a voice-activated computer.

I can't replicate Rick's experience because technology has moved so far; I feel I might as well plagiarise some of his research so we don't both waste a big chunk of our lives. What if I were to try and ignore his work and start from scratch using the Internet, only to find next year that my entire family history is available as a brain implant?

On the other hand, I do want to feel a sense of achievement. I am going to find out how to do this online, but I'm going to have Richard's two huge ring binders of stuff by my side as my guardian angels. And when I'm getting good at it, I'll have a crack at the Hardy dynasty, because Rick didn't get far exploring the shameful bastardy in my bloodline.

Let me begin digging online. I check out Annie, who was a Hitchin girl, daughter of Henry and Sarah Aylott, and born 1874 or 1875. Oh blimey, Hertfordshire is absolutely full of Aylotts. But crucially, I find that Alfred Hardy's dad, the alleged bastard, was called Charles. So let's pursue Charles and Alfred together. Here they are on the 1881 census, living on Wendover Street in Basingstoke. Charles is 32, married to Jane, 31. Both were born around Basingstoke. The kids are Francis, who is a girl, aged 16 working as a servant, Charles junior, who is 11, and nine-year-old Alfred. Both the boys are 'scholars'. I love the fact that school children used to be called scholars as an occupation.

In 1891, Alfred is 19 and a pattern-maker's apprentice. That makes sense because later on he's a pattern maker. This is like time travel. His dad is doing something to boilers. I can't make out what Charles junior does. There are lodgers. One is Henery Hatter from Bedfordshire. What a great name. Is Henery a variant of Henry or is it a mistake originating in the song about Henry VIII?

I jump forward to 1901. Lionel is one. The family live in Nightingale Road in Hitchin. I google the address...it's for sale! I could go there posing as a potential buyer. Or propose a new property/ancestry show to Channel 4 called *Secret Genealogist in the Attic*. Minor celebrities try to buy their grandparents' homes and return them to their original squalor.

I look up Charles and Jane Hardy in 1901 to see if they're still alive. They are, and they've also moved to Hitchin. Well, I've established one thing. Five of my eight great-grandparents were born in the south-east of England. I haven't yet found Becky's dad, or either of Herbert's parents on a census. I've noted that Herbert's grandmother Charlotte Bridle was from Borough but I'll hang fire on finding out about his parents, and build anticipation in the hope that one of them was an Inuit or some kind of animal.

What about Douglas Hardy, my great-uncle who died in police custody? Looking him up, I've found he's on the family tree of someone else. So I'm emailing them to find out the connection. I continue to look for him but find only his birth in July 1903.

I keep scrolling through Hardys until I find someone called Ronald Allan Hardy, born in Hitchin to Alfred Hardy in May 1906. Clearly Grandad had another brother. Excitedly, I search for him. Here he is in the register of deaths. He died in September 1906. His age is listed as 0. I look at other deaths. Many of the deceased are aged 0. I feel deflated and stupid. Of course the boy died. Otherwise he'd have appeared in the 1911 census.

And I feel sad for my great-grandparents, whom I never knew, and my grandad, whom I did know. Shouldn't I have known he had two brothers – lost two brothers? Maybe there were so many infant deaths then that it wasn't something people brought up years later. But Grandad would have remembered, being seven and presumably proud of his new baby brother. Maybe the boy was sick from birth. Should I say anything to Dad? I decide to call Richard and see if he knows anything more.

Richard doesn't know. So I ask him if he knows why Grandma's father, who he tells me was called Thomas, is alive but not living with his family in 1911 and who the 'Nurse Child' might be. He suggests I email Brian, the cousin in America, since he has done so much work researching the Monk and Jones lines, Thomas Monk and Eliza Jones being the parents of my grandmother, Becky, and his grandmother, Esther. So I email all the way to America.

CHAPTER 6

Brian Replies

rian emails me back. He thinks Thomas Monk, our
shared great-grandfather, was probably ill in hospital
in 1911, but doesn't know where. As for the 'Nurse
Child', he raises two possibilities: the family had a live-in
nurse who was not in on the night of the census; or they
minded the child while a friend, or paying parent, was at
work. Frederick is only one month old. My own thinking is
that our great-grandmother, Eliza, was a midwife and was
caring for a sickly newborn.

More importantly, I'm now officially in touch with Brian.
He says he'll call me on Saturday about 6 p.m. UK time. He
is an incredibly warm, friendly and helpful man. He tells me
that, inspired by the work Richard had done when they met
at the family reunion – the one at which the Americans
confessed to having no idea who the Hardy family were – he
embarked on his own quest to trace the Monk and Jones
families, as well as his other ancestors. He says he has spent
'almost fifteen years and thousands of hours doing this'. This
means a number of things. One, there is a mountain of stuff
already done, which is useful. Two, it means it would be silly
for me to cover the same ground. Three, I can use his work

and still have three other sets of great-grandparents to investigate. Four, that will take bloody ages.

While Brian is on the phone, I run some of Becky's family legends by him. The one I always liked best was that our great-aunt Eva was a bootlegger in New York. Brian says that, as far as he knows, Eva was never in New York. Neither can he shed any light at all on the Christopher Wren story. But what about Eliza Jones's father, Matthew, having been head gardener on the Duke of Norfolk's estate? I refer to notes Richard took when he interviewed my grandma:

> The two men had a close relationship and were often seen wandering in the grounds deep in discussion. One of the Duke's plans was to build a Roman Catholic church in Arundel. His dearest wish was that Matthew would become a convert to RC. He was a devout Protestant and stuck to his beliefs, even when the church was completed.

Brian is dubious. In the 1841 census, aged 20, Matthew is indeed a gardener. But in 1851, he is a 'labourer of beer and lodging house keeper'.

I suspect bad penmanship when it comes to 'labourer of beer' but why would the head gardener on a large estate go off to run a boarding house at the age of 30? Bad back maybe? Nonetheless, Brian is certain that Matthew worked on the estate, which means a visit to Arundel Castle seems in order. I promise to send Brian pictures of gravestones, if I can find them, so that's a day out when the weather gets warmer.

So what about Thomas Monk, Grandma's father, having been a royal bodyguard? Richard's research yielded up the certificate of his marriage to Eliza in 1876. He is indeed a policeman, living in Fulham, London. But Brian says that he was a dockyard labourer in 1871, a general labourer in 1881 and a greengrocer thereafter. This strikes me as fishy. Clearly he can't hold down a steady job, but to go from being a copper to a labourer suggests to me that something went wrong in the course of his duties. To my knowledge, no members of the Royal Family were assassinated at that time, something that might have caused the Met to think Thomas wasn't cut out for the job. Perhaps Eliza was worried about him or the hours were unsocial, but if he left the force of his own volition, couldn't he have got a better job than 'general labourer'? Was he laid off? Were hundreds of bobbies made redundant because of a lack of crime in Victorian London? I'm sure a *Daily Mail* leader writer would favour that view of history. It's an interesting line of investigation and it's cop stuff so it'll be like opening a cold case, and there can be flashbacks or reconstructions, so that'll be good.

What about Becky's big story, the one about the Monk family land in Kent? Brian can't shed any light on this. I decide to compare the documents I have with Becky's account, as recorded by Richard in 1983. I say goodbye to Brian, who is going to email me a load of stuff as soon as he gets off the phone.

So how does the reality match up with Becky's fables? Before finding out, I might as well tell you the whole story, as it's almost certainly more fun than the truth.

According to my grandmother, her grandfather was the elder son of a wealthy landowning couple who lived in Sevenoaks in Kent. The mother favoured the younger son, and wanted him to inherit the estate. Her elder son fancied himself as a horse-rider and entered a wager with another young man. They arranged to 'borrow' two horses – at that time horse-stealing was punishable by death.

His mother heard of this wager and arranged for the law to apprehend the elder son for horse-stealing at the end of the race. His brother discovered what their mother intended to do and went to warn his brother. The only solution was for the elder brother to run away to sea. A friend had a boat and was willing to take him on.

In the absence of the elder son, the estate passed into Chancery on the death of his father (isn't this *Bleak House*?). The younger son, who had no children, could not inherit because it could not be proved that his brother was dead. Meanwhile, my great-great-grandfather rose to the ranks of captain, and his son, Becky's dad, was born at sea.

After the birth of Becky's father, her grandfather went back to sea without his family. He went down with his ship. Becky's father, Thomas Monk, tried all his life to claim his inheritance but although he possessed various birth and marriage certificates, he was unable to gain it. He spent a lot of time at Somerset House (the old records office) and at Lewis's the solicitors. In the end, totally disillusioned, he destroyed all the evidence in his possession.

This implies that all records of this remarkable story were lost. But the originals of certificates of births, deaths and marriages were kept at Somerset House and will now be at Kew. I'm afraid this story mightn't take much unravelling. I decide to do some digging of my own before looking at what Richard and Brian have done. Let's begin with the births at sea.

It seems to me that to give birth on a boat you have to be a passenger, or a prisoner of some kind, and I'm sure sea captains don't traditionally bring their wives on voyages. That would obviously have to be the rule, because, wherever in the world a sea captain sails to, his wife is bound to say, 'Well, why don't I come along and we can make a trip of it?' It wouldn't matter to her if he were taking slaves to the New World – 'Marjorie says Florida's lovely' – or convicts to Australia – 'You could drop me off at New Zealand; my sister's been on at me to visit since she and Graham moved out there.' Without a no-wives rule, there would have been chaos.

I google 'wives on board' and hope I don't pull up a porn site. Oh bugger. The Historical Maritime Society tells me I'm completely wrong and loads of women have been on ships, some as prostitutes, some as maids, some masquerading as men – which I thought you could only get away with in a Shakespearian comedy – and a great many as wives. Wives even served in the Battle of the Nile in 1798; one gave birth on the *Goliath* in the heat of battle. Rather marvellously, the last line in this exhaustive study reads: 'As re-enactors, we are doubly fortunate that women can take an active role on board ship and still remain women without having to dress up as men.' Apart, presumably, from the ones playing women who dressed up as men.

My thanks to the re-enactors and now I want to see if there are any cases of women spawning on ships closer to the time when my great-grandfather was born.

Nothing. But I still want to see how far I can get on the web before cheating by diving into Richard and Brian's research. So, armed only with the names of Thomas and Eliza Monk, I am able to track his birth down to Sheerness on the

Isle of Sheppey in Kent in 1848 or 1847. Might it say he was born in a town even if he was born at sea?

I would like to find everything for myself (well, I'd quite like it), but I can no longer pretend I don't have a bunch of birth, death and marriage certificates in the stuff Richard gave me, and the emails from Brian that are arriving even as I write. Foraging in the big blue folder, I find the wedding certificate of Becky's grandfather, Thomas Monk. He married Frances Gambell in 1840 on the Isle of Sheppey. Both signed with an 'X'. Would the son of a landowner have been illiterate? It does say he's a seaman. On the marriage certificate, his address is indeed a ship, the HMS *Ocean*. Frances's dad was Thomas Gambell, a shipwright, probably in Sheerness, which was a major shipbuilding port at one time. Thomas Monk's father, Edward, was a dredgerman – a man who trawled for shellfish. I wonder, how many dredgermen owned large country estates in Sevenoaks? That appears to be that for the lost land.

Brian has done a mountain of research. Edward was born in 1788 and his wife Harriet Gane in 1798. Looking back at my Christopher Wren research, I see that, 'My only remaining leads are his great-granddaughters Henrietta Wren (1739–1805) who married Clement Newman in 1771, and Sarah Wren (1751–1836) who married James West in 1774, and had a son, James, who married Anne Roberts and "had issue".' So I'm looking for a Roberts or possibly a Newman. Becky told us it's the Monk line that leads to Wren. The only way that could be right is if Edward's mother, Mary, was the daughter of Henrietta and Clement Newman, and gave birth to him aged about sixteen. I suppose it's possible. I'll have to come back to it.

For now, here's the birth certificate of Grandma's dad, Thomas Monk junior, born 27 September 1847, and registered by his mum on 6 November. His mum's address is Chapel Street Place in Sheerness. Well, that doesn't mean he wasn't born at sea; I'm still hoping that's true. Brian has researched the HMS *Ocean* and found that from 1838 to 1848, it was a guard ship in the harbour at Sheerness, so perhaps Frances came aboard to drop, there being a doctor available. Or maybe Thomas senior forgot his sandwiches and she gave birth while bringing them to him.

Here is the marriage certificate from 1876 that says Thomas junior's a policeman in Fulham, and has his wife Eliza's dad, Matthew, down as a gardener. So 'labourer of beer and lodging house keeper' was definitely a sabbatical and he went back to gardening.

Where to now? Let's try and find out about Thomas Monk the policeman. No one's done anything on this and Brian really hopes I will. I might as well start with the Metropolitan Police website.

CHAPTER 7

The Met

I go first to the History of the Met website and am drawn to the Book of Remembrance. I am immediately struck by the number of officers who have died while on duty or as a result of their work. I'm looking at the years 1829 to 1899. An alarming number of officers drowned falling into rivers, canals and docks while on night duty. I make it 22. Most of the other deaths were also accidents, including falling downstairs. The comedian in me impels me to make a joke about that being the traditional explanation for prisoners' injuries, but I don't feel like it. A younger Jeremy Hardy might have joked about comical-sounding deaths of policemen; but I'm becoming increasingly sombre about all death. I'm with John Donne.

The one death that did raise a smirk was that of the constable who choked after swallowing his false teeth while running to assist an arrest, but he's probably someone's ancestor, so let's not name him.

Over 60 of the deaths resulted from deliberately inflicted injuries. That's nearly one a year. I'm interested to see how many have been killed in recent years, because I like to think we're a less violent society today. Scrolling back 25 years from the present, I make it eight murdered; the famous ones being Yvonne Fletcher, who was shot outside the Libyan Embassy in 1984, and Keith Blakelock, who was hacked to death on the Broadwater Farm estate in 1985. I was part of the campaign to free those convicted of PC Blakelock's murder, Winston Silcott, Engin Raghip and Mark Braithwaite. All had their convictions quashed in 1991. They had clearly been wrongly convicted, otherwise I wouldn't have got involved.

I got involved because of meeting Sharon Raghip, Engin's partner, in 1990. She had befriended Breda Power, daughter of Billy Power, one of the Birmingham Six, the Irishmen who were wrongly convicted of the Birmingham pub bombings of 1974. By 1990, when I had only been involved in the Birmingham Six Campaign for a few months, there was already a momentum toward the campaign's success; it was just a matter of keeping up the pressure, and diligence on the part of the legal team. The campaign to free the Tottenham men was not making anything like the same progress.

Sharon realised she needed to remodel her campaign along the lines of the campaign to free the Six, a small part of which involved getting me to organise benefits of the kind I was arranging for them.

For the next few years, I was always organising a benefit for one campaign or another. I still perform at benefits but I make sure someone else is organising them. It took over my life for a while. I think I did some good work as a campaigner. I even started one campaign and ran it from home, but I reached a point at which I thought I was going to lose the ability to do anything else, and I didn't want that to happen.

A feature of all of these campaigns was the misbehaviour

of policemen, either in fitting people up or in failing to investigate or prevent murders. More recently, I have been raging about the killing of Jean Charles de Menezes. But I have also had dealings with individual policemen and women who've been helpful, and considerate, and good. I have had police protection when threatened by neo-Nazis. More recently, Katie and I decided to leave a march against the Israeli attack on Gaza because we were getting crushed. Two very nice officers helped us over the barriers and another said, 'You're a very funny man, I've paid good money to see you.' I'm sorry but, when you're a comedian, a remark like that outweighs all other considerations. I don't know if that man was one of the officers who later battered people in the crowd, having 'lost it' or whether the officers who did that were all bastards to start with.

At any rate, looking at the deaths of all the men and women on the Met site, I see that most of these deaths were accidents, and an extraordinary number of them in recent years involved motorcycles. I remember an incident in 1997, around the corner from where I lived then. A motorcyclist collided with a lorry and died. I found out afterwards that he was a policeman. I look at the deaths for that year on the site. Two constables died in crashes that year, one of them on his way to the Notting Hill carnival. The carnival is held over the August bank holiday weekend, and I'm remembering that the crash near my house was on a bank holiday Monday, a few days before the death of Princess Diana. I google Diana and find she died on 31 August. The policeman died on 25 August. It must be him.

I associated the two deaths because I was quite affected by the death of that policeman, and largely unmoved by the death of the princess. It wasn't that I didn't care at all; she was a person. But I had already wept for a stranger when Diana died. I wept after seeing the failure of the people trying to save the injured motorcyclist near my home. Someone covered his face. I'd been hovering near the scene, wondering if there was anything I could do, while knowing there wasn't. I think what upset me was the thought that there was I, a stranger, witnessing the last seconds of his life, and yet all the people who loved him were completely unaware that they would never see him alive again. And the fact that all the human goodness that surrounded him at that moment could not undo such a sickening piece of bad luck.

I'm very fortunate not to have seen much death in my life. Perhaps if I had, the motorcyclist wouldn't still be in my mind. I've only seen one other dead person, and that was Linda – except it wasn't; it was just her body. I loved her very much and I'd know the difference.

I suppose I should get back to trying to find out about the police career of my great-grandfather. It is feeling like a very trivial matter in the light of what my unfocussed research throws up. But surely, the point of genealogy is to put us in touch with our common humanity. God help us if it's to do with genes.

Let us look at the section marked, 'Timeline. 1870-1889', since Thomas was a policemen between those dates. This is the entry for 1870:

The standard height for Metropolitan Police officers is raised to 5ft 8ins, except for Thames Division, where it is 5ft 7ins.

Here is 1871:

As a result of frequent larcenies of linen, the Commissioner Edmund Henderson said, on the 21 April, 'Constables are to call at the houses of all persons on their beats having wet linen in their gardens, and caution them of the risk they run in having them stolen...'

Obviously, a low-crime year. 1872 is much more interesting.

Police strike for the first time. Various men are disciplined or dismissed, although these latter are later allowed back in to the Force.

Blimey. They struck. There have been occasional rumblings in recent years about possible strike action. I've often pictured striking policemen on picket lines, huddling around braziers, when over the hilltop on horseback come ex-miners and anti-capitalists to baton the merry fuck out of them. But this next bit is relevant to our search, as it's about recruitment. 1874:

A survey of recruiting over a two-year period showed that of those who had joined the force, 31% came from land jobs, 12% from military services, and 5% from other police jobs. The remainder came mostly from manual jobs. The majority of recruits and serving officers came from outside of London.

1876 is the one year in which we know Thomas to have been a policeman. This is what we learn about that year.

8 January the following order was released: 'Relief from duty during severe weather – during the present severe weather as much indulgence as possible is to be given to the men on night duty, due regard being had to public safety.'

And the papers rage about the effects of snow on public services in 2009, as though it was not ever thus. There is one other interesting entry in the time before Thomas leaves Fulham. It is for 1877.

Turf Fraud Scandal exposes corruption within the Force

Please don't say my great-grandfather was a bent cop. I click on the link. Three detectives were arrested. None was called Thomas Monk. So he's in the clear for now. Let's see what staff records the Met still has.

Metropolitan Police staff records have not survived in their entirety.

These are the words that greet me. What follows does not bode well. Here's what is available:

Numerical registers, September 1829–March 1830; alphabetical register, 1829–1836; alphabetical registers of joiners, September 1830–April 1857, July 1878–1933; attestation ledgers for February 1869–May 1958 (MEPO); certificate of service records for January 1889–November 1909; registers of leavers, March 1889–January 1947; an incomplete nominal index of officers covering the surnames with the initial letter of A–Brazier; an index to officers who joined the Metropolitan Police between 1880–1889.

Notice how my great-grandfather manages to fall into none of those categories.

I wonder if I should contact the Met to find out if there's anything more, but wasting police time is an offence. I then wonder what is the most trivial question anyone has ever asked the police and contemplate ringing 999 to find out. I try clicking on the National Archives link, which takes me to the public records office in Kew where, it turns out, everything is. I feel as though entering the site brings me closer to the day when I shall physically go there. It's not far to Kew, and when the weather's nicer I might take a turn around the gardens, perhaps even see the pagoda that my father used as a bomb testing chute in the war. That's actually quite interesting, isn't it? Notice how I slipped that in.

Yes, there is much to recommend Kew as a place, although I'm worried that once I enter the records office, my life will start to resemble the fictional wasted years of Thomas Monk in Chancery, as concocted by Grandma Becky. But I must bite the bullet. I'll ring them first.

A lady answers, and she is helpful. Very helpful. This is a great day. She says that yes, they have all the police stuff and I can just turn up any time but to bring ID. That is something I was bound not to do if she hadn't told me to. I can see myself standing at reception in tears pleading that, just because I haven't got a utility bill with me that doesn't mean I don't exist.

I'm quite excited now. If I go after the morning rush hour – there is a portal between 10 and 12 – I could make it in 40 minutes. That's if they have parking. If not, it's the train and it'll take an hour, but I can read on the train. Soon my travels will begin again. I shall go to Woking, to Arundel, to Hitchin and to Kew. Imagine the adventures I shall have, and the people I shall meet.

But before then I want to have another look for Douglas. I'm feeling disloyal, being all friendly with a police website, when the police were partly responsible for my great-uncle's death.

Unfortunately, the web furnishes me with no information on Douglas Edward Hardy other than his date of birth. I can't even find the mystery person who's put him on their family tree now. She must have got scared when I emailed her. Perhaps she knows too much and my contact with her has jeopardised her safety.

What to do now? Clearly I need to leave the house soon, both for research purposes and mental well-being.

CHAPTER 8

Mum and Dad

Yesterday, I went to see Mum and Dad. They were long overdue for a visit. Visiting them, of course, now involves research, but this was the first time that I have taken a notebook. I simply don't have Dad's capacity for retaining information. He has the most extraordinary memory. I don't know anybody else with such a huge memory. Mark Steel can remember phone numbers for ever after hearing them once, but doesn't retain absolutely everything in the way that Dad does.

I realised yesterday that the thing I often said about my grandparents – that I wish I'd recorded their recollections when I had the chance – applies to my dad. I'm going to have to take a tape recorder and interview him, or at least let him talk. His tendency to pursue every possible tangent is the subject of family humour and occasional irritation, and I have probably inherited it. A time will come when I want just to play a tape and hear him ramble about the history of Hampshire watercress production, all the breweries and farms of the Basingstoke area, and all the amusing things that happened in the course of his long working life.

Sadly, I have missed the opportunity to do that with

Mum. She has been ill for a long time, and reminding her of her mortality seems tactless, but Dad would probably relish being asked to talk on tape and would be philosophical about the reasons behind it.

I want to find out more about Dad's uncle Douglas. Another of my realisations yesterday was that, since my dad has a phenomenal memory, he is probably a more reliable source of information than the Internet. I'm sure if I'd read any of the books or articles about tracing one's roots that I have collected, the first piece of advice is 'ask an older relative what they know about your ancestors'. I don't know if it's just my dad or if it's a generational thing, but my dad knows more about his grandparents than I know about him.

So of course he would know about his uncle Douglas. Why have I been playing detective online when I could have got full details from Dad in a second? And in the second after I asked him, a rather important newsflash occurred: 'Doug died in early '48, in Winchfield Hospital.' Not in a police station. He did fall off a bar stool, in the North Camp Hotel, which is still there. I can go there to see whether it still has the brass rail on which Douglas hit his head. He was not drunk; the pub had just opened, although he *was* a drunk, as well as a philanderer. He was taken first to the Cottage Hospital in Farnborough, and, later, when it was ascertained that he had brain damage, to Winchfield. He was not arrested – 'at least not on that occasion' – and the police were in no way culpable for his death.

Many years ago I told someone in an interview that my great-uncle died in police custody. I am, as I've already said, unhappy with myself for saying it because it wasn't relevant and I was saying it – let's be honest – to show off. Now I find out it wasn't even true. So who told me?

Mum. Mum told me that story years ago, when her memory was very sound. She must have just got hold of the wrong end of the stick. She never knew Doug. She hadn't met my dad at the time of Doug's death. She probably heard the story some time in the fifties and had mixed up the details by the time she told me sometime in the eighties. Maybe the police took Doug to hospital and thought he was drunk. Maybe hospital staff thought he was drunk. And perhaps that contributed to a delayed diagnosis of the brain haemorrhage. And Mum got on very well with dad's father, Lionel; maybe he told her other stories of drunken incidents involving the police.

In any event, I suppose I'm pleased it was just an accident, and that no malice or neglect was involved. And, although it shouldn't make a difference, the tragedy seems to be softened by the fact that Doug does not sound like a particularly nice man. It should not be relevant; he was a human being. But the fact that he probably didn't leave a huge hole in lots of people's lives does seem to matter. This was just after the Second World War, when tens of millions were slaughtered. A drunk whose family didn't like him doesn't seem such a loss. That sentiment is against my philosophy but I can't shake it off so I may as well be honest about it.

I say his family didn't like him, but his mother survived him by four years, and mothers always love their sons. He also had a widow, Lileda. She was a department store heiress who had served in the Canadian army during the war. They met in Aldershot. Doug had been divorced by his first wife, Betty Forbes, the daughter of a Scottish wholesaler of coal.

She was a singer known as 'The Scottish Nightingale' but I can't find any record of her. She and Doug ran the Reliance Tyre Company in Aldershot. She divorced him because of his dalliances with chorus girls. I'm not sure whether Dad means that literally or whether it was assumed in the 1930s that all loose women were chorus girls.

Lileda's father gave Doug a job, and the couple moved back to Canada, until her dad sacked him and they moved back to Farnborough, where they shared a house with his mother, Annie. Lileda ran a newsagent's and tobacconist's on Netley Street. Apparently the building is still there.

Doug continued in his feckless ways until the fatal accident. I suppose there will be some record of it in the *Farnborough News*. There was an inquest. I could try to find out more, just to see if there is anything about the police and First Aid, just because I like to think that Mum got more of the story right than seems to be the case. Maybe I'll carry out a little more research when I go to Farnborough.

So that's Doug. Parts of it read like a movie, except that in a movie a man's head can be hit hard by a metal bar and he wakes up with no more than a sore head. Indeed, in a movie, a person can be clobbered over the head with any object and be harmlessly stunned. A person can even be knocked out by a vase, so long as it breaks. That's always bothered me: surely if it breaks, it's not that hard. And why don't the fragments cut or scratch their head? I always take things too literally. Maybe Mum's version of Doug's death was a metaphor.

I want to go to Farnborough with Dad. The trouble is, he's a full-time carer, so someone else will have to look after Mum. Which is fine as long as he has an enjoyable day out.

I'll do a reconnaissance day first; find his grandfather Alfred's grave so I can take him there. Then we could just drive around to see the different places where he lived.

I was born in Farnborough, although I only lived there for one year, on a council estate. I assume that it was after I'd been called Jeremy that we had to move, to Mytchett in Surrey, where I grew up. I always say, if asked, that I was born in Hampshire. But I shouldn't be ashamed of Surrey. Grandpa Herbert was from Croydon, and Nan was from Betchworth. Croydon isn't Venice, I'll warrant you, but it's funny and unglamorous and some cool people are from there. Betchworth, I've never been to, but I'm going to take a train there, because the porter's cottage where Nan was born is right on the station, Dad says.

The public perception of Surrey is that all of it is posh. It's all suburbs and golf courses, and full of people who've moved out of London because they're scared of black people. In reality, it's Hertfordshire, Kent and Essex that brim with white-flight migrants, and I have, as yet, found no ancestors in Essex. So far, my grandparents and great-grandparents (I've still got two of them to go) are from Sussex, Surrey, Kent, Herts and, of course, Hants. I say 'of course' because I paint myself as a Hampshireman, as does Dad.

Dad, himself, was born in Sussex, in Burgess Hill, a place I only know from a Betjeman poem. And the family was only there for a while. Dad's parents, Lionel and Audrey, met when they both lived on Park Road in Farnborough. Nan was a secretary in the Aldershot tax office. I have the clock they gave her when she left, as married women were obliged to do. Lionel was a clerk, and Dad thinks he might also have worked at the tax office. They also both played in the same dance orchestra.

Audrey's uncle Ted got Lionel a job in the coal office in Burgess Hill. Lionel took a flat there, and Audrey moved in when they married. Dad was born the following year. I forgot to ask Dad when they moved back to Farnborough. But they were back well before my aunt Muriel was born in 1931. They moved in with Grandad's parents, Alfred and Annie, in a flat in Camp Road, then a house in Peabody Road; but Alfred got increasingly ill, took early retirement and died a few months after Muriel's birth. Towards the end of his life, he was bedridden, and Dad remembers going in to see him in the morning before school. Alfred always ate a boiled egg for breakfast and would crack the top off and give it to Dad. Dad says he was a very nice grandfather, always playing with him until he was no longer well enough. And he was tall and handsome, his nose more Roman than that of Dad's other grandfather, Albert Hewett, which was 'beaky', like ours.

By the time Alfred died, of course, the Great Depression was in full swing. It was not a good time for the family. Lionel had a succession of brief clerical jobs and was a postman for a bit. He also, as Dad puts it, shared one characteristic with his brother: a propensity for drink. Both my grandfathers had this problem. I doubt it was uncommon among men who had been in the trenches in the Great War. Lionel and Herbert were both deeply damaged by the experience. Then they had to face unemployment in the thirties.

I would have been shocked if I had been told about the drinking as a boy. My grandfathers were such proper men. And both drank still, in moderation. I used to do a drunk act to entertain (I thought) the family. It was an imitation of

Dave Allen playing a drunk. I had never seen a drunk in real life. I'd seen them in films, but Dave Allen's was the best portrayal and he was on telly all the time. I think I probably did Jimmy Cagney as well. All impressionists did Jimmy Cagney in those days and young boys' impressions were always impressions of impressionists' impressions.

On one occasion, after doing my Dave Allen drunk act, for some reason I asked, 'Have you ever been drunk, Grandad?' The room fell silent, which was rare, and Grandad said softly, 'Not lately.'

My father is fiercely proud of my grandad and prefers to talk about how good his father was at everything and how much he could have done if only he had more ambition. We talk about Grandad's war, the Great War. In the second war, he was a platoon commander in the Home Guard, which he described as being much like *Dad's Army*. I know that it wasn't and that the Farnborough area suffered its fair share of bombing. But his experiences in World War Two wouldn't have been nearly as extreme as his days in France. As I've said, he joined up aged 15. His father had already enlisted. There is a very faint picture of the two of them together in uniform, Lionel looking ridiculously young; his dad, Alfred Hardy, looking rather dashing. He is indeed a tall, handsome man, with a neat moustache. I don't know why, but I hadn't expected him to look like that. Actually, I do know why: we don't do dashing in my family.

Alfred was brought back from France to use his skills as a pattern-maker at the new Royal Aircraft Factory, at Farnborough. Dad says that the story goes that, when the Royal Flying Corps was renamed the Royal Air Force – the RAF – a problem arose. RAF was also the acronym for the

Royal Aircraft Factory. Someone suggested that the easiest thing would be to call it the Royal Aircraft Establishment or RAE as the F on the sign at the gate could be turned to an E with one stroke of a paintbrush.

But, whereas Alfred was brought home – Dad also thinks he'd been gassed – Lionel spent most of the war in the trenches. Initially, when his true age was discovered, he was downgraded to a drummer boy; but it was not long before he was promoted again and sent to the front, partly because he was a crack shot. Dad told me a slightly different version of the story I remember about Grandad's sharp-shooting insignia. The way I remember it, Grandad cut the insignia off on the boat on the way to France, to avoid being made a sniper, 'Not being a very brave chap.' The way Dad tells it, and he's probably right, all snipers were told to remove their insignia because, if they were captured, the Germans would cripple their hands. Lionel did remove the insignia, and did serve as a sniper, a job he can't have relished.

Dad says he was one of the best shots in the army, and I have no reason to disbelieve him. It's naïve to imagine he could have dodged sniper duty by cutting a bit of material off his uniform. He wouldn't have liked it and I dare say it left emotional scars. Dad says his father never spoke of the war at all; and the stories my Grandad told me were funny anecdotes, tall tales and old jokes that he told as true stories. I hope I never asked him if he'd ever killed anyone, because obviously he had.

Lionel wore his poppy for Remembrance Sunday, and he wore a British Legion pin; at least, I think he did. Men of his age always did. But he never struck me as a militarist – quite the reverse. All boys of my generation seemed to love the idea of war, probably because none of us had any idea what a war was really like, a problem shared by today's politicians. Grandad was still a boy when he became part of a real war. He lied about his age, so he was undoubtedly keen, but I'm sure the reality was not a memory he relished.

To this day, I'm always baffled when ex-soldiers say they 'enjoyed every moment' of their time in Iraq, or Kosovo or Northern Ireland. Surely, even if you think a war just, it's a horrible thing to be part of. I know Grandad thought so. As I grew up and lost my boyish militarism, I became aware that he didn't have much that was positive to say about it, other than how good the boots were or how he had some funny scrapes.

It was at the time of the Falklands that I fully realised what he thought. The whole area was celebrating the war, the military being very dominant. There were the barracks at Aldershot, and the shooting ranges at Ash, Sandhurst and Deepcut were nearby. I was at university in Southampton, which, being the embarkation point, was abuzz. And coming home for a weekend, just travelling the two miles from Ash Vale station to Mytchett, I realised how many army families lived locally. Houses were bedecked with huge Union Jacks and bedsheets emblazoned with slogans such as 'Welcome Home our Brave Son, Kevin', as much for the neighbours as for Kevin.

And it was all sick. Thatcher and Galtieri, two leaders previously hated in their own countries, had sold this charade of a war to hungry publics in an effort to save their careers. When it's said that 'we' won the war, I demur. I think Argentina was the clear winner. They got rid of their lunatic, authoritarian, nutcase of a ruler. We were saddled with ours for several more years.

Grandad did not seem to approve. Certainly he did not approve of the jingoism, and the reflected glory bathed in by soldiers' families. He told me a story of being home from France and hearing someone speaking to a neighbour who had lost her son there. 'You must be so proud,' said the well-wisher. 'Proud? Of course I'm not proud,' said the grieving mother. Grandad was not a pacifist, but he saw no glory in war.

I would like to know more about my other grandfather's view of war, but I think I might have left it too late to ask my mother about it. I can't quite believe I haven't been more pro-active in asking her stuff before. Alzheimer's means a gradual bereavement. We're losing more of her all the time. When I've seen Mum over the past year, I've mostly wanted her to talk to exercise her mind.

And I don't want to hassle her about family history. Tons of research has been done on her mother's side by Richard and Brian. But I don't think all that much is known about Mum's dad's side. I'm not that sure Mum ever did know that much about his family, indeed, she never knew any of her grandparents, but I would have liked to find out interesting things to tell her while she could still absorb them. I just wish I hadn't left it so late.

Before trying to find out more about Mum's father, I'm looking over a bunch of documents I got from Dad. I've got the birth certificate of Nan's dad, Albert Martin Hewett, born 17 June 1875, son of Henry and Charlotte Hewett, formerly Watford. It says that Henry's a baker and that they live in Crondall. The Crondall bit I also knew, although I had no idea where it was until I looked it up just now and it's ridiculously close to where Sue and Rick and my parents live. Sue's always offering to take me there and I say, 'Yes, we must do that' as though we'd have to set aside a week. Basically, she can take me there anytime and show me our great-great-grandparents' home and their graves.

I also have the certificate of Albert's marriage to Clara Emily Hammond on 7 October 1899. Her dad, James, is a bricklayer. Albert's a porter at Betchworth and the Hammonds live in Stoke-Next-Guildford – more Surrey ancestors. Dad said, 'I've got a picture of Clara somewhere,' and disappeared for a while before returning with a framed portrait. It is a photograph, slightly retouched. She looks glamorous in a Victorian way. Being a beauty she got free pictures done in return for the photographer's right to use them. I realise I have a photo of her in a folder Rick lent me. I didn't know who it was, as the picture was tucked inside the wrong sleeve. But it's definitely Clara and it was taken by a Mrs Read, who has letters after her name, which must stand for Fellow of the Royal Photographic Society. Her studio was the Rosedean Studio in Farnham Road, Guildford.

Sadly, I also have in front of me Clara's death certificate from 1962, and Albert's from 1960. Both died aged 89. Clara was the only great-grandparent alive when I was born. I see that she was living at Park Road then. That's where Nan and Grandad lived for most of their marriage and where I used to go and see them as a boy. They must have taken Clara in when Albert died or when she became ill. I'd quite like to know that she met me.

On a happier note, I have Albert's baptism certificate from 1875 and Lionel and Audrey's wedding certificate from

1925. Albert is now a signalman. Dad remembers spending time in the signal box at North Camp with his grandfather as a small boy, and being impressed by how strong his arm muscles were as he pulled the levers. Albert was also very bright, though untutored, and an active union man. He was a real countryman, like most railwaymen of that time, who had been pushed off the land by mechanisation, although he himself had been apprenticed to his father, the baker, and not taken to it. Dad says he was hugely popular and at his funeral railwayman came from all over and told funny stories about him, and then apologised to Clara for causing her any embarrassment, but she didn't mind.

Clara was a tough cookie. Dad says the only person she was scared of was her sister Sophie, whom I've seen in pictures, and who was a tiny thing. Clara was a matriarch, in charge of the money and very good with it. Marjorie, Nan's sister, who married quite late and lived at home until then, dared not admit to buying new clothes, or if she did, she would lie about how much the clothes cost, because her mother would upbraid her for any perceived profligacy. Clara snapped up bargains and would also sell things at the door, so items of value were constantly appearing and disappearing. My aunt Muriel, Dad's sister, remembers there being a Landseer at the house for a while. And the Hewetts lived very well on a railwayman's wages, mainly because of Clara's knack with money. They even managed to buy their own home.

My grandparents' marriage certificate shows that Lionel's dad, Alfred Hardy the pattern maker, became a theatre manager. There you go: I do have theatrical blood. Dad says it was the garrison theatre in Farnborough. He had to give up pattern making at the RAE because of the sawdust in the workshop, probably complicated by having been gassed during the Great War. And he ended up managing a theatre. Well, it's not the Old Vic, but it was a theatre. Dad says his grandad was an educated man and very intelligent.

Annie Hardy, Dad says, was also bright and quite well educated. She was not only a telephonist in Hitchin, she was *the* telephonist in Hitchin, although she later suffered from hereditary deafness. In Farnborough, she ran a sweet shop and tobacconist's, supporting Alfred when he had to retire early, and supporting the whole family during Lionel's long periods of unemployment. The shop was open every day except Christmas Day, when she led the family to Alfred's grave to lay a holly wreath after he died. She tried to keep the business going during the Second World War, but ran out of things to sell. Physically, she was scrawny with a hawkish face, but she was very kind. She decided to move out of the shared home on Park Road when Muriel and Dad reached the age when they should have their own rooms. She moved to a bedsit in the house on Netley Road where Doug and Lileda joined her. When she fell ill, she moved back in with the family, and Nan nursed her until she was taken to hospital for tests in the autumn of 1952. She was diagnosed with a brain tumour and died a couple of weeks later.

One other titbit from Dad: the Hewetts never lived in Frimley Green. They lived at the Ash Vale end of Mytchett, and Mytchett was at that time considered part of Frimley Green, not yet having achieved independence. I knew we were in the orbit of Camberley because, for years, when writing down our address we wrote 'Mytchett, Near Camberley, Surrey', even when including the postcode. The

Royal Mail must have been grateful for the directions. But I didn't realise there was another tier of authority between us and Camberley.

Well, that's it for Hardys and Hewetts now. My big adventure, the quest to uncover the origins of Alfred's father, Charles, must wait. For now I am going to chase up my mum's dad, Herbert Stagg.

CHAPTER 9

My Own Herbert Research

I'm doing well this morning using the 1911 census and the ancestry site and nothing else. I didn't even look at my grandpa Herbert's birth certificate, even though it's in a bag by my side.

You remember that I found him in the 1911 census without any help? Actually, I can't now remember how I did that. I'd had no idea he was living in Portsmouth then. I work backwards from 1911. In 1901, his mother, Harriet, is 'Head of Household', which suggests his father is dead. I can't make out what Harriet does for a living but it begins with a 'P'. Oh, it's publican, so St George's Hotel is a pub. Herbert was raised above a public house, not something Grandma Becky ever mentioned.

The 1901 census says that Harriet was born in Portsmouth, as though I need more ancestors from bloody Portsmouth. Her parents, William and Charlotte Bridle, are living with her. I remember the name Bridle easily because of the Brioche debacle. It also tells me William was from Andover, also in Hampshire.

In 1891, in Croydon, Herbert's father George is still alive

and selling watches. He was born in Croydon. So that solves the mystery of the last of my great-grandparents. Three were born in Hampshire, two in Surrey, one in Kent, one in Sussex, one in Hertfordshire. My blood is not looking like a rich cocktail of diversity. I could fold a map of England very small and still fit everyone on. If I have any interesting heritage at all, it must be less than an eighth. But hey, how many people can claim that? Racists would envy me.

William Bridle is at the same address but I don't know where Charlotte is; just out, I suppose. I don't think they went in for trial separations or me-time in those days. Or pampering. But you'd think the census-taker would ask if anyone else lived at the address. What's the point in an exhaustive list of everyone in the country who happened to be in at that exact moment? Are those listed as 'Visitors' just people who'd popped round? Did they declare a one-off curfew and do the whole country in one night? Do I have to check every house in Britain to see whom my great-great-grandma was visiting? That would be ridiculous; instead I check everyone in Britain with a name anything like Charlotte or Bridle and still can't find her. Maybe she had a migraine and told William, 'If anyone calls, I'm not in.' What if she was on her way home and they just missed her? Idiots. Still, at least civil servants walked around with huge wodges of paper in those days. Today, they'd put it all on one memory stick and leave it on a bus.

William is an ironmonger. I've never been sure what mongering is, but I know you can really only monger iron, war, fish, scares, rumours and whores. Ellen, his other daughter, the future Mrs Flower, is a dressmaker. Well, that's creative. I wonder if any dresses she made still exist anywhere in the world. That's a genuinely fascinating thought. But how the hell am I supposed to find that out? I'm on my own here.

Looking at 1881, still on St John's Grove is William, mongering away like a bastard. Charlotte's in. Harriet is a milliner, and it turns out her actual name is Charlotte Harriet. They used to do that a lot. My aunt Joan was Lillian Joan, her mother Frances was Rebecca Frances. I've always disliked my name, but I've had the integrity to stick with it. I could be James – Jim, even. I like Jem, the traditional diminutive of Jeremy, but it seems to have fallen out of use, perhaps because it sounds like 'Gem'. My family still call me Jem, and my friend Andy Hamilton does. And Linda did. It's a sure way of getting me to like you, should we ever meet.

I can't find 1871, but I find 1861, when William and Charlotte are living in bloody Portsmouth, William ever mongering. I also find 1851, when William is 18 and a baker's apprentice, which obviously didn't work out, which in turn is good for me because I've already got one great-great-grandfather who was a baker, and I need all the diversity I can muster. In 1851, he's living with his parents George and Eliza in Andover. Eliza is 45 and a charwoman. George is 57 and his occupation is 'Formerly Hatter'. In 1841, Eliza's not working but has a stack of kids at home and George is hatting. I'm pleased to find a hatter in the family; perhaps it explains all the mental illness.

There's something else I should tell you about Grandpa. He was a widower when he met Grandma. His first wife died giving birth to their son. The boy was raised by Herbert's aunt, so I presume that's Ellen Flower, the dressmaker. He was called Harry, and my mum was very fond of him. He was a pilot, shot down in the Second World War.

My sister Serena found his grave in France or Belgium a few years ago and told Mum. She burst into tears. I've found his death in RAF records in 1943, his birth in 1915, his parents' marriage in 1913, and his own marriage in 1939. I've ordered certificates. I see that his mother, Grandpa's first wife, was named Hendy. I'm going to try and find out more; I feel she deserves some recognition.

I didn't actually make it to Croydon today. I still haven't made my pilgrimage to St John the Baptist's Church to look at gravestones which the sacrilegious bastards moved when they also knocked down the house where my Grandpa was born. I'll go tomorrow. I got distracted. My plan was to print off these census pages and then go, but I've decided to organise an event to commemorate the death of my friend Rosemary ten years ago, so I've been preoccupied with that. I'll tell you about Rosemary tomorrow.

CHAPTER 10

Rosemary

This story is possibly a tangent, I'll admit. But I've been thinking a lot about death and policing, and reading back over stuff I wrote for the *Guardian*. Part of the purpose of recording family history is to honour those who went before us, those we have lost. And the politics of Ireland are informed by British colonisation and the resistance to it; and are, as such, closely entangled with history, ancestry, birthright and identity.

Moreover, I have to admit that I used to think I would like to be Irish, because I wished I was *something,* perhaps not appreciating that I already was. And I used to spend quite a lot of time in Ireland. It lost a lot of its appeal for me when Rosemary was killed.

Rosemary was blown up in her car on 15 March 1999. She was a well known Catholic solicitor in Lurgan and Portadown. I got to know her when my newspaper column had strayed from the levity that the paper desired and into campaigning journalism, or, if that sounds self-congratulatory, propaganda. I was using it as a platform. Ireland and policing had become particular interests of mine since my days in the Birmingham Six Campaign. Once the *Guardian* took me on, in 1994 or 1995, it wasn't long before those concerns infiltrated what was supposed to be a jaunty look at current events.

At that time, Catholic residents in Northern Ireland were increasingly protesting about the Marching Season, when the Orange Order, the Apprentice Boys and affiliated societies, parade their historic victories over Catholics with much pageantry, festivity and bile. Special fun is to march though Catholic streets and delight in atrocities that took place there, such as the betting shop shootings on the Ormeau Road in 1992.

Portadown was, and I'm sure still is, an intimidating place for Catholics. The thoroughfare that ran through the main Catholic area was Garvaghy Road, down which Orangemen march on their way back from Drumcree Church. The Garvaghy Road Residents' Coalition was trying to stop them, and its legal representative was Rosemary.

She also represented Republican suspects and was loathed by RUC officers. She complained to the United Nations, the US Congress and human rights groups that RUC officers had sent her death threats via her clients. A great many people believe that RUC officers colluded in her death. But most of her work was low profile. And varied. She represented travellers, the most marginalised section of Irish society, and she represented Protestants. One Protestant family she represented might have become higher profile had she lived. They were the relatives of an RUC officer murdered in the seventies, very likely, they suspect, by fellow officers.

But the cases for which Rosemary was known were those of Garvaghy Road, Republican suspects and Robert

Hamill. Robert had been kicked to death the previous year in a random sectarian attack, and no one was convicted of his murder. According to eye witnesses he was attacked in plain view of a Land Rover in which sat four armed RUC officers, although the officers deny having been able to see the incident.

I started to write about the case a lot. And that meant speaking to Rosemary. I met up with her in London and very soon was on the phone to her all the time. I spent a weekend with her in February 1999 when I went to perform at two benefits; one for Robert's family campaign, and another for the Pat Finucane Centre in Derry. It was the tenth anniversary of the murder of Pat Finucane, another Catholic solicitor.

It was a solemn anniversary but the weekend was great *craic*, as they say. The sobering aspects were the deaths of Robert and Pat, and the very great danger surrounding Rosemary. Those close to Rosemary talked to me about her refusal to take full precautions for her own security. She would not even park the car in the garage because the kids played table tennis in there.

The car sat outside the house in her cul de sac, and on the Monday morning, we got in it and she drove me to the airport. As I got out, she told me, 'Give me a ring to let me know you got back all right.' Three Mondays later, she got in the car after a family weekend in Donegal, in the caravan she was always trying to get me to go to. She drove down the slope to the main road, turned right toward Lurgan town centre where her office was, and the car exploded. Her legs were blown off but she was alive.

I was in Putney Church filming a documentary about

the English Civil War. Great political debates took place there before Cromwell shut down the English Revolution and ruled like any tyrant. He is, of course, especially hated in Irish nationalist folklore. I was on a break when my friend Lin Solomon, a journalist who is now a lawyer in New York, rang to tell me what had happened. Five minutes later, she rang again to say Rosemary had died. The director put me in a cab.

Rosemary was due to come to London in a few days' time to help me and Lin and another activist (now also a lawyer) Paul May, to launch the Robert Hamill campaign in London, with others including my ex-wife Kit. We met up without Rosemary, and ran quite a good campaign for Robert up until the British government called a public inquiry into the circumstances surrounding his murder. I'd like to think we helped secure the inquiry, but more significant was the fact that it was on a Republican shopping list. Sinn Féin was trying to cut a deal with the Blair government and it needed to show ordinary Catholics that progress was being made on civil rights. So the government appointed a Canadian judge to determine whether inquiries should be held into the cases of Robert, Pat and Rosemary. In the interests of balance, the judge was also asked to look at three cases in which Unionists and Loyalists sought inquiries. Robert, Rosemary and Pat all got inquiries, which are still ongoing. They are all being blighted by attempts at whitewash, but anyway.

We'd decided when Rosemary was killed that we couldn't wrap up her case and Robert's into one campaign, and that the best way to honour her memory was to concentrate on Robert. The cases were inextricably linked but very different in the specifics. Some Irish activists set up a Rosemary Nelson Campaign in London but it didn't seem to get off the ground. I helped a bit, but, in a way, I found it easier working on Robert's campaign because I hadn't actually known him.

Our campaign for Robert was a cottage industry. My main input was the newspaper column and organising benefits. I spent almost all my time on the campaign until we got the inquiry, and then I just couldn't do it any more. Paul and Lin were also veteran campaigners, and both wanted to move on and start new careers, using their skills in a professional context rather than wrecking their old careers by spending all working hours campaigning.

I thought that once the inquiries were in the bag, our work in England was done; not that things would run themselves but that the focus would be in Ireland and that there wasn't much for us to do but stay in touch. I have stayed in touch with Robert's case. But for some reason I progressively lost touch with most people around Rosemary.

Looking back, I think I wanted to cut myself off. Increasingly, I wanted to cut myself off from Ireland, except on a social level; I have great friends there. But, and this will read very badly to those who have been affected deeply by 'The Troubles', I'm not Irish, so I could walk away. I think I'd had a crush on Ireland and I was over it. I'm one of those well-meaning progressives who get called 'honorary'. I have been An Honorary Irishman. I have been an Honorary Jew and Honorary Palestinian, simultaneously in fact.

Moreover, Irish people, at least those with whom I mingle, are great talkers and tellers of history, and drink in pubs in which people play musical instruments without being barred. They seem more overtly 'cultural' than we are.

English people seem to know little of our history. We don't know where anywhere in England is, apart from Liverpool, which is pretty much Ireland, and we just have spasmodic, unfortunate bursts of Englishness surrounding war and sporting events, when the country gets decked out like a Loyalist estate. We seem to be either culturally dead or horribly jingoistic, or both.

I've never gone completely down the road of fetishising 'national liberation'. There is some bit of left-wing ideology which says that, because independence movements are progressive and revolutionary, it's right to support the inherent nationalism. And this becomes idolatry. Oppressed people are so welcoming and rhythmic and clever with fabric. So lefties will drape ourselves in Palestinian keffiyehs and say how passionate Latin music is, and love African-looking vegetables, and say how marvellous the Irish are with words, as though any of that's the point. It shouldn't matter if people are unfriendly, tongue-tied clodhoppers, whose poetry doesn't scan and whose needlework is all over the place – if they've got a case, they've got a case.

But I think I was rather in love with Irishness. And then Rosemary was killed and it all stopped. I felt scared, I felt stupid, I felt hurt. Many people I knew had suffered terrible loss, injury or injustice but none had yet been killed. And then one was. I still wanted to keep in touch with people. I still wanted to continue Rosemary's work, and I did. I did a lot on Robert's case. I did little else for two years. I also helped and wrote about other campaigns in Ireland. I still loved the Pogues and the Dubliners, and all the great Irish comics, like Kevin McAleer, Ardal O'Hanlon, Tommy Tiernan, Michael Redmond, Dylan Moran, Eddie Bannon,

Kevin Gildea, and Ed Byrne. But the joy of setting foot in the country was gone.

I miss it now because I don't go there often, but Ireland was sort of spoilt for me. Maybe that's very solipsistic but this book has a very introspective theme; it couldn't be more introspective, when you think about it. And I'm trying to be honest. I'm not doing the 'I was a naïve leftie but I grew up' thing that people do when they're rich or drunk enough. All the campaigning I did was right and just, and I had great times and met great people. And I'm still very close to some of them. But one of them was murdered, because of the whole bloody historic mess she was part of. Because of history and ancestry and identity. Yes, ultimately because of Britain, but I can't escape from Britain. My whole life is wrapped up in Britain.

But, as I say, I continued Rosemary's work, or a small part of it, and for a while I kept in touch with some of the people who knew her. And I'm getting back in touch with them now, because it's time. We must mark the tenth anniversary of her death, and I realise I've missed people, so I'm in touch again.

So that's why I didn't get to Croydon. I'll go now, once I've been to the gym.

CHAPTER 11

Croydon

By the time I'm out of the gym and showered and dressed and I've dealt with phone calls, it's nearly three and I've missed the empty roads slot. Between ten and noon, there's a quiet time on the road. After 12, the traffic steadily builds to the school run, which I am about to hit.

I also realised I left the house without a map or any kind of directions to the area I'm going to explore. So I go to Smiths and get a new A–Z. I hope to save time by not consulting it until I'm at a loose end stuck in traffic. The problem is, as I soon realise when I'm stuck in traffic, that I've also forgotten my reading glasses. So I can't see the map. I try looking at it in long bursts in lengthy queues, for my eyes to somehow refocus, but I just can't see the grid references in the back or the smaller road names on the maps.

I can just about make out what looks to be the area containing St Thomas the Baptist Church as I remember it from its website. And, studying very hard, I can make out Church Street, a turning off the road I'm now on, so I figure I'll turn down there and try to find a church. I turn off the dual carriageway and, immediately, as is always the case in Croydon, I am faced with the choice of a one-way system or a multi-story car park. I go for the latter, the entrance to which is the most tightly coiled helter-skelter of a ramp I've ever climbed. It is the Centrale Car Park. Not the *Central* Car Park – the *Centrale*. It has a continental flavour – well, a pretzel franchise. Parking is a pound an hour, which isn't bad for the London area, and I figure I can at least park up, get my bearings and walk the very streets my forebears might have walked. And buy some glasses. It's no use; I just can't see.

I resent continually buying new glasses. But I'm always losing or breaking them. I used to have proper prescription ones with coated lenses to protect my eyes from the harmful emissions of computer screens, but they fell off during a radio recording and two other comedians stood on them, so now I buy cheaper ones and lose them. Normally I get them from Boots, although I found a decent pair in Sainsbury's recently. I'm sure my grandparents would have been utterly bemused by the idea of going to Sainsbury's for glasses. But then, they probably got theirs from blacksmiths in those days.

I enter the mall; there will be a Boots, I'm sure. At first, I wonder what Grandpa would have made of all this and then remember that, since he only died in 1973, he wouldn't have found shopping centres all that weird. So I try wondering what his father would have made of it. I manage not to be distracted by H&M or Uniqlo. There is something seductive about a mall; somehow, the fact of being under cover makes me feel capitalism has my interests at heart. When I ask someone where Boots is, I don't feel like a lost weirdo, but more like someone in a reference library or hospital, entitled to guidance. But this Boots does not have glasses. Only in their larger branches – because spectacles are a mighty purchase, after all. So I do without, and find my way outside using a combination of touch and daylight, although it's already getting dark, being February.

I walk back down Tamworth Road in what I think is the right direction. I see a Victorian school building and wonder whether Herbert went there. It's now some kind of college. I walk around it but can't see a date. I start to feel like a lost weirdo, so walk on. I find some more traditional shopping streets, but my path is blocked by the construction of a new tramline. They started putting trams back in Croydon a few years ago. 'They' aren't the same they who ripped the old tramlines out, but I hope they see the irony. I circumvent the digging and notice a small chemist, so small it's a wonder I can see it at all. They couldn't possibly have reading glasses, but they do and they're only four quid, so today is shaping up brilliantly. I can always use a spare pair if they're only four quid.

I see a church spire so head in its direction. I see what I think might be the memorial garden but it turns out to be the grounds of Croydon Palace – which is a historic building and not a bingo hall as it sounds. Actually, although it's now a school, it used to be the palace of the Archbishop of Canterbury. There's a sign saying one can visit it at certain times but none of those times seems to be now. I'd probably need an appointment and a more convincing reason, and be obliged to spend an hour with a guide. 'Any chance of a quick shufti?' probably isn't the right approach. But it's nice to see it, because it makes me feel like I'm on holiday and I'm only a few miles from home. And, more importantly, it's very old. Most of Croydon is very new, but this was here long before my grandfather, or his father, were born.

There are a few old bits of street that don't really go anywhere, and I wonder if one of them used to be St John's Grove, where Herbert was born. I head round to the church grounds.

The church is Croydon's Parish Church. This area is the Old Town; I think the only old bit of Croydon. Six Archbishops of Canterbury are buried here and Henrys VII and VIII and Elizabeth I visited. Very likely, Herbert was christened here. It's a nice church, medieval but mostly rebuilt after a fire exactly a century before the havoc wrought by the town planners on my great-grandfather's likely resting place. In 1957 the bastards desecrated the graves of every local person buried here when they moved the war memorial to accommodate the widening of Church Street. They even cut some of the headstones stones to the shape and size of paving slabs. And what did they do with the bodies? The website said 'special tombs' were moved. I wonder if other people are still beneath me where they were laid to rest or whether they dumped the coffins and bones somewhere else.

The schools are out now, and it's clearly a place where teenagers come to hang out, there are broken Smirnoff Ice bottles aplenty. I feel reflexively scared, before remembering that, until my daughter left school last year, I was quite often surrounded by enormous children without being afraid.

I feel a bit odd wandering about looking at the gravestones, under the gaze of young people snogging. All the headstones are very worn, especially those that have been turned into flagstones. I can make out a few names, but I don't even know if Herbert's dad died in Croydon, and I already know the date he was born, so, in the unlikely event that I find his headstone and I can make any lettering out, it won't enlighten me much. I can see my great-great-grandparents' graves in Crondall without spending a whole day peering at hundreds of worn-out stones.

Across the dual carriageway is the vestige of a road that probably used to run up to the church: St John's Road. It might have been St John's Grove then. It's about a hundred yards long, and all the houses are so messed-about by pebbledash and PVC windows that I wouldn't be that pleased to find that one of them was where Grandpa was born. Having said that, they had quite likely decayed into slums before the pebbledash and the PVC windows came along. I decide to have a longer stroll around the immediate area and then head home.

As I walk back past the church, a youngish man approaches me on a bike. He asks if I'm doing a show tonight in Croydon, and I say that I'm not and explain the purpose of my visit. He then says that he's a distant relative of mine, the great-nephew of David Haswell. The name rings a bell, but for a moment I can't think who David Haswell is, except that I have a strong feeling he's on the Monk side.

'David and Doris; they live in the New Forest,' he prompts.

'Oh yes, I know,' I reply. David is one of Mum's cousins, brother to Sam, of Sam and Doreen.

'I thought you might be doing a gig here,' he goes on.

'No, no,' I reply and repeat what I said about Herbert having been born here. I say the words, 'the other side' as though that renders his great-uncle irrelevant. I'm not trying to get rid of him; I'm just disoriented because I was entirely focused on the Stagg family and I'm in Croydon, which is all about the Staggs, and he's thrown me. I should get his mobile number but I just stand there bewildered and he says, 'See you, then.'

I have always shot myself in the foot. I blow almost every opportunity that comes my way. If someone rang me at 7.25 with a tip-off as to what tonight's lottery numbers were going to be, I'd think there was time to bleach the dishcloths before running to the petrol station to buy a ticket. Here's a man I'm related to who has approached me while I'm in the very act of tracing my roots, and my embarrassment and awkwardness prevent me from seizing what might be a great opportunity. I can ring my sister Sue later and ask about David, but this man won't be in front of me then.

I somehow imagine that, if he is of significance to my search, I'm bound to bump into him again. So I just say 'See you,' as he pedals off. I don't even get his name. I rededicate myself to the Stagg quest as though impelled by a determination not to be distracted. Here I am, trying to concentrate on my grandfather, and someone has confused me by talking about someone else. I quickly block the moment out and devote myself again to Croydon.

Many of the shops are old buildings. Some are jewellers and I wonder if they have always been jewellers, since that was Grandpa's dad's profession. As I turn from Church Street on to Surrey Street, I see pubs that George might have drunk in. Then I double back onto the High Street, which is rather grander, and from there I see the Clocktower, which is a very grand municipal building. I decide to give it a look. The only other buildings I know in Croydon are Lunar House, the unmistakeable immigration office building that looms over and dominates the town centre and is visible from space because the sheer heartlessness of the people who work there makes it glow with indifference; the lovely old Warehouse Theatre, which they are closing because of its popularity and success; and the famous Fairfield Halls. I have played at both venues and also seen shows at both. The Warehouse was a delight, the Halls dreadful. They have less soul than Paul Young. One evening, Katie, Betty and I went to see Japanese drummers there and they turned out to be Scottish, which ruined it. They were very good and everything but imagine one of the guards in *Tenko* being Mr Mackay from *Porridge*. Great performance but unconvincing in context.

In any event, when I think of Croydon, I unfortunately think of the Fairfield Halls. But today, I see Croydon in a whole new light. The Clocktower turns out to be an arts venue, housing a library, a cinema, a gallery, a performance space, a café and a museum. I think that the least I can do is have a look at the museum, or the part of it covering the time before my grandfather moved to Portsmouth.

It's only a small museum but I like it. There's a large map from 1800, which shows that it really was all fields. There's a section of air pipe from the London and Croydon Atmospheric Railway, a bizarre-sounding system of moving trains by air-pressure. The trains were moved by a piston underneath that was held inside a tube with a sealable leather valve at the top. Leather, that's brilliant. If there'd been fridges in nineteenth-century Surrey, they'd have had leather seals. Anyway, air was pumped out of the tube in front of the piston and into the tube behind the piston to suck and push it along, thus moving the train. This seems completely nutty, especially as the steam locomotive was already successfully in use. Indeed, the experiment, begun in

1843, was abandoned in 1847. But I like them for trying. I doubt northern engineers would have been impressed by effete notions of shifting heavy machinery by means of air, but here in Surrey it must have been considered an agreeable fancy worth toying with. And anyway, we (we?) had the first railway in the world in Croydon in 1803, pulled by big shire horses. They don't have big shire horses up North, only broken down pit ponies.

I learn about Croydon's first mayor, Jabez Balfour, who was disgraced and jailed after swindling thousands of people out of their life's savings. His building society used their money to buy his own properties. I suspect he'd get away with it today.

The next room begins in 1900, so I don't bother with much of that. I think my connection with Croydon ends around that time. And I want to go home now. Since I'm on my own, and I'm not going to a hotel to change before going out to dinner, it's time to stop being on holiday.

Carrying on down Surrey Street, I stumble upon a sixteenth-century building, something to do with John Whitgift, the Archishop of Canterbury after whom every other thing in Croydon is named. I'm getting a bit fazed now, and the building looks unreal set against the pedestrian precinct and the entrance to the Centrale mall. It occurs to me that, if I didn't have a girlfriend at home, I might buy clean pants and socks for the morning and check into a hotel, in order to continue experimenting with living as a tourist. Then, I see how easily my life could slide out of control if there were nobody waiting for me at home, and I'm glad to be getting out of here.

Remembering my domestic responsibilities, I resolve to

swing by the big Sainbury's in Streatham to get vinegar. And I also remember that I need to call my sister to find out about David Haswell. I park and call Sue who reminds me that David is the son of my grandmother's sister, Zina, better known as Auntie Cissie. Apparently, Cissie came to my grandparents' golden wedding anniversary in 1967. All I can remember about the occasion is Auntie Eva, another of Grandma's sisters, looking elegant and severe, and my uncle Desmond, Auntie Esther's son, dancing to the 'Spanish Fly', by moving one foot to the other at the same time as clapping. I thought this was an actual dance step I should learn, and got him to show me.

David Haswell, Sue tells me, has some old family pictures in his loft. She is in touch with him but has never gone down to the New Forest to see him. I'm very happy to go and see him and Doris but not sure I'm the best person to be asking him questions. Sue gives me a number, so I have now by-passed the great-nephew on the bike but I do feel bad about not being more responsive to him. I think I am probably the last person who should be relied upon to research anything.

CHAPTER 12

To Arundel

I didn't set out to go to Arundel this weekend. Saturday was a beautiful morning and Katie had mentioned that our friend Daisy was screening her film about the actress Liz Smith at a documentary festival in Brighton. So I said, 'Let's just go,' as though that was incredibly, spontaneously romantic. I did suggest we get a nice hotel for the night, which was quite a romantic gesture. And I also added that we could always go to Arundel the next day, even though I wasn't supposed to be working.

Brighton is the nearest seaside town to London, a fact that defines it. I have always been ambivalent about it. I like the English seaside. I like chips and piers and amusement arcades and shingle. I like that it's near and I like that it's quite arty, and we know a number of people who live there. But it annoys me. Everyone is so bloody pleased with themselves. 'I couldn't live in London,' they avow, as though that makes them special in some way. Why boast about something you can't do? I can't seem to avoid walking in dog shit, but I'm not proud of it. And then I think, 'No, you're right, you couldn't live in London because wearing that hat, you'd be shot dead the minute you left the house.'

It's in Brighton's favour that eccentricity, albeit cultivated eccentricity, is celebrated. The population is a wonderfully cosmopolitan and diverse collection of middle-class white people. They're so tolerant, with nobody to tolerate. So they tolerate people practising circus skills in public.

I'm being mean. There's lots to admire about Brighton. They're just all too bloody pleased with themselves for my liking. But we had a nice afternoon on the beach, sunbathing with coats on because it was freezing. It's been good to have a break from London, and by the next morning we are ready for a break from Brighton. So we take a leisurely drive westward and inland to find my Sussex roots.

I have been in Arundel once before, I think. I remember a picnic, which almost certainly involved hard-boiled eggs, the old-fashioned ones with the black yolks, the kind that you don't see any more. I was probably stung by nettles if not by wasps. I was often stung by wasps as a child, because my family seemed to think that an overflowing litter bin always was a good place to pitch a picnic site. I don't remember very much, if it was Arundel. I don't remember the castle, only that there was one. And I don't remember the town, but I know I was told that we had ancestors from the place. At that time, the only things that interested me about ancestors were the Christopher Wren connection and the thing about Grandma's grandfather being a Welsh coalminer. How that thing was supposed to square with the fact of his having been head gardener here, I don't know, but I probably wasn't listening properly.

The castle is the first thing you see as you approach the town. It's one of those castles that are hard to date because it was started in the eleventh century but went through various phases of building and rebuilding up until 1900. The present Duchess of Norfolk lives there, so it will have rope across some bits. We park in the first car park we come to as I'm worried we won't find a space anywhere else, it being Sunday lunchtime. In the summer that would probably be the case; it's quickly obvious that it must be a very popular town in high season. It's very pretty in the way that makes you worry you're getting old for thinking that.

It's a lovely town that somehow hasn't been ruined. The only obvious sign of globalisation is Pizza Express, and I don't mind Pizza Express. Of course, food is our immediate concern. It's 2 p.m., but places seem to be serving all day. There are even two Indian restaurants and a Chinese. We walk down an inviting street and find the Bay Tree, which is very busy but they say they'll be quieter in an hour and a half so we say we'll come back.

We walk up the high street, going steeply uphill. Soon we hit a stretch of the castle walls. The estate clearly dominates the town. There's a gate but it's locked. We find a cemetery and have a quick nose around, but I think there's a proper way of finding graves. Katie asks some people on the street if they know the way into the castle. The people are extremely warm and friendly, in a way that suggests they love living here and are happy to share it with others. They think the castle is closed off-season but tell us where the main entrance is, back down the hill and round to the left at the river. Katie always asks people things, I never do. I don't know why I so dread social interaction, but I know it's not healthy.

I try several times to get hold of Sue or Rick on the phone. I haven't brought a note of where my ancestors lived. But walking back past the street where we are going to have lunch, I see the sign Tarrant Street, and I remember the name. It's where Matthew Jones, my great-great-grandfather, according to my cousin Brian's research, was a 'labourer of beer and lodging house keeper' in between being a gardener for the duke. What if he lived in the very building where we're having lunch?

We walk back down the high street to the river and follow it towards the Wetlands Centre. A man is on duty at another of the castle gates. There's some sort of corporate function on, but he confirms that the castle is closed until April. Katie tells him I'm writing a book. He doesn't look impressed. The movie *Young Victoria* was filmed here recently, and they will have had catering, so a man he doesn't recognise purportedly writing a book is not going to bowl him over. Nonetheless, he gives us a leaflet and indicates a phone number saying we can ask to speak to the archivist.

We reckon that if we ring and ask to meet the archivist, we might get privileged, all-areas access before the castle opens to the public. I'm happy to come back. For now, I'm quite content walking along, saying hello to the ducks and seeing how close I can get to a swan before it breaks my arm.

Soon it's time to eat, so we go back to the Bay Tree, where the lady is genuinely pleased that we returned, but not in a way that suggests her restaurant is often stood-up. The other staff are also friendly. We're doing something wrong in London.

Rick finally picks up the message and rings. He goes online to find out were Matthew Jones lived. He texts back to say the 1871 Census says King Street, and the 1881 Census specifies 55 King Street. It's lucky he texts because we're enjoying our lunch, and the fact that this is a pleasant way to spend a Sunday afternoon is in danger of taking over from my research.

We get directions for King Street. It's a lovely walk, though all uphill. King Street appears to be one long terrace on each side, which is good because, if no houses have been demolished or knocked-together, the numbers should be the same as they were in 1881. We make our way up the odds side, finding that all the houses are still houses of the same period, fairly untouched.

But of course, passing number 53, we find a gap. There's an alley, then the backyard of a pub. I despair, and ring Richard to find out if he has any more information. Katie, having more initiative about her, runs into the pub and comes back two minutes later to say the pub and its yard have been there for two hundred years, which means they have not replaced anything in the time since 1881. Furthermore, down the alley, there are some more houses.

So down the alley we go, to find a little row of cottages tucked behind the last few houses on King Street. It's a narrow alley, and we quickly become conspicuous to a couple relaxing in the front room of the first cottage we come to. My instinct is that we should run away because it feels as though we are doing something that borders on trespass. Katie's instinct is that we should knock, because otherwise we will look even more weird.

So I knock. The door is opened by a personable man in his fifties, who doesn't say, 'What the fuck do you want?'

I mumble, 'Is this number 55?'

'Yes, it is.'

'Er, hello, I'm doing my family tree and I think my great-great-grandfather lived in this house.'

In his position, I'd be thinking, 'That might be true, but it's mine now. I bought it fair and square. Who do you think you are, turning up here, laying claim to it? Lots of people have lived here; it's an old house. You're not even very famous. I won't be able to call my friends and say, "You'll never guess who showed up here just now. Only some bloke off radio panel games, that's who."'

But they ask us in. The man is slightly shy, as anyone would be in the circumstances. His wife is much more animated. Once it is established that the back of the house is an extension built in the 1980s, Katie has a new handle on the situation. More interesting than my genealogical breakthrough is what's been done to the place, how sympathetically it's been done, and how much storage they have. I suspect she's getting ideas for our place, and that, in the car on the way home, I'll be treated to: 'I was thinking we could turn the flat into a nineteenth century cottage and then build a new kitchen and utility room on the back and have a guest bedroom upstairs.'

The women are immediately poring over the extension, leaving us two men alone, not really knowing what to say to each other. What is clear is that people love living in Arundel. They don't mind that it's awash with visitors. They accept that that will happen in a beautiful historic town. They appreciate the town and its conservation, unlike many people in rural areas, who are apt to say things like, 'That huge toxic waste dump will be the best thing that's ever happened to this village.'

We start to communicate a little, the husband and I. The fact that I am writing a book seems to convince him that I have some direction in life. And he is interested in the history of his home. In its original state, the cottage would have had this one not-very-big main room downstairs, which would have served as living room, kitchen and probably bathroom; a humble dwelling, then, but a solid and warm one, with a decent fireplace. Upstairs are two small original bedrooms and then the extension with its ample storage, third bedroom and bathroom. The women are enthusing, and I wonder if Katie will now try to convince me to make an offer.

They have old deeds, apparently, but can't lay their hands on them at the moment. They are happy for us to come back another time to see the records once they've found them. The lady also works in the public library and is more than happy to help in any way. One thing they do know is that the building used to belong to the Duke and was occupied by his servants. So that all makes sense. My grandma's version of events, according to notes taken by Richard, is that Matthew spent the end of his life in a 'club' owned by the Duke, not wanting to live with any of his children. But in 1881, at least, he was living here with his son, Mark. Grandma also claimed that it was the Duke's fervent wish that Matthew should convert to Catholicism, but that Matthew held fast to his Protestant faith. I suspect that, in those days, you'd dance naked around a bust of St Thomas Aquinas, if the boss wanted you to.

We have imposed for too long on the good people of King Street so, assuring them that we will indeed return, we thank them and leave. It's too dark to get much of a photo now but there will be another time. We're fifteen minutes overdue on our parking ticket, but I doubt that parking wardens are patrolling the car parks of Arundel at quarter past six on a Sunday evening in February, looking for transgressors to punish. In London, we'd be sprinting down the hill ready to plead with armed police not to blow the car up.

The next morning I ring the castle at ten, and manage to speak to the archivist, who recognises my name and voice, which is what I was hoping for. I'm not sure how much it impresses as the archivist says, 'We get a lot of requests like this' at least three times in the course of the conversation, and is quick to stress that, 'You will have to pay.' Nonetheless she is very helpful; and, it turns out, she used to live in Streatham, and doesn't say, 'It's a shit hole, isn't it?' So she must be on the side of the angels.

Her name is Heather, and she books us in for 1 April. The fee will be £15 for half a day, £20 for a whole day. They should have records of Matthew's wages. I mention the possibility that he was head gardener and Heather tells me, 'We get a lot of people who say that.' In any event, I have time to prepare properly for the visit and find out how to locate graves. I should imagine an older person would be booking the train tickets now and planning their sandwiches. But I live on the edge.

CHAPTER 13

A Slightly Interesting Fact

I n one of Richard's folders is a press cutting from the *Aldershot News* in 1959. It's about the diamond wedding anniversary of Albert and Clara Hewett, my nan's mum and dad. There's a picture of them standing next to Nan, who's standing next to my dad. In front of them is my sister Sue aged eight, handing them a bouquet of flowers. I don't know if local papers still print reports of wedding anniversaries; I suppose it depends how many stabbings they have to cover. I do look at our local papers occasionally, but seldom get past the stabbings.

Anyway, there's a hook to this news story: four generations of the family are present. It's two years before my birth but Sue is there, and the attendance of Serena and the three-week-old twins is noted. It also says Mrs Hewett is crippled by arthritis and in a wheelchair. Grandad once told me his mother-in-law 'enjoyed very poor health all her life'. But Albert is described by the paper as being very active. His career as a signalman is mentioned, as is his 39 years with the St John's Ambulance Brigade. It is the latter role that gives rise to the slightly interesting fact: he met the Empress Eugenie several times. Now, I can hear you asking, 'Who was the Empress Eugenie?' I know the answer to that for two reasons: I'm from Farnborough and I did History A-Level.

This is now a test of what I can remember of my education. Empress Eugenie was the wife of Louis Napoleon Bonaparte, the nephew of Napoleon. Louis became Napoleon III when the Second Empire was established, after the reign of Louis Phillipe, I think. The family was driven from France by the Prussian invasion and the revolution of 1870, which is when the Communards took over Paris. The family relocated to Chislehurst in Kent, where Louis fell off a horse and died. His son, the Prince Imperial, joined the British Army and died at the Battle of Isandhlwana, which was a famous military debacle and caused great embarrassment what with an imperial heir getting killed. I can't remember much about the battle or when it was, but I'm pretty sure we got a pasting from the Zulus. All of the above is from memory and could be wrong.

Broken-hearted, as such sentences always begin, the Empress had Farnborough Abbey built so her husband and son could be buried there. You can see the abbey if you stand outside the house where I grew up. Eugenie had bought Farnborough Hill, a large house previously owned by the Longman publishing family. I'm unclear about the sequence of events at this point but I got very excited when I learnt at school that the town of my birth was inextricably linked to the Bonaparte dynasty. I came home full of questions, and even took my girlfriend up to the abbey to see the tombs, which is possibly why that relationship didn't last.

But my father, pleased that I had taken such an interest in

local history, filled in the details about Farnborough Hill. Nan and Grandad told me that up until her death in the twenties, the Empress was a famous local figure and that crowned heads of Europe used to arrive at Farnborough station to visit her.

What I glean from the *Aldershot News* is that, during the Great War, she turned her house into a military hospital, and that Albert met her in his capacity as an ambulance worker. I'm guessing that soldiers shipped to Southampton were brought by train to Farnborough where he picked them up, when he wasn't controlling the level crossing at North Camp. But I'm speculating somewhat here. Actually, it's more likely that soldiers were treated first in Aldershot and then convalesced at Farnborough. What am I saying? I have no idea; casualties must have been pouring into Southampton constantly, and taken to all sorts of hospitals.

I do a bit of searching about Farnborough Hill and find that since 1927 it has been the home of the convent school founded by nuns from the order that Eugenie installed at the Abbey. Being a private school, it completely dominates the search results for 'Farnborough Hill' but eventually I find some history and ascertain that the house was commandeered by the army in the Great War, rather than being offered up by Eugenie. The *Aldershot News* chose to be more deferential to her in their account.

And the important thing is that my great-grandfather, who died only a few months before I was born, met the niece-in-law of Napoleon Bonaparte. Dad once met Prince Charles, or rather received an honour from him. I can't remember what the honour was now, though I have seen it. But Grandma is still in the lead with Paul Robeson, I reckon. This has me trying to think who is the most famous person I've ever met. I'm thinking Burt Reynolds. There might be someone more famous I've met for a second and forgotten about...no, I don't think so. I'd say in terms of international fame over a long period, it would be Burt.

But Empress Eugenie is pretty good, I'd say.

CHAPTER 14

Back to Croydon

Sunday was the anniversary of Rosemary Nelson's death. And last night was the meeting I organised to commemorate it. I suppose it would have been nice to be surrounded by her friends but most of them are in Ireland. My main focus was on ensuring I did her credit at the meeting. I dug out old articles I'd written about her and things about Robert Hamill, realising how much I had forgotten. I used to be able to give a 20-minute speech about Robert with no preparation at one time.

I set off about 5 p.m., ringing my main speaker Pádraígin Drinan from Streatham Hill station to see if she was in town yet. I say my main speaker but the others were the very famous lawyers Gareth Pierce and Imran Khan, so I had a pretty strong line-up to introduce. But Pádraígin was a close friend of Rosie's; and well up-to-speed on, and very angry about, how the inquiry into her murder is going. I was not too worried about how out-of-touch I am at the moment because she's completely on top of it.

So of course, at the last minute, she couldn't come. She faxed everything she'd planned to say to Gareth, but I felt there'd be a huge hole in the evening. As it was, both Gareth and Imran were superb and I was pretty good too. We were in the seminar room of a very grand barristers' chambers in Lincoln's Inn Fields with a not-huge but very bright and attentive crowd, most of whom were lawyers. The exceptions – in that they are not lawyers, rather than not bright and attentive – were some stalwarts of the Irish community in London, notably my friends Gavin Carroll, and Jim and Mary Redmond. I spoke with some very interesting lawyers after the meeting, but was glad to retreat to the pub with Gavin, Jim and Mary to toast Rosemary with an early St Patrick's Day Guinness. I felt I'd done all right by my friend.

Today is St Patrick's Day. I celebrated it for years, so steeped was I in Irish politics and culture. But I haven't really celebrated it since Rosemary died. Paul May, Lin Solomon and I arrived in Ireland on St Patrick's night ten years ago, the night before Rosie's funeral. That night in Portadown, the Orange Order decided to have a particularly loud drum practice in the Orange Hall by Garvaghy Road. They said it was a St Patrick's Day celebration, despite the tradition of Protestants shunning the festivities. Some Catholic youths went down to the hall and started yelling. Orangemen came out and threw legs from toy dolls, in reference, one can only assume, to the fact that Rosemary's legs were separated from her body by the bomb blast.

On the news while all this was going on, we saw the Sinn Féin leadership with their Unionist counterparts at a St Patrick's Day peace process shindig in Washington. Gerry Adams was shown with incredibly bad timing, tapping his knee while watching a group play the Orange favourite 'The Sash My Father Wore', in a spirit of cross-cultural respect. I felt the entire leadership of Sinn Féin should return for Rosemary's funeral, but they would have said, and many would have agreed, that the peace process was too important. They're over there again today, meeting Obama, and trying to ride out the present upsurge in activity by Republican dissidents.

Anyhow, in between trying to get the laptop mended and getting ready for the meeting, I got back into the ancestry site to have another go at my Grandpa Herbert's family in Croydon. I hadn't had much luck before but, this time, I found Herbert's father George, aged 19, living with his father and elder brother, both named Charles, in 1881. Charles senior is a builder employing four men and one boy. Dammit, I've already got Surrey builders on Dad's side; I want some toreadors and grave robbers. Nonetheless, more excitingly than you can possibly imagine, there's an address on Duppas Hill Lane, which still exists. I also found the family in 1871, complete with a mother. She's Mary from Cliffe in Kent. I've already got plenty of Kentish blood, but never mind. At that time, George's father appears to have been a 'Bowkeeper'. I also found George aged two days old in 1861, when his father is what looks like a 'Beer Shop Carpenter'. Couldn't they have printed in the nineteenth century? They must have thought, 'We'd better do indecipherable, swirly long-hand; they'll love that in the future when calligraphy's a lost art.' If this were the telly, they'd find me a handwriting expert. Humph could probably have figured it out for me; he was a wonderful calligrapher. Oh well, beer shop carpenter will do for now.

I might have some parents for Charles Stagg, called George and Susan, and a brother, called Alfred. Susan's from

Wiltshire. Blimey – west of Portsmouth. I'm becoming exotic; except, of course, I can't be sure it's the right Charles Stagg. But I'm excited to have found Charles, as Richard hadn't found him, and I'm fired up about Duppas Hill Lane.

I head again to Croydon, this time using satnav, which brings me a different way, ending up on the opposite side of the dual carriageway from the church. St John's Road doesn't look any better for it being a beautiful spring morning. I turn up toward Duppas Hill Terrace but am met by a No Entry sign so turn round and have to pay at a meter to park. I can't quite imagine parking is at a premium here, but perhaps shoppers used to park here to avoid paying the pound in the Centrale car park. It's not near enough to a station for commuters to be a problem. Perhaps it's people researching their family trees.

I make my way on foot, clutching a printout of the 1881 census and an *A–Z*. The dual carriageway is on my left, then curves round to the right and is in front of me, Duppas Hill Lane coming up on the left. And, of course, they've knocked down all the houses and built flats. I feel more crestfallen than I would expect to, but it's a nice day so I go to the church to take some pictures and have another look at gravestones.

I find a Daniel Stagg. He might be distantly related but I can't be arsed to find out at this point. I make my way round to the garden where cremated people live, looking at all the headstones in the brilliant light. Then I see a parish office that has a doorbell so I ring it and the vicar answers. I sort of know they don't hold records in churches but I might as well ask him where they are held. Woking, he says, and then says he knows who I am and invites me in. He takes my number in case the secretary who's not there knows any more. He says he thought for a minute I might have brought the BBC with me. John Hurt was filmed here being shown some old records, for the programme in which they discredited his theory that he's Irish. I take some comfort from the fact that someone else's search for an interesting history forced them to Croydon.

The vicar doesn't say, 'So what's Sandi Toksvig like?' But then, I don't say, 'What's God like?' either. He's very nice and I'm quite keen to press on as well, so the fact that he doesn't want a long chat isn't too deflating. So I head back to the car, trying to get some pictures on the way, but my camera's rubbish.

I think I might finally be finished with Croydon.

I've received the certificates I ordered relating to Herbert's first marriage and son, Harry. Herbert married Margaret Mary Hendy, a 19-year-old neighbour, in March 1913. She died in childbirth in 1915. Harry became a civil pilot and married an 18-year-old typist called Jean Thomson Hawker in 1939. Harry was shot down in 1943. I found Jean marrying Edward Long-Collins in 1951. He died in 1985 and she moved to Plymouth, where she died in 1994, aged 73. We should have found her years ago; she was my uncle's wife. Herbert's sister, Ellen Flower, who raised Harry, seems to have turned Jean against Herbert and his second family, and all contact was lost after Harry was killed. I would have liked to go and see her. Well, I say that now. I don't know how I would have felt 15 years ago. I'm sorry to say that I might not have been that interested then.

I don't know what to do next. I've been spending ages

trying to make sense of the Aylotts. I'm confident that the parents of Annie, Grandad's mum, were Henry, born 1842–3 and Sarah, born 1837. I know that Sarah was born in Loddon in Norfolk and think her maiden name was Bell. But I've been straying on to other people's family trees again and Hertfordshire is awash with Aylotts. At one point, I thought I had a line going all the way back to 1701, before I realised they were the wrong Aylotts. I can't remember how I got there but I think it was from somebody else's family tree.

I'm reaching a point at which I'm not sure I feel differently whether a bloke in the eighteenth century is my ancestor or not. I am descended from 32 great-great-great-grandparents. I can't pursue them all, and I have no reason to believe any of them was particularly exciting, except in that human life is something of a miracle. The ancestors geographically furthest from where I sit now seem to be in Norfolk. That's fine, I like Norfolk. I'll look up where Loddon is and probably go there.

If I were to find out that one of my forebears was John the Baptist or the inventor of steam, I suppose the fact of their genes being in me would be more remarkable. If anything, I am slightly surprised that so many of them seem to have had practical skills. I've got a pattern maker, a watch maker, a gardener, a signalman, a baker, a hatter and various sorts of engineers. There are builders in Guildford. There are labourers, and the archivist at Arundel told me that 'Labourer' on a census was a lazy way of recording working-class people, so such people might well have had their City and Guilds.

The only person who seems to have had difficulty holding a job is Thomas Monk, Grandma's dad, the one who was a labourer, a copper (but only for a bit), a labourer again and ended up a greengrocer. I suppose that could be seen as a progression, with a bad patch when he lost his way and joined the police.

Anyway, the Hardys, Hewetts, Staggs, Monks, Aylotts, Hammonds, Bridles and Joneses all seem to have been solid folk. No one seems to have done anything terrible. And no one does anything at all like what I do. I'm going to have to start narrowing the search.

I'd like to find out more about the Staggs because there isn't much on them. I want to find out about Thomas's police career. I want to find out about the sea-faring Kent people on the Jones side. I want to see gravestones. I want to try to find the houses where my parents were born. I want to visit Hitchin, Betchworth and the Isle of Sheppey, places I've never been. I want to go to Portsmouth, Crondall and Borough. I must at least speak to the Surrey History Centre. I've got to find David Haswell in the New Forest. I might go to Loddon because I've googled it and it looks nice. I'd like to put the Christopher Wren thing to rest. I also need to explore the mystery of the identity of my great-great-great-grandfather, who sired the bastard Charles Hardy. And that will probably be enough because this project is taking bloody ages.

CHAPTER 15

Back to Arundel

I t is 1 April. No, really, it is; I'm not joking. We had planned to go down to Arundel last night and get a hotel, so as to maximise our time there, but for various reasons, it didn't happen. Neither did we set off early this morning to be there when the archives open at ten. This was partly because I had done no preparation at all for the trip. I don't mean a picnic; we weren't delayed because we were making a big cheese roll to share and gathering fruit and nuts to snack on, although we did do those things, obviously. But I'd forgotten to do important preparation, things that might stop me looking like a bloody idiot when we get there.

Fortunately, I've recently been printing off everything I find online and I have census returns for Matthew Jones from 1861, 1871 and 1881, in a carrier bag with loads of other bits and pieces. But Matthew was born in 1817 and I have nothing about him from before 1861. I find the emails that Brian sent me from America, including the one which had Matthew down as a 'labourer of beer and lodging house keeper' in 1851. It also has all the dates of birth of his children, his siblings and his parents, Isaac and Elizabeth. I realise that I have never checked as to whether anyone else worked at Arundel. Quite likely Isaac worked there; and I have a notion that Matthew's daughter, Eliza, Grandma's mother, was a young maid there. But now I'm making us late, which is probably worse than being ill prepared. I can lie about how slipshod I have been but I can't lie about being late, save to say the traffic was terrible, which is the first thing I say whenever I arrive anywhere, even if I arrive by train.

Thankfully, the journey is a breeze, which is good because, if there were traffic, we'd be really late. At about half past eleven, we pull off the A27 and the implausibly grand castle comes into view. It's almost too big and striking for this modest, rolling countryside. It is, of course, largely a mock-Gothic Victorian creation, which gives it a slightly Walt Disney atmosphere, but it does have a proper Norman bit round the back.

It's a glorious day and the castle does look spectacular, so we stop for Katie to take a picture, which gives me the chance to ring Heather, the archivist, to say we'll be there in five minutes, which is fairly pointless because we'll be there in five minutes. We arrive at about 11.45, which at least is before the main gate shuts at 12, making it all much more of a palaver to get in. As it is, the gate's wide open and we say to the same man who was standing there last time that we have an appointment in the archives; and we are allowed to walk up the winding path to the castle entrance. I'm glad it's another two days before the public are admitted; it feels as though we're doing something important. Disappointingly, we don't come to a portcullis or huge oak doors with a big knocker, just a side door with a buzzer and a security camera. We are buzzed in. We leave the lovely warm spring morning and are in a castle. I think castles are for winter. They are cold and dark. Without blazing torches and roaring log fires, they are bleak places, however magnificent.

Someone tells us to report to security. A moment ago, I felt like a guest of the Duke; now I feel like a prison visitor. But suddenly we are met by the reassuring sight of a phalanx of schoolbags. There's obviously a party of kids here somewhere, looking forward to swapping sandwiches and crisps from their lunchboxes. Actually, I don't know if primary school children still eat sandwiches, or whether they suck a purée of cheese, bread mulch and mayonnaise out of tubes.

The security man intercepts us and tells us that Heather is coming down to meet us. I expect to find her intimidating, but she is very pleasant, and walks with us to the security desk to pick up our passes, which makes me feel invited again. She apologises for the security. It is a recent development, not, as I've imagined, a product of post-9/11 hysteria; it is a reaction to a robbery last year. An art heist from a castle sounds like the basis of an enjoyable crime caper; but of course everyone here will have been very upset by the robbery and taken it very seriously.

More stairs, for which Heather apologises. Heather is not a bit irritated that we're late; a little baffled perhaps, because we're paying twenty quid and it's our own time we're wasting. She leads us on a long trek down corridors, through the banqueting hall, past the schoolchildren who are being asked if any of them knows what a banquet is, and up more stairs to the compact office which houses the archivists. Here we meet an academic called Deborah who is researching documents in Medieval Latin. I feel unworthy.

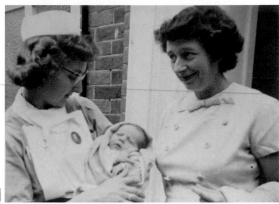

As a baby, with the midwife and my mother

The Hardy siblings, Simon, Serena, Joy, Susan and me

With my dad

My mum as a toddler in Portsmouth

Dad, as a boy

Mum and Dad's wedding day: (left to right) Lionel, Muriel, Audrey, Dad, Joan (who always hid), Rebecca, Mum, Herbert, and the best man Dennis Gridley

My grandfather Lionel, aged 15,
with his father Alfred, as they leave
for the Great War

Grandmother Audrey

Audrey with her mother, Clara

Lionel and Audrey in later
life, with me (saluting) and
my brother Simon

Herbert and Rebecca

Mum and her
mother Rebecca
on Malta

In Valetta on Malta

Grandma Rebecca, apparently
opening the gift of a watering can

My great grandfather Alfred Hardy, with moustache lying back (front row, second from right)

Great-grandmother Clara, the Guildford beauty

Her husband Albert

Albert and Clara in later years

Clara's parents - James and Clara Hammond

Albert's parents, Henry and Charlotte (née Watford) Hewett

In Crondall, Henry and Charlotte's grave

Rebecca's father,
Thomas Monk

What's left of Chapel
Street, Sheerness, where
Thomas was born

Rebecca's mother,
Eliza Monk (née Jones)

Matthew Jones with a daughter and granddaughter

Harriet Jones (née Coombes)

Arundel Castle gardens, where Matthew worked

Outside 55 King Street, where Matthew lived

We also meet Heather's colleague, Margaret Richards. Thankfully, it transpires that the two of them have already dug up some references to Joneses. There is a large ring binder ready for our inspection, along with a number of large and heavy books. We are allowed to take one item at a time from the main office into the side room next to the kitchen where the photocopier is. Margaret suggests that we put strips of card next to anything we want copied so that she can do it all in one go for us later on.

The fact that we can only have one thing at a time means we can't have a pile of stuff each, so Katie instead rings the parish office at the church to see if they have a plan of gravestones. They don't and don't remember any Joneses. Heather tells us it's quite likely my ancestors had no headstones because most ordinary people at that time couldn't afford them. I have promised Brian in America I'll try to get pictures of the gravestones, and I won't have time to scour the graveyard today by the looks of things, so it's a relief that I can knowledgeably tell him they're very unlikely to exist.

Heather asks if we'll wish to join them for lunch at 1 p.m., when we must in any case leave the building as we cannot be left alone in the archives. It's really very nice of them to ask us. We have brought a picnic, but decide that can be our dinner on the way home. Heather plans to show us some of the gardens after lunch. All this means that we're going to spend very little time poring over documents.

It's just as well, then, that they seem to have done much of our work for us. The ring binder is Margaret's 'Quick Glance File' that contains, among other things, the names of former staff. These are all life-size copies of original documents, each held in a plastic sheath. Tucked in front of each copy is a typed sheet giving a transcription of the key facts. Margaret has inserted bits of card into some of the sheaths to alert us to things that may be relevant. I can see that the first bit of card, in the middle of the file, flags up Matthew Jones, but I am determined to start at the beginning in case she's missed anything, which, of course, she hasn't. As lunchtime looms, I turn pages faster and faster until I get to the bit she's highlighted.

And here we are: a list of employees from 1856. Matthew Jones is one of the garden labourers, paid 14 shillings a week. He has five years' service and has a wife, one boy and three girls aged three to nine years. Grandma had told us he was head gardener. He's not even an under gardener, of which there are 11. He's one of 30 labourers. The head gardener is George McEwan who earned £100 a year, had been seven years in the position and was recommended by the manager of the Botanic Gardens at Kew.

I calculate that Matthew is already 39, so the chances of his making his way from labourer to head gardener are a bit faint, especially since, according to the census, he's still a labourer in 1861, 1871 and 1881. So, that's one family story down the drain for sure. I knew, but quite wanted to see the evidence for myself.

Lunch is timely in the circumstances, a family legend lying in ruins. We all head to a pub on Tarrant Street, where the Joneses once lived. We are joined by Sarah, another archivist and John, who says he is a librarian, but is actually an architectural historian and author of a seminal study on the Dukes of Norfolk. He is wearing a pinstriped suit of the kind bankers have been told not to wear today, because there are anti-capitalist demonstrations in the City. He is tremendously posh but in that honest way that's very endearing. Proper, old-fashioned posh. I much prefer posh people to sound like characters in a Noël Coward play. Today's posh people are usually so pleased with themselves that they can't even be bothered to speak well.

In the pub, Katie talks to Deborah who, she concludes, is every bit as brainy as her research suggests. I talk to Heather, who is also very brainy. She grew up in Croydon and Streatham and is not at all posh. She went to school in the Archbishop's Palace. She read Classics at university and is a very experienced researcher. I know that, given two weeks, she could find every single one of my ancestors as far back as the first to walk upright. She probably does it for house-bound neighbours: drops in some essential groceries and a complete family tree. Actually, she could make a fortune doing such work for the idle rich, but I'm sure would be insulted if anyone were to suggest it. If, however, someone were to say to her, 'I'd love to research my ancestry but my work with Kenyan Aids orphans takes up all my time', she'd have it done for them by morning.

She doesn't make me feel that my search is trivial; social history seems to be her passion. I suspect she's happier helping someone whose great-great-grandfather was a labourer than helping people who are convinced they are related to the Duke. She is also interested in the fact that my grandpa was from Croydon. I mention the moving of grave-stones and demolition of houses to make way for the memorial garden, and she remembers them doing it.

After lunch, the others rush back up to the archives, as the pub was slow with the orders and it's gone two. Heather takes us to see the gardens, which brings us past the unusual Norman double bailey. I can't remember what the bailey of a castle is for. It's something I would have known at one time, probably at an age when I was pretending to lay siege to castles with a plastic sword and shield.

Heather has already shown us some maps of the estate and gardens, but being in the gardens is the first time since Malta that I've really felt physically connected to this process. It's probably because gardening is to do with the ongoing renewal of life. Or something. The gardeners today are doing the same work Matthew did.

Heather realises before I do that I should meet the gardeners who are here today. Gerry Kelsey is the Head Gardener. He's a Londoner originally but loves it here. He's interested in my research because he's interested in the history of the gardens. It happens that Matthew joined at a time when major work was being done. The high street was actually moved and houses demolished. Hot houses, which have recently been restored using the original Moroccan glass, were built for the growing of exotic fruits. Pine pits were dug for pineapples. Fresh fruit and vegetables were sent to the Duke's other houses and even to Covent Garden, Gerry tells us, before steam ships came along and pineapples could be brought from the Caribbean in a fortnight.

Beneath us are boilers, built to heat the glasshouses. Tunnels were dug, leading under the high street to the fields on the other side. If we come back on another day when he's got time, he'll take us down to see the tunnels. I am a boy with a plastic sword again.

Isobel McKinley, the Deputy Head Gardener, appears.

She, like Gerry, is a true character. People think of Margaret Thatcher as a character, in the sense that it would be better if she had been fictional. But Gerry and Isobel are characters because they buzz with life. They love it here. They love it, I think, not because they feel privileged to be working for a noble family, but because it's their garden.

I once did some filming in a stately home. All the staff seemed to me to be rather small and remarkably servile. Unkindly, I referred to them as the Oompa-Loompas. One of them told me that their master did a lot for the community. For example, there was once a danger that a local primary school would be closed. His Lordship raised the matter in the House of Lords and the plan was scrapped. 'Nine other schools were closed instead,' beamed the Oompa-Loompa.

Isobel is from Essex. Now she lives here in the gardens, in a strange sort of medieval gatehouse thing, where she'll make us a cup of tea next time we come. She has extremely long hair, but it's all tucked inside a khaki army hat, like the ones they wore in *M*A*S*H*. I could say, 'Go on, then, show us your really long hair' but it's enough to know it's there.

Isobel immediately engages Katie on the subject of gardening. We have a very small, badly planned garden with a patio that's painted pink and a few things in pots. Neither of us has any gardening skills at all. Plants die if I look at them. We've had quotes from landscape gardening firms but they just show you brochures with paving stones in them.

Isobel recommends things that might do well in a shady, clay-soil patch of ground in Streatham. She recommends veg, including some that's beautiful, like chard. She gives us a handful of rocket that's growing like a weed. She plucks off some sprigs of rosemary and tells Katie to put them in water so they'll root. She shows us the papaya and peaches in the hot house. She says the peaches are lovely. I ask if the gardeners nick them all, and she says, no, the public do. Anyway, I realise it wouldn't be nicking if the gardeners took them, because, if this garden belongs to anyone, it belongs to them.

She shows us the pane of glass on which a gardener called Scutt scratched his name in 1897. His descendant Stuart works here. Stuart appears and is interested in Matthew because generations of his forefathers worked here. He is a 'Mullet', the local name for one born and bred in Arundel, probably derived from the mullet in the river.

Heather reminds us that our time to look at documents is running out. We have to be gone by the time the last person leaves the office at six. We tell everyone we hope to come again, and see the tunnels and have tea with Isobel in her funny gatehouse.

It's about half-past three before we get stuck back into the archives, but because of the preparation done by Margaret and Heather, we're ahead of the game. We find Luke, Matthew's brother, who worked here for many years as a sawyer and woodman. We also find a Scutt working in the gardens at the same time as Matthew and flag up the reference so Margaret can copy it and Heather can give it to Stuart.

Further on in the file are references to a widow, Elizabeth Jones. Matthew's mother, Elizabeth, was widowed by this time. References to Widow Jones stop in

1862, when Matthew's mother died. She appears to be one of the people mentioned in Duchess Minna's book. The Duchess paid a lot of philanthropic visits and recorded them all in a book in her own writing. There are also records of the charitable donations she made to the needy. I ask Heather if we can see the originals, and she asks me to note down the references from the blue folder so she can find them. The fact that I actually have to find and note down the references and bring them to Heather makes me feel I'm doing some real work in this process.

Each original document is bound with a ribbon of white cotton, which I learn is archive tape. Pulling the bow open does feel like research. Duchess Minna's book mentions Joneses as people visited in Bond Street and King Street, both places where my ancestors lived. In King Street, it's Mrs Jones, very likely Elizabeth, thereafter referred to as Widow Jones or Widow Elizabeth Jones. And here are the handouts. She's one of the 'poor persons' who received two shillings on 1 August 1859. She got another two and six on 7 November 1860. And on Friday 21 December 1861, she's one of those who received gifts of fabric: three yards of flannel. Naively, I ask Margaret why Duchess Minna gave out flannel to people. To make warm skirts, is the answer.

It is the view of the archivists, and they are probably right, that the Duchess felt it was her Christian duty to help the poor. It doesn't seem like a vain fancy, such as Marie Antoinette dressing as a shepherdess or Haile Selassie scattering coins from a moving car. Neither does it seem like the desire of the contemporary rich and famous to do their bit for charity as a passport to goodness. It seems like a solemn responsibility to help those less fortunate. The fact they were less fortunate was considered part of the natural order of things. There was no belief that, if you really want something, and work really hard, you can achieve anything. The Victorians knew the truth that you can work really hard and really want something, and still not get it; it's just how things are. In fact, they believed something that Conservatives today believe, but would never admit to believing: that it is entirely right that some people are poor. There was no question in their minds that it was inevitable that some people should be poor. To believe otherwise was seditious. But there were those, like the Duchess, who thought it God's will that they should alleviate some of their inevitable suffering with acts of kindness.

Perhaps I am romanticising the Christian morality of the Victorian upper classes. Probably. Perhaps I'm a little grateful that the Duchess of Norfolk helped my great-great-great-grandmother to keep warm in the last months of her life. Elizabeth lived to the age of 82, which is pretty good for those days. And Matthew's wages of 14 bob a week weren't bad for a labourer, so she probably saw some of that.

Heather asks if the Joneses were Catholics, because the Norfolks tended to favour them. Arundel was a haven for Catholics, who had been discriminated against since the Reformation. The Duke's good works in terms of welfare and education seem to be partly acts of solidarity and partly aimed at evangelising. There is one bit of Grandma's fanciful story that rings true for Heather, the bit where the Duke tries to convert Matthew. Heather thinks that's quite likely, even though Matthew was just a garden labourer.

The Duke wasn't averse to be a bit of friendly persuasion when it came to the Roman Catholic faith. I rather hope Matthew never got the push for standing his ground. Since we don't know how long he worked here, it's hard to tell.

There is one more book to look at. It's the directory that lists all the documents. If there is more information about the estate workers in other years, this directory will say that those papers are here somewhere. But it's 5.30 and we need to be wrapping things up. We ask Margaret to do our copying and we need to pay for that and the twenty quid. Heather has asked to copy the picture of Matthew that Richard gave me, and I'm very pleased to have been of some use. Plus she knocks off the cost of two photocopies for me by way of remuneration. My bill comes to £24 and I make it £25 as there's no change in the box. I get a handwritten receipt, which I like. You get them at the hardware shop on Streatham Hill as well, but this seems more special.

We have to go. John is leaving now to get his train back to London. He can save Heather the trouble of escorting us off the premises. We tell Heather we will see her again, thank her very much, then scurry after John who walks very fast. We say goodbye to him as the door next to the main gate closes behind us.

In the car, we ring the nice people whose house we invaded last time. I did ring last night and spoke to Linda, who said she'd be in after 5.30 and would get the deeds out. But now she says she's glad I've called because they only go back to 1949. I ask if we could still pop round and take a picture of the house in daylight. She says that's fine.

We pull up outside and ring the bell. Linda answers but is on the phone and is happy for us to take the picture.

Then she shuts the door. We're tired and quite glad not to be offered a cup of tea, but also feel slightly rejected. I think we've got carried away with how nice everyone's been. We've started to think, 'What are we going to say if they ask us to move in with them?' But time passes. I expect dozens of people have knocked on their door looking for ancestors since we did. Perhaps some of them misbehaved and ruined it for the rest of us. Perhaps it's an important phone call. Anyway, why should she offer us a cup of tea?

We have a wander down Bond Street where Eliza Jones, Becky's mother, was born in 1856. The houses all look old enough for one of them to be the right one, so we get some pictures.

Katie fancies seeing the sea before we go home. The nearest beach is at Littlehampton. The sun sets while we're driving, which is bad timing as it's one of those good sunsets when the sun goes bright red. It's hidden by the trees and gone before we reach the sea. Katie saw a four-bedroom house in Littlehampton advertised in one of the papers recently. It was on at about forty quid or something. You can kind of see why. There's not much here, but we walk around from the sea, along Pier Road that faces the harbour, and get a craving for fish and chips.

I always fancy fish and chips at the seaside and it's always disappointing. Why do people imagine that, just because fish live locally they will have instructed people as to how they should be cooked? But we both have a craving and there are two chippies. We go into the first one and have the nicest fish and chips I've eaten in a long while. The only thing I would do differently is to put bottles of proper ketchup on the tables. What petty-minded bastard invented the sachet?

But all-in-all it was worth getting up today. And you can't always say that, can you?

CHAPTER 16

Loddon

My dad is spending a week's holiday in Wymondham, in Norfolk with my brother, Simon, two of Simon's children, Matthew and Joan, and Joan's boyfriend, Ben. I've asked to join them, spend the night and lead a party to Loddon, the birthplace of Dad's great-grandmother, Sarah Bell.

Dad always had an interest in archaeology, which he passed to Simon, who became an archaeologist and passed the interest to Matthew. Joan is happy to go along for the ride as Simon rushes from one site of historical interest to another. I have already made them late today. Simon has planned a route up to the north Norfolk coast, which is very beautiful. We will do Loddon tomorrow.

Simon is on a mission to see a number of churches and priories and the site of a Roman fort, with a couple of brief stops at the places I had recommended. I realise as I lead the party from the car park at Wells-next-the-Sea through the woods to the beach, that my family delights in ancient monuments, so a sandy beach on a day that's suddenly turned very chilly, when there are several more archaeological sites lined up, is a bit of a distraction. I've also forgotten that Dad can no longer walk all that far; and all the distances are much further than I remember them being. Wells is a place that Katie and I like. Now I've brought them to one of our special places and it all feels a bit wrong.

I persuade everyone that it's worth driving on to Holkham where, I have forgotten, you have to park up and walk through the woods to be met by a mile of flat nothing before the beach starts. I fear I have wasted even more of their time. I hope that we don't lose the light before they're able to see all their priories.

On the plus side, everyone's up for going to Loddon tomorrow and I'm catching up with family. I feel rather proud of my brother, as he explains slight bumps in fields as the foundations of Roman outbuildings. And it's nice that his kids are proud of him too. Even Ben seems quite happy, as he picks up bits of earthenware and takes them to Simon to be told they are fragments of medieval crockery or Roman roof tiles.

I realise that I am ill prepared again. I know that the mother of my great-grandmother Annie Aylott was Sarah from Loddon, and I remember that I somehow worked out her name is Bell, but I can't remember how, and that's as far as I got. I ring Richard to ask him to go online and find out more, but he's at my niece's. This is quite embarrassing now. Simon is building his day around me tomorrow. He's a very organised man and an expert historical researcher. But I have very little idea of why we're going to Loddon tomorrow except for a notion that that's what you do when you're doing history stuff: walk around places and that.

Fortunately, by the time we get back to the holiday barn conversion Simon has hired, Richard has come through with valuable information. And in the meantime, Simon got lost on the way home, so I feel less incompetent by comparison.

I was right about the name Bell. Richard hasn't discerned how I worked it out but has found it to be true. I did supply him with a date of birth, calculated from census returns. And he has found Sarah Bell, born in 1837, and her parents John and Sarah, living in Bridge Street in the village of Aldeby in 1841 and 1851, between a tea-dealer and a watch-maker. John is a butcher. We look up Aldeby on the map and it is a tiny village about ten miles from Loddon itself.

In the morning, Simon has already detected a problem with what Richard has told us, which is that according to his local maps, there is nothing in Aldeby for a bridge to go over. But I decide to set off before the others, hoping that, by the time they catch up, I will have something to show them. And I have satnav so I won't get lost. It is a misty morning, rendered lovely by the sun's attempts to shine through. I'm glad I'm in my own car; I feel like I'm on a quest.

Aldeby is tiny. Really tiny. And there is no bridge and nowhere that looks as though a bridge could once have been there. I park by the Church of Mary the Virgin. It seems unfair still to be calling her 'Mary the Virgin'; we were all virgins once and as far as we know she did go on to have other children after Jesus. I walk up the hill out of town. Agriculture seems to be the only activity apart from prayer. There is no shop, pub or post office. I meet a man who's dressed like a farmer, who confirms that there is no Bridge Street and says he doesn't know the name Bell. He says there are a few more houses up the hill that are a couple of hundred years old. I walk up there and they are post-war council houses. In fairness, he never claimed to be a local historian.

This is clearly the end of the village so I walk back down to the church. I like being on my own, but I'm also glad that I've got back-up arriving any minute. Perhaps some locals will start to harass me, and then Simon, who is a large man, will turn up in his rented black Volkswagen Sharan, my dad walking behind him giving instructions as to how much of a beating he should give my tormenters. I have no idea why this fantasy comes to mind.

I check all the standing gravestones for Bells and then start on the horizontal ones, many of which are partially or completely overgrown. After a while, I see Esther, the wife of James Bell, and start to tear away at the grass, which has grown over the stone like carpet underlay. There is little soil under it; I just tear it away in great pieces. If anyone asks me what I'm doing, it will be okay because I am clearing a neglected grave, although I realise that the grass has preserved the engraving well and now I'm exposing it to the elements.

Eventually, I have cleared all the lettering and can read the whole stone. I have always wanted blow dust off an inscription in this way. For a moment, I am Indiana Jones. The engraving tells me that Esther, the wife of James Bell, and their daughter, also named Esther who died at 19, were buried here in 1832 and 1829 respectively. There's even a poem:

A tender mother to her children dear
Who loved till Death has placed her here
Though many years in trouble grief and pain
But now the silent grave her bones contain.

I reckon that in a village this size, these must be relatives. In fact, these could be the mother and sister of John Bell.

Simon arrives and the kids join the search. Dad goes to inspect the church for more evidence of Bells. Joan comes to help me clear the rest of the grave, and notices a key fact. In my enthusiasm to find a Bell, I haven't noticed that clearing away the stone properly has revealed that the name is actually Bee. Now I am annoyed. What kind of a stupid name is Bee? Bastard Bees and their shitty poem.

Simon, being the person who should have undertaken the task of tracing our ancestors, has managed to find a lady who has access to the vestry and who pulls out a map of all the graves in the cemetery. This is the moment for the cameras to roll if we had cameras. We scour the map pretty thoroughly and find no Bells. Lots of Belts and Balls, but no Bells. And the lady is sure she's never seen that name anywhere. Arse.

I am running out of time because, stupidly, I've agreed to do a radio programme tonight. But we decide to go to Loddon after I check the satnav and find there is a Bridge Street. Having the satnav, I lead the way, although my standing in this situation is at zero.

It's not a long drive but would be one with a horse and cart, so it seems unlikely that John Bell commuted to his butcher's shop. He either lived and worked in Aldeby or Loddon, and Loddon seems more likely at this stage. We park for free for two hours by the church, which provides some small consolation. It's a much bigger and better-preserved graveyard and offers some hope. To me, that is; not to its residents.

High Street becomes Bridge Street as we walk down

towards the river. Aldeby was a complete red herring. Most of the buildings look like they were once businesses and would have been here at the right time. Many have out-buildings behind. We come to the river, which is the end of Bridge Street and the end of town; over the Bridge, Chedgrave starts. The river today serves as a conduit for pleasure craft on the Broads. I vaguely hate the boat owners but mostly wish I could spend the rest of the day on a boat myself.

The others are agitating in favour of lunch. I like the look of the tiny Rosie Lee's Tea Room, although I should skip lunch and get on with some work. The Tea Room is run by a warm Indian lady. I have undyed smoked haddock and a poached egg on toast. I feel slightly cheated because it's lunchtime and I think there should be some mashed potato and maybe even spinach. On toast is fine for breakfast but, at two o'clock, it feels as though someone has said, 'What should we serve with smoked haddock and poached egg?' and received the reply, 'Fuck it. Put it on some toast.' But it's very nice and the lady's very nice and if we didn't spend most of an hour here when I'm running out of time, I might think it was a good idea.

I lead an advance party of Dad, Joan and Ben back up Bridge Street towards the church. Dad notices Mutton Cottage. It takes me a while to get the significance of the name: it might have been a butcher's shop. Why is everyone else better at this than I am?

By the car park, Joan has noticed, is the library. Dad says they might have trade records. I make him ask because he's old and authoritative, but they don't have them. All records are in Norwich. So we have a nosey round some graves and then enter the church, which has a local history exhibition up some stairs. There are loads of old photos of shops in the nineteenth century. There's even a book for sale – by means of an honesty box – but it's £7.50, which seems a lot because it's only one those flimsy sorts of local book that doesn't look like a proper book. So Joan, Ben and I each grab a copy and pore over it looking for a butcher called Bell. Despite its flimsiness, it's a mine of information, but none of us finds what we're looking for.

And now I'm completely out of time. Simon accompanies me back to the car park because he's made me a sandwich so I've got something to have for my tea. I mention that Dad seems faintly irritated by my research. Simon tells me it's not that he's irritated; he's just not interested in ancestors he didn't know. Now I feel a fool for interrupting his holiday. And I realise that, if someone had told me two years ago that my great-great-great-grandfather was a Norfolk butcher, I probably wouldn't have cared. I think that perhaps my two years' younger self was wiser. I get in the car and eat my sandwich straight away.

At about six, I hear the bleep that tells me I've got a text. I'm stuck in heavy traffic so I have a look. It's from Simon. It tells me they found and uncovered a tombstone bearing the words, 'Memory of Helen, the beloved daughter of John and Sarah Bell, who died 22 July 1865 aged 14 years. Blessed are the dead which die in the Lord. Also Thomas Burton Bell who died in infancy.' Helen might be on the 1851 census, and that should mean these are the right John and Sarah. I feel slightly less of a fool, and comforted that my brother could be arsed to spend the afternoon helping me.

In the morning I go online. There is a Helen in 1851; she's

six months old. I am pleased. Then I realise I have barely registered the awfulness of children dying. I don't think I like the past very much. That only leaves the future.

CHAPTER 17

Wizo

Wizo died. I thought about him the other day while I was driving back from Loddon, seeing a sign for Bungay. I haven't been to Bungay since I did a gig there in 1985 as part of a tour called Three Line Whip, with Arnold Brown and Claire Dowie.

The legendary comic and promoter, Malcolm Hardee, had asked Arnold and me if we'd like to form a package and we both said we were big fans of Claire and wanted her to join us. I went through a Thesaurus, looking at the word 'Three' until I came across 'Three Line Whip', which with hindsight was a terrible name. But it did have Three in it.

Malcolm booked us to play in strange places where he knew people and had vomited over various parts of their houses. We played in Matlock Bath in Derbyshire, where we learnt that a man had recently been arrested having sex with a sheep in a phone box. For months, Claire delighted in telling audiences that my response was, 'In a phone box?'

Wizo was our tour manager. He was a mate of Malcolm's. They had known each other since they were six, and had been in prison together after stealing a car belonging to Peter Walker, who was a minister in the Heath administration. It was the time of the Angry Brigade, the short-lived anarchist organisation that carried out a number of bombings in the early seventies. The theft of Walker's car was seen not as Taking and Driving Away but as terrorism.

In autumn 1985, Wizo, Paul Wiseman, was at a loose end. He'd been doing some gigs with Malcolm's *Greatest Show on Legs* and was generally doing a bit of this and a bit of that. Malcolm suggested he drive us for a few quid plus petrol. I think we only paid Wizo £15 a day, and he was happy enough to have that on top of his dole. He liked travelling around, always knew interesting things about places and would make us go on day trips between gigs. He would tell us about how he'd enjoyed Borstal, the fresh air and the library books. He loved poetry. He also regaled us with stories about his past with Malcolm. I told him he should turn the stories into a play or film.

Wizo moved to Australia a number of years ago. He went there to escape enormous debts, and some quite dangerous people whom he had upset; and he didn't come back until the slate was wiped clean. He loved Australia. He quoted Betjeman as saying the light was like being inside a diamond. He remarried, overcame his excessive use of alcohol and drugs, and generally lived a less manic life. He tried to persuade Malcolm to join him there, so that Malcolm wouldn't destroy himself. But Malcolm stayed in Greenwich and destroyed himself. He fell in the Thames and drowned because he was so drunk. Some people saw it as a really *Malcolm* way to go, because he was so larger-than-life, but I just thought it was a lonely, cold and terrifying way to lose a life. Wizo knew Malcolm better than anybody did. He loved the boy he'd met at six years old, throwing stones at cars. He wasn't so impressed by Malcolm's role in the world of comedy. I think he saw it as part of what destroyed him.

Wizo flew in for the funeral. I think it was the first time he'd been back to Britain. His hair was white and he was missing a tooth but he seemed to be in good shape. He'd been doing his family history. He'd always believed his dad was Jewish. It had never been talked about, but that was quite common in a lot of working-class London families. Being partly Jewish or partly Romany was a source of shame. But Wizo celebrated his Jewishness and claimed to be of the religion while in prison, so that his family could bring in food that they said was kosher. Doing the family tree, he found out his father was actually not Jewish at all. He was of Scottish descent, and related to the big dairy company. That's what Wiz said, anyway.

He had also written up a load of stuff about his earlier life with Malcolm and talked about the play I'd suggested two decades before. I thought he should work with Arthur Smith on it. Arthur – or Brian as he is known to friends – is from the same part of south-east London as Malcolm and Wizo, and I thought he'd have a better feel for it. Wiz was going to come back over for a longer visit, but I suppose he got sick with cancer, and now he's gone.

So why am I telling you about him? I suppose because this book is making me look back over things, and because a lot of it is about people who are long-dead, and I feel I should pay tribute to some of the people who've actually played a part in my life. There seem to be a lot of people in my life who are dead now. I think you know you're getting old when people ask for directions and you say, 'Well, you know where the crematorium is…?'

CHAPTER 18

Borough Market

It's a Saturday in early June but the weather has turned cold and wet. Since we want to get out but be under cover, it seems a good time to visit Borough Market. You might recall that my great-great-grandmother Charlotte Watson was born in Borough. She was the maternal grandmother of my grandfather Herbert who was born in Croydon. Neither Croydon nor Borough are far from where I live today, and although I hoped to find an ancestor from somewhere exotic, I'm starting to like the fact that none of them seem to be.

I'm always deeply sceptical when someone claims to feel a real attachment to something they've only just discovered about themselves. It's mostly projection. If you tell a man he's adopted he'll say, 'I always knew I was different, that I didn't fit in.' By saying that, he's telling you he's special. If you tell him his birth parents were merpeople, he'll say, 'I always knew I had this link to the sea. We had this goldfish I was particularly close to. My adoptive parents were lovely and did their best for me, but the fact is the sea is my home. I never knew why I liked to spend ages in the bath and why I always order the crispy seaweed when I get a Chinese, but it makes sense to me now.'

I suppose that, as an adopter myself, I am sensitive to displays of possible disloyalty by adopted people. I once read a strange interview with the Tory education spokesman, Michael Gove, who would now be my MP if I'd never left Mytchett, in which he spoke about feeling out-of-place intellectually with his adoptive parents. The thrust of the article was about the Right's belief in rescuing a handful of brainy oiks so as to ensure that the remaining poor are genuinely undeserving and that the undeserving rich are backed-up by the intellectual muscle of deserving arrivistes who have enough inside knowledge of the poor to lord it over them efficiently. That's not how Michael Gove put it but then I'm not sure that Conservatives themselves truly understand their own opinions.

In fairness, he speaks warmly of his adoptive parents and says that he would not want to seek his birth family because of the hurt it would cause his mother. He's mainly trying to promote his education policy and it seems to be the interviewer who is fixated on adoption. Mr Gove quotes Alan Bennett as someone who also felt out-of-place with his parents, and Alan Bennett was not, to my knowledge, adopted.

I'm straying from the point. I was talking about projection. John Hurt always felt he was Irish and he made his home in Ireland. When the telly programme did his family tree, and it turned out he wasn't Irish at all, he was devastated, as though it mattered. Even though I'd love to find an ancestor who was Irish or Jewish or African, I also know in my rational mind that it wouldn't mean anything, and might even be a misprint.

And yet, weirdly, because I've always felt I'm an outsider in London, not being from here, even though I've been here more than half my life, I was pleased to find out Herbert came from down the road in what is now pretty much part of south London, and that his grandmother actually came from London proper. I didn't immediately know why I was pleased until it occurred to me that I feel more entitled to be here. I would be appalled by the suggestion that anyone else has no right to be in London if they weren't born here, and yet I seem not to have extended that sense of fair play to myself.

And I realise that I feel quite relaxed nosing around in Arundel, or Loddon or anywhere else I've found an ancestor, because I have an acceptable reason for being there. It's not that I feel a new bond with the places; it's more that I don't really feel comfortable wherever I am, but if I have a reason that seems to justify my presence, I feel less embarrassed.

Borough is the area on the south side of London Bridge, in the Borough of Southwark, once part of Surrey. (See, even in London, I can't shake Surrey off.) The Romans began the first market when they built the first bridge. Since then, the area has had a fascinating history, trust me.

The short version is that London had no other bridge until the seventeenth century, so traders from the south and the continent headed to Southwark. I read in one place that there was no other route for continental produce to reach London, which strikes me as wrong. Since they were at sea anyway, wouldn't it have made sense to nip round to the Thames estuary and on to the port of London, and not have to make the overland trek from Dover?

In any event, it seems as though the first market was on the bridge. Then it got moved further down to what is now

Borough High Street because it caused congestion. Then it got moved again for the same reason and it's been where it is now, just south of Southwark Cathedral, for 250 years. Its main function was as a wholesale market until the foodie revolution. Now it's one of those places about which one says, 'It's ridiculous, I've lived in London for 27 years and never been here.'

It's very easy to get to. We can take the 133 bus all the way from Streatham Hill. We figure that, as it's a Saturday, we'll get the full experience. I think I might be putting too much pressure on this occasion; we're finally going to Borough Market to find out what all the fuss is about. And my great-great-grandmother Charlotte Watson was born there. I don't even know if she was more than a baby when she left. I've discovered by sending for her marriage certificate that her father, Thomas Watson, was a millwright, but I don't know if he was a millwright in Borough or even from here. Charlotte was only 17 when she married and by then was living in All Saints Road in Portsmouth. I know nothing about Charlotte's connection to Borough other than that she was born here. There is nothing I can actually look for, so the entire weight of this part of my family's story is being borne today by a swanky food market that has been cracked-up to be really special. Surely it can only disappoint.

For years, I've meant to come here. I know Linda used to come here. She loved nice things. Her origins were unglamorous and she took nothing for granted. She would spend excessively on all the pleasures in life. 'Working-class fecklessness' she called it. She also loved the flowers in Columbia Road Market, somewhere else I've always meant to go since she told me about it.

I start the experience with three very nice oysters. I like oysters a lot, but I hardly ever have them. Conversely, I don't much like porridge and I have it every day. There are lots of nice-looking things to buy but we make our way to the area where vendors put out samples to taste. Clearly, many people come here to graze and never buy anything. But we tell a fresh pasta lady we'll come back, with every intention of doing so. She has put out little morsels of ravioli, and pesto on tiny bits of bread, as have other pasta people. She says the pasta was made yesterday, which a real foodie will tell you is not fresh at all.

You can get pasta made only hours ago in Soho. But Borough Market does have something special about it: it makes you feel like a tourist in your own city. You feel like you're doing something a guidebook told you to do, to get a real sense of somewhere, somewhere that's brilliant because the locals go there; yet we *are* the locals but somehow don't feel like we are.

Everything is very expensive. And most of it is delicious. Whether they can afford to put out free samples because they're raking it in, or they have to charge the earth because they're giving so much away, I don't know. But you could quite easily fill your belly here for free, or spend a hundred quid on a sliver of parmesan and one olive. And, oh my Lord, the Arabic food stall is to be martyred for.

We pass by Southwark Cathedral, which I've also never been in. We give it the once-over. In a strange parallel with the market, there are stalls arranged around the edges inside – I can't remember what those bits of a church are called. The side bits, anyway. It's a kind of Christian marketplace, set up in a way similar to the stalls at a party conference or university freshers' week. We are handed a brochure by some Anglican nuns who smile in a really lovely way. I've always liked nuns, and I suspect they have a laugh. These nuns don't look glassy-eyed or mad. They don't look like people who speak of God's love with hate in their hearts. They look at us in a way that suggests they genuinely love us as fellow human beings. Anyone who would sneer at these women is missing something. I like that they are people contemplating something bigger than themselves. I'm not saying I want to hang out with them, but I wouldn't want to upset them either. So I hope they never come to one of my gigs.

I'm out of the cathedral and back in the temple of gluttony. I see the biggest oysters I've ever seen and demand one, without even looking to see where it's from. It is a ridiculously big oyster and the little spoonful of vinegar and diced onions with which I season it seems inadequate. I want more onions on it. So I add another spoonful, and another, not realising that I am about to try and swallow something the size of an omelette that is now sitting in a cupful of vinegar. Clearly oysters are a rare treat for me; otherwise I'd have thought to scoop up some onion without bringing a whole load of vinegar with it. My punishment is a face bathed in industrial acetic acid that proceeds down my front while I try to use my jaws to hurl a huge mollusc into the back of my throat, like a heron trying to down an oversized salmon. I am just so cool. It's good to contemplate something bigger than oneself, but not to try and eat it.

Time to get out into the street to let the breeze waft the stench from my shirt. We run into Warren, who was Linda's partner and is now with Deborah. Her mum has come down from Newcastle and they are showing her the sights, one of which is me, for I am now one of the sights and smells of London. But they don't seem to notice that I've turned into fish 'n' chip paper, and they've got to rush because they're off to the Tate. But it was good to see Warren and Deborah. He looks well and happy and that's good.

We have a little look around the neighbouring streets, which are a mixture of bohemian and council, and then we collect our pasta and strike out in the direction of the South Bank, walking along which is one of my favourite things to do in London. Only now does it occur to us how many times we've walked within yards of, or right past Borough Market. On the positive side, we've saved a fortune over the years by not knowing where it was.

And I'm always happy on the South Bank. Today, I can also say I've got in touch with my London roots. Having lived in London for 27 years, I can now say that I am one-sixteenth a Londoner, except that saying something like that is as stupid as trying to swallow an oyster that's bigger than you are.

CHAPTER 19

Finally to Kew

I'm here. It should have taken 40 minutes by car, but as I entered the Wandsworth one-way system, I remembered something about bringing ID, rang directory enquiries, got through to Kew and found out I did need a utility bill and my passport, just in time to come back round the one-way system and go home to get them.

So I've missed the 11.30 a.m. daily tutorial and have to fend for myself on arrival. At least I find the place okay, despite having forgotten to bring an *A–Z* or satnav. The building is signposted from the main road. I thought it would be right by Kew Gardens and would have a pleasing approach. It's nowhere near the gardens, it's actually tucked round the corner from the Retail Park. The car park with 'limited parking' has loads of space, although waves of people appear from the direction of the train station. I should, of course have come by train, but I'm very glad I wasn't waiting at Clapham Junction when I realised I had none of the documents I need.

It's a hideous building and absolutely enormous. It should be grand, considering it holds our nation's archives, but it's just big and ugly. I'm not equipped to describe the architectural style, so let's just say it's shit. I'll probably discover it's considered a masterpiece and has won loads of awards but somehow it manages to be forbidding without being impressive.

I panic slightly on arrival when I realise I have absolutely no idea what I'm doing. I spoke to someone ages ago, who recommended I 'just turn up', and there are instructions on the website, but my brain is full and instructions won't go in. I figure the best way forwards is just to walk in and then question everyone I come to who might be a member of staff until I get to something I can look at.

First stop is the main library bit where loads of people, most of whom are very nearly ancestors themselves, are looking things up on computers. I walk straight up to some people behind a desk and tell them I am looking for someone in the Metropolitan Police in the 1870s. A lady looks on a computer and finds out pretty much what I found out from looking at the Met site. The only difference is that she thinks the attestation records might bear fruit. I have no idea what attestations are but she gives me the file number and tells me I can order it once I've registered. Registration is done online. You type in your name and address and then go and wait to present ID, be photographed and be issued with a pass that lasts for a year and enables you to order documents. While I'm queuing, the lady who suggested the attestation ledger comes up and gives me a list of annual Metropolitan Police service orders for the period I'm interested in. There might be something in one of them.

Successfully issued with my Reader's Card, I go back to the computer and order some documents, which will appear in the reading room in an hour. You can order three at a time.

Then you have to wait. Rather than play around on the computer until it tells me my documents are ready, I go down to the café and get a big coffee. I've already had lunch while driving because Katie gave me a sandwich when I went back to get my passport and the gas bill. But I'm sitting in the café and *BBC News 24* is on a big telly with the sound off but subtitles. I'm trying to ignore it because the main story is that Britain has elected two fascists to the European Parliament. I really can't bear it. My only hope is that the strain of appearing respectable will unravel the British National Party, but I am ashamed and angry that this has happened. I just don't believe that people are unaware that it is a fascist party. But at least I'm in the right place to establish my racial purity, should I need to.

My documents should be nearly ready. First, before entering the Reading Room, I have to put most of my stuff in a locker, which is free. I can keep a few sheets of paper (printouts of Brian's research), a single notebook and a pencil with no rubber on the end. I guess that's to stop me rubbing out historical things, even though there's nothing to stop me setting fire to the building. There's no saying I don't have a box of matches in my pocket, although I don't.

The reading room is to the right of the library. I have to swipe in using my new card, and my belongings, which I have transferred to a clear plastic bag, are thoroughly searched. While I was ordering my documents, I was prompted to book a seat in the reading room, and even offered the option of a table near the window, in case I want to photograph anything. The documents are left in the pigeonhole that relates to the seat I've booked: 44E. They're proper old documents like the ones at Arundel.

But this is not fun like Arundel. I find it hard to express how much I don't like it here. And I don't want to get to like it here. People obviously do. I expect they come every day and make new friends, but I don't want to get involved. You can't in the Reading Room in any case. It's a silent room and you have to have your phone off or on silent. I ought to enjoy the focus on work, and the fact that I won't be interrupted, but I long to be interrupted by someone from the outside world. In the normal run of things, I crave the opportunity to work with no distractions, but in reality it's torture.

I begin with the medal records for the Royal Army Medical Corps in the Great War. I want to see if there is any more information than I was able to glean from the Internet. I have a printout of Herbert's record showing he received the three usual medals nicknamed Pip, Squeak and Wilfred. One of the ladies who helped me said the big book I'm looking at might tell me more about his service record. It lists the RAMC men who received Pip and Squeak. The book is organised alphabetically up to a point, which is to say the letter S comes after T but the names beginning with S come up in no particular order. I leaf right through the S section and find nothing. So I go through it again. If I looked closely at the thing I have printed off, I'd see that page 5671 is actually listed, but I don't. Nonetheless, eventually I find Herbert on that page. This confirms he received Pip and Squeak and tells me nothing else. I remind myself that this is the name of my grandfather, whom I knew, typed in a ledger in 1919, that it's the real thing and not a copy. Then I think I should take a copy of it, but that seems to defeat the whole purpose of seeing the real thing. I could probably have ordered a copy without ever seeing it. So I just look at it for a while.

Again, if I looked properly at the printout I have, I'd see that somewhere there's a record of the other medal, Wilfred. Herbert's on page 3 of that book, so I'd have very little turning to do. But I'm doing two ancestors at once and have my maximum of three documents. And I'm not concentrating properly. I know I'll come back here, probably. And I suddenly don't care what's written down about my grandfather, for the very reason that I did know him, and whoever issued these medals or recorded the information did not. He was my grandpa, not theirs. We often talk about people being reduced to the status of statistics and, in a way, that is the activity that this building celebrates. Also, I've seen the medals, and touched them. That's probably why I feel no need at all to look up the record of my great-uncle Mattie's medals: I have the real thing on the shelf above my desk at home.

But I suppose I should look up Grandpa's other medal. And look for Lionel's. I hadn't even thought about my other grandfather's medals, perhaps because no discussion about them has ever taken place in my hearing. Yes, I'll have to come back here. More than once. Maybe the weather will be nicer and the building will grow on me. I'll get here early so I'm not in a rush. And the staff are helpful and pleasant.

I've looked at this book for quite a long time now. So I start looking at the police Service Orders for 1876, the year when my great-grandfather Thomas Monk married and was, according to the marriage certificate, a policeman. It occurs to me that I should give the medal book back in case I need to order anything else, since I'm only allowed three at a time. Then it occurs to me that I ordered three documents and I've only got two. I'm missing the attestation ledger. So

I give back the medal book and ask about the attestation ledger and am told it's probably upstairs in the Map Room. I go up to collect it, thinking I'll bring it down, but it's huge, which is probably why it's in the map room and I have to look at it there. I hope my stuff is okay downstairs and start trawling through the names of people who were sworn into the Met between 1871, when Thomas wasn't a cop, and 1876, when he was.

While I'm looking, one of the strange-looking men who patrol the library in blue blazers, grey slacks and headsets approaches with these big polystyrene wedges to protect the spine of the book. I suppose if I'd done the tutorial, I'd know these things. He doesn't say anything, just puts the wedges in place, silently, like an over-attentive waiter putting a napkin on your lap.

I get to June 1871 and then decide to work backwards from the end instead. Somehow, I figure that if he was a definitely copper when he married in November of that year, statistically it's more likely that his name is close to that date. This is probably not the case. I try to scan the names thoroughly but it's difficult because I'm trying to do it quickly. I try moving my head, as though it's a camera panning down, and then start moving my whole body, as though I'm somehow more likely to catch the name if I put my back into it; rocking backwards as I move down a column of names and forwards as I move up the next column. I must look mental. I spend about an hour doing this but don't see the name. I try looking only at first names for speed's sake, then think Thomas might have used a middle name first, so I focus on surnames. Either way, if it's there I can't find it, and I'm not doing this for another hour.

So I give the book back and return downstairs, to realise I left the Service Orders book open and that everyone else has their books propped up on the wedges. For a while, to avoid drawing attention to my mistake, I carry on reading without wedges, trying somehow to create the illusion that, with this book, you're not supposed to use them. Then I reckon I'm not getting away with it and fetch some.

This book is quite interesting, mainly because of the huge turnover in police. I know from the hour I've just wasted upstairs what a lot of recruits there were, and I can see here that men were resigning or being dismissed all the time. Loads of coppers were sacked, almost all for drunkenness and its attendant behaviour. Constables using 'disgusting language' to a superior, not showing up for their shift and being found drunk at their lodgings or in a pub. One is found 'in a field in an indecent position with a female'. Given how pissed they all were, it's no wonder so many drowned, patrolling docks and river banks in the dark.

On 19 January, PC 359, Monk, receives a reward of eight shillings. But on 10 April, PC 300, Monk, is fined five shillings and cautioned. It doesn't say what for, but I'm thinking PC 300 is the more likely to be my great-grandfather. But I can't be sure either of them is and the book is big, so I cut to his wedding day to see if any leave is mentioned, but find nothing. So I flick through a bit more and realise it would take a couple of hours to do this properly and that I'd need to do this with ten more books, and I've already got two different PC Monks, so I can't be sure of anything. Maybe when Brian comes over next month, we can trawl through them together.

If this stuff were online, it would be more like a leisure

activity reading it. Well, that's how I feel trapped in this environment. If I were at home with my computer, it would probably feel like work. But the point is, I'm not enjoying this reading room. How would a chatty person cope in here? I'm usually quite happy to be quiet, and even I find it oppressive. Worse than a silence rule, there's an *expectation* of silence.

I would stick it out for longer but we've got tickets for the cinema. We're going to see a new film about the collapse of fish stocks. Mightn't sound like fun to you, but in this situation, I feel like a schoolkid on the last day of term who's being taken to see the new Harry Potter. So I return the book, swipe out and retrieve my belongings from the locker. I validate my parking ticket and am cheered to learn that parking is free. I bet people come here just for that reason.

At the cinema, we run a gauntlet of people with leaflets about sustainable fishing. Greenpeace have set up an information booth and are giving out a guide as to which fish can be eaten safely, basically pollock. There is also a suited man from Waitrose giving out a booklet entitled 'The Very Useful Guide to Fish'. It turns out Waitrose put money into the film. Furthermore, the company claims that all their own-label fish comes from sustainable sources. Waitrose is expensive enough for me to believe that all their fish has been put through university.

It's a beautiful and effective film, the sort of campaigning documentary that brings you to the edge of despair and then tells you there is hope if we act now. But it also does for the idea that farming fish protects the seas. Farmed fish, obviously when you think about it, live on ground-up fish which is caught for them. It takes five kilos of anchovies to produce one kilo of salmon.

Basically, we shouldn't eat salmon at all. Or cod. And I learn the reason for these infestations of jellyfish that appear on local news broadcasts: we've eaten all the fish that eat jellyfish. For the same reason, the sea is filling up with plankton. And 'line-caught' fish are not landed by keen anglers and humanely despatched with a little wooden truncheon, there are thousands and thousands of miles of baited lines in the sea. Although the lines don't do the same damage as the vast nets that actually scrape the seabed, ripping up everything.

I'm reminded that my great-great-great-grandfather, Edward Monk, the one who was supposed to be a landowner in Kent, was a dredgerman of that county. This means that he used nets scraping the seabed. I remember reading something from that time, expressing concern about the sustainability of oysters.

I will, however, have some oysters when I go to Kent, because I'll be getting in touch with my Monk roots; and as the Japanese say when they hunt whales, I'll be doing it for research purposes.

CHAPTER 20

Grave Times

I've been to see Mum and Dad who were way overdue for a visit, and I thought on the way back I could go to Crondall, where Nan's ancestors the Hewetts lived, and Victoria Road Cemetery, where Grandad's dad, Alfred Hardy is buried. I want to see graves. I don't know why but a memorial to someone seems to be the most solid affirmation that they lived. I haven't found any other graves and I've been saving these ones up because I know they are there.

Crondall, it turns out, is quite substantial. It is the sort of perfectly gentrified Hampshire village that would not be out of place in Suffolk. It has one shop which is perfectly decent and clearly doing its best to get people through the door; but I suspect that nobody uses it except when they have run out of something. We might be in the country, but it looks like Waitrose country to me. However, it's clearly a lively community because a troupe called the Crondall Entertainers are doing a stage version of the *Titfield Thunderbolt*. I think they should be called the Crondall *Players*; the audience should be the judge of whether or not they are entertainers. And I really don't approve of anyone who thinks a film should be made into a play. It's completely back-arsewards and never as good as the real thing. I saw that *Brief Encounter* thing and it was irritating. The woman playing Celia Johnson's part was very good, as were the special effects, but if Noël Coward had wanted special effects, he'd have written *Private Lives II, Final Impact.*

I was supposed to come here with my sister Sue because she knows where all the relevant places are, but I mainly wanted to visit Mum and Dad today and just see if I had time to fit in Crondall as well as Victoria Road. I'm quite excited about Victoria Road because I've spoken to a nice lady called Kelly at Rushmoor Borough Council who gave me exact directions of how to find Alfred Hardy's grave. If I can find it, I can take Dad there sometime.

Crondall is en route. I don't feel the urge to moon around in a soul-searching way, as I did in Norfolk, because Crondall isn't that far from where I grew up and Sue already knows where everything is. I go straight to the church and have a quick search of headstones to see if I can find any Hewetts. Failing to do so, I ring Sue, who, it turns out, is not well, which compensates for the fact that I didn't tell her I was coming; she wouldn't have been able to meet me anyway, I rationalise. From memory, she talks me to the grave of Charlotte Maria Hewett and Henry Hewett, Nan's dad's parents. It's a large stone in good nick, but I suppose it's not that old. They died in 1920 and 1934 respectively. His name was added beneath hers. He was a lay minister so his parishioners might have chipped in for the stone, and he was also a baker, which was probably quite a remunerative profession in those days.

Next to Charlotte and Henry is Charlotte's father, Thomas Watford. His name is only just visible. The surface of the stone is flaking away and soon the grave will be anony-mous. Maybe that will take decades; I don't know that much about erosion. But Thomas's name looks very fragile. Thomas came from Farnham, where I went to school. I have a very ambivalent attitude to Farnham. Finding out that one of my bloodlines runs to there must be some sort of punish-ment for never really accepting who I am.

Susan tells me to walk back down Church Street to find a house that Nan told her about visiting as a little girl. I know that Thomas and his wife lived on Church Street many years earlier but I don't know if it's the same house. My eldest sister is incredibly good at giving directions over the phone, especially considering that Nan died eighteen years ago, so it must be a very long while since she pointed the house out to Sue.

It's the first house in a pleasant terrace that's set back from the road and up on a bank with its own little path running in front. But the owners have put a really big new number 1 on it so I don't tarry. I don't think I can face a conversation with someone who's put a really big number 1 on the door: 'I think my great-great-grandparents lived here, and I'd love to see how much of a bollocks you've made of it.'

Instead, I continue walking back down to The Borough, the main street. There are a couple of terraces of cottages, one of which was Albert and Charlotte's. Sue has narrowed it down to one of the terraces but she's poorly so I don't bother her again. I'll come here with her another time. It'll be good to have an excuse just to hang out with my sister.

I feel I should immerse myself in the local culture by buying a delicious handmade delicacy from the shop, but Crondall is not so rural a place as to have its own variation on the pasty, so I buy a packet of peanuts, which would most likely have been considered ethnic food twenty years ago. Today the village is populated by folk in Range Rovers who forsake local traders and stock up in Farnham.

I feel slightly protective of this once-great civilisation from whose loins I am partly sprung, so I decide to be especially nice and polite to the shop lady, because I've noticed they do that in the countryside. And I am moved by a notice saying, 'We take dry cleaning!' The exclamation mark was possibly put there by one of those people who use exclamation marks when they're writing postcards about uneventful holidays in Dorset, but it has an added poignancy, I think. It doesn't just denote the fact that a food shop doing dry cleaning is a tad surprising; rather, it has an air of desperation: 'Please shop here – we'll do anything. We'll get you crack or prostitutes if you like!'

I walk the long way round to the car so that I've done a circuit of the village, and I have a last look at the graves, before heading off. To my shame, I decide to satnav it to Victoria Road, because it's twenty years since I drove round Farnborough, the town of my birth. I am going home. Indulge me and imagine this is momentous.

The journey takes me over the top end of Farnham. Today I feel a slight attachment to it, which is something I have not felt since I moved to London. I don't know if it was visiting Crondall or visiting my mum and dad, but I feel a general sense of belonging to this area.

I pass the outskirts of Aldershot, where Sue still lives and where my nieces, Laura and Hattie grew up; and where the crematorium is. All my grandparents ended up there. Aldershot is also where I spent many a dreary Saturday afternoon shopping with my parents. It's where I once saw a trumpet for twenty pounds in a junk shop window and walked around the block deciding whether or not I wanted to learn the trumpet enough to pay twenty pounds. When I returned, I'd decided I did, but it had been sold, which is why I can't play the trumpet. How different my life might have been.

I pass the big roundabout near the Hall and carry on past signs for the Military Town. The army was ever-present during my childhood. The woods where we went for walks were often crawling with soldiers in full camouflage. They'd appear out of a bush and run past looking slightly embarrassed. If you walked further, you came to the firing ranges. The only thing to stop you from wandering into the ranges was the occasional red flag. Sue once rode her horse, Tom, up there, and managed to get right into the area of the ranges without seeing a flag. Suddenly, bullets were flying over her head.

I don't think many bullets ever hit the targets. We found loads. We found them way behind the steep bank of sand that was supposed to catch the misses. Some had gone over it and some had gone round. Some were just dropped on the ground still in their cartridge. Allegedly, it was possible to fire them by clamping them gently into your dad's vice and banging the cartridge with a hammer. There was no PlayStation then; kids had to make their own weapons in those days. Boys even found unexploded mortar shells up there. We had to be given talks at primary school about the dangers of returning home from the woods with unspent ordnance in our satchels. All in all, the presence of the security forces made for quite an insecure environment.

Aldershot itself was like a town under occupation. I had a joke about it when I first started, 'You can always identify the army off-duty, because other skinheads don't wear corduroy trousers.' It was quite a good line 26 years ago. The local papers were full of crimes perpetrated by squaddies, and the squaddies always got off very lightly, either because they had just got back from a tour of duty in Northern Ireland, or because they were about to embark on one. They had to 'let off steam' which involved all manner of horseplay from criminal damage to gang rape. These were the peace-keepers we sent to the Six Counties.

But I always enjoyed the Army Show when I was younger. We still thought of the army as being the people who had fought the Germans. In fact, I think I believed the army was still fighting the Germans until I was about six. I would have been eight when the troops went into Northern Ireland, ostensibly to protect the Catholics. I remember playing soldiers with lads up the road, and the two sides being drawn up by my friend Mark Brown. I recall clearly Mark's words, 'We'll be ve army, you be ve Cafflicks.' The honeymoon hadn't lasted long.

I'm getting close to the roundabout at which Aldershot turns into Farnborough. There is a sign for North Camp. I remember that Dad's uncle Doug received his fatal head injury in the North Camp Hotel, so I suddenly turn right on the roundabout to look for it, then remember that Alfred's grave is my priority and turn round in front of the fire station. According to the satnav, I'm only a few minutes from Victoria Road. Soon, I'm passing the RAE, where Dad, Lionel and Alfred worked. I'd forgotten how huge it is. It has always been a very important part of British aviation. All I can tell you about that is that the SE5 was built there, when it was still the Royal Aircraft Factory. If I remember correctly, the SE5 was a First World War bi-plane. I don't know if the Sopwith Camel was developed there, but that's my favourite aeroplane name. I used to love British warplanes. Lancasters, Buffalos, Mosquitoes, Spitfires. I read about them in those boys' magazines in which the enemy pilot received injury uttering the words 'Aaargh, Himmel!' Dad would have been an RAF pilot had he not been short-sighted. He'd probably have got shot down, and I'd never have been born.

The RAE is also the only place I've worked in what you might call a job. I was a car park attendant for a week during the air show one year. I considered my objective to be fitting in as many cars as possible. I was less concerned about leaving gaps between rows of cars to enable people to drive out. I'd like to be able to say I've never had a job at all, because that would be quite an achievement; but my one week there does mean that four generations of Hardys worked at the RAE. And it was a chance to find out that the air show is mostly an arms fair, not just a chance to see Spitfires in flight as I'd imagined.

We're going past places with loads of memories. I'm trying to work out why I remember driving around all of the roads to my right, which don't really go anywhere. Driving lessons, that's why. We started off here because it was near to Mytchett, and then progressed to the test route in Aldershot. I took my test three times. Passed every time. My instructor once laughed when he saw a black woman. 'Is that your girlfriend?' he chuckled. I just said, 'No', because she wasn't.

There's the Tech, where Sue did her A-Levels. Coming up is the site of Queensmead shopping centre. Queensmead used to be a street before it was a precinct; more recently, it was demolished and it's flats now, apparently. It was where we did our family shop because Sainsbury's was there. See, even in the sixties we were neglecting our village stores.

On the right is a dental surgery where once was the dentist we went to as kids. He was a nightmare Welshman called Mr Williams who gave us more fillings than we had teeth, often with no anaesthetic. He was always especially rushed when Wimbledon was on. He loved Wimbledon. There's the doctor's surgery. Doctor Turner smoked during consultations, but was ahead of his time because he practised osteopathy, which was only just starting to replace hanging.

And here's the Clockhouse roundabout. The Clockhouse is famous. In Farnborough. But it's not very old. It's just a clock house. I turn left and I'm on Victoria Road. I'm heading towards Cove. Cove is where Grandma, Grandpa and Joan moved to be nearer Mum when she left Richmond to marry my dad. She thought she'd shaken them when we moved to Mytchett, but Joan found a house opposite. Cove was also the home of the Nazi nail-bomber, David Copeland. I felt embarrassed when he was arrested, as well as feeling other more relevant things.

On my right, I find the cemetery. I know the entrance is on Union Street because both Dad and Kelly from the council told me, so I turn right and drive round the back of the cemetery. I'm near the station now. I used to go to Southampton from there when I was at university; and sometimes I got the train to there from London when my parents still lived in Mytchett. This area actually does feel like home and I'm not happy about it. I would take you to the hospital where I was born but it's flats now.

Here's the entrance. It's only a small cemetery and very orderly, but I'm glad to have Kelly's directions: 'Take the path straight ahead of you, turn onto the first path on the right, then count six graves in. The grave on your right is number 169. Turn in to the right and count along to number 175, which is Alfred's.' I wasn't expecting there to be actual physical numbers but there are oval metal plaques hammered into the ground. The number 169 is still visible, as is 173. So two graves along must be 175, Alfred's.

It has no headstone, just a stone rim going round it. The one next to it is similar and I can see engraving on the top end of the rim. Alfred's is too overgrown to see the engraving. I could tear away at the grass, but I remember from my failed search for Bells at Aldeby that the grass and soil will be protecting the engraving, so I decide to leave it. The grass is quite short and neat and there are no weeds, so it looks quite nice. I know he's down there, Alfred Hardy. That's enough.

I want to go home now, but first I'm going to try to find the North Camp Hotel, so I head back to the turning and make my way down towards North Camp. I ring directory enquiries to try to get a number, as it occurs to me that it's very likely to have closed down or be under a new name. They can't find it. I see a sign off to the left pointing to 'Shops' so I head down there and park up. I'm about to call Dad and then I see that I'm outside a pub called the North Camp Hotel. Twenty minutes on the meter is 10p, so I figure I'll have a drink and a pee within twenty minutes and then head off.

There's no bar rail. There are a couple of bits of Victorian moulding, but other than that, nothing of the original interior remains. Nonetheless, somewhere in here, Doug Hardy hit his head on a bar rail. I feel I should have a drink to him, but because I'm driving, and his drinking was a problem, I'll raise a glass of Coke to him. He was a wrong'un but he was still my grandad's brother, chorus girls or not.

I feel I've done right by him. And I've paid my respects to a number of ancestors today. I feel quite whole. And I do feel weirdly at home.

CHAPTER 21

Betchworth

I start the day full of positive feelings about trains. I've decided to go to Betchworth station where my nan was born. And I figure that, if I get the train, I won't be tempted to try and tick any other boxes. If I were to drive, I might try to take in Stoke-Next-Guildford or Burgess Hill. I'll be stuck in Betchworth, so I might as well soak up the experience.

Plus, from Streatham Hill it'll only take an hour and twenty minutes, even with three changes. I've been using the car too much and it probably wouldn't be quicker. I say this despite the fact that last night I forgot to change trains at Clapham Junction, ended up in Selhurst and had to wander around Thornton Heath looking for a cab office. And you know what that's like.

And, of course, when I arrive at Clapham Junction this morning, I can't find my train to Dorking where I'm supposed to change, so I miss it and have to wait for an hour and a half for the next train. The only consolation is that the next one involves only one change, at Redhill, which shaves two minutes off the hour and a half. Plus I bump into my friend Jan and have a moan and there's time to get a coffee. I figure I'll get the first available train to Redhill and wait *there* for an hour and a half, for the sake of variety. I've had lots of long waits at Clapham Junction, but when in life will I ever have a reason to experience Redhill station for 90 minutes? I've been through it plenty of times on the way to Gatwick. I've even done a couple of gigs in a huge, horrible municipal barn of a venue, but when have I ever taken the time to appreciate the station and absorb its charms?

I'm not a glass half-full person, I just try to find compensation for adverse situations. For example, it's probably just as well I missed the Dorking train. I have bad memories of doing *Just a Minute* there. Plus, if I had got that train, I'd have been rushing and flustered and might've looked at a schizophrenic the wrong way and been stabbed. I'll get letters for writing that. Several letters. All from the same person.

Anyway, I won't waste the time I spend at Redhill. I've brought the laptop and I need to call my friend Suresh about a benefit I'm doing tomorrow. Clearly missing the Dorking train was meant to be. The fact that, if I'd driven, I'd be in Betchworth by now doesn't matter. I'd probably have crashed. Or run out of petrol. Or picked up a schizophrenic hitchhiker and had to drop him off at more than one place.

Fuck. I'm at Redhill and it's a shit station with no cafés at all. Clapham Junction has shops and everything. This is rubbish. Oh hang on, I've picked up Wi-Fi. I can productively check my emails. Now it's disconnected again. That was weird; it was on while there was a train at the platform. Did the train have free broadband? How come no train I ever get has free broadband?

I discover that the train to Betchworth takes only seven minutes. What's the point in waiting an hour and a half for a train that takes seven minutes? That's fucked up. I could probably walk it, except I'd get lost. And the whole point is to arrive on a train, because that's how you should arrive at a station, especially when your great-grandfather was the signalman there. However, if I had decided to drive, I would have forgiven myself because my great-aunt was killed by a train. I did actually think about that fact quite seriously. It might be quite a weird place to go. But I'm trying not to be morbid or write myself into a tragedy that took place a century ago. I'm trying to celebrate my nan's birth and the fact that my great-grandfather was the signalman at Betchworth. He didn't stop being a signalman; he got transferred to North Camp, to where every bloody train that leaves here seems to be going. I could probably go there and back and still make the Betchworth train.

I probably should go to North Camp station at some point, but I doubt the old signal box is there. And I know that Nan was born in the station cottage at Betchworth and it's definitely still there. So I can justify the fact that I drove right past a sign for North Camp station the other day without even stopping.

Time goes by very slowly on Redhill station. I need a pee but I'm putting it off because it seems like the kind of station at which that will require a huge and complex quest. Someone will probably say, 'We don't really have facilities for that kind of thing. We used to but people kept peeing in them. Try the public library in Reigate.' But finally I give in and go in search of the gents, which it turns out is adjacent to this very waiting room. Furthermore, behind them is a little coffee kiosk where I buy a flapjack and a smoothie. Now I hate the station less. Plus my train is now in, some time before it's due to leave, so I can get on and sit in comfort.

The train starts up and quickly passes through Reigate, whereupon Surrey goes all rural. This could be Sussex. And now we're in Betchworth, drawing to a halt as we pass over the level crossing once managed by my great-grandfather, Albert Martin Hewett. In all likelihood, we have also just passed over the spot where his daughter Hilda was killed.

I get off and right there on the platform is the cottage in which the family lived. It's obviously been knocked about and added to. Part of it served as the signal box for a while. Probably the bit that now houses some older people sitting at computers. I hope they are the local historical society using council archives but it turns out that they are Assured Indemnities Limited and that their office is private. Damn them for living in my nan's house. But then, Nan would have had only faint memories of this place, and not happy ones.

I want to know when Hilda died, so I ring Dad to see if he knows, but he's not sure. I thought the copy of her death certificate I have – and forgot to bring – was taken from one he had, but I must have borrowed it from Richard. Dad clearly has genuine feelings for the aunt he never knew. He tells me Hilda and his mother were playing together. Hilda was the elder sister and it was believed that she had thrown Audrey out of the way of the train. If that's the case, I owe my existence to young Hilda Hewett.

Dad says she's probably buried in the churchyard, which hadn't even occurred to me. He says there might be a children's section. For a moment, I think he means a reference section for schoolchildren, with colourful explanations of death in felt. So I say, 'Dad, I'm 48' and then very much wish I hadn't. But Dad is trying to get lunch on the table anyway, so I quickly take my leave.

There is one large house next to the station, and apart from that, nothing; no indication of what and where Betchworth itself is. There's no one to ask, save the worried-looking staff of Assured Indemnities Ltd who are peering out at me, perhaps suspecting me of being part of al-Qaeda. I can't see where the town would be, but there's a steep chalk escarpment on one side of the tracks, so I think it more likely that there's life along the road on the other side, as it winds downhill. I follow my nose, which usually gets me places pretty fast.

It's not sunny but summer is under way now. Beside me on the path are grasses as I tall as I am – not that tall – and bursting with seeds. Other things to do with the reproduction of plants are floating on a very light breeze and probably causing the itching in my eyes and running of my nose. I haven't had hayfever before, but then I never had asthma until my forties, so who knows what the back half of my life has in store?

I cross a roundabout which has a signpost to Betchworth, suggesting that I'm not there yet. I pass a large garden centre and then a Rolls Royce and Bentley service centre. Then houses start to appear. There is serious money here. I feel a daft class animus towards these people. How dare they be rich in a place where my great-grandfather worked on the railway?

It's not really a town, it just spreads out around the intersections of various roads. I guess which way to go and eventually find a signpost, a proper one on a little traffic island of its own. It's painted white and has finger shapes to assist direction. One of the fingers points to the church. It's still quite a walk. This is one of those ridiculous places that are nowhere near their station. It's probably nearer another town's station, an amusing fact that the locals delight in telling strangers.

The church has a posh furniture workshop on one side and, on the other, a forge that I'm guessing makes things for decorative purposes. Shit, there's a funeral on. I'm not local and I look like a scruff. The hearse is there with the back open and mourners are gathering. I will have to walk through them to get into the churchyard. I could go to the pub and wait for them to go in, but I don't know how long that will take and I'm expecting a tortuous journey home. I should have driven. I'm not doing this again.

I'm carrying a smart laptop bag so I reckon I look slightly professional and entitled to be here. It's God's house after all, not theirs. The funeral does mean I can't go in the church or look for anyone who could help me find the grave, but I'll have a go at finding it myself. The only thing that puts me off is the presence of the undertakers, who maintain a distance that is neither discreet nor respectful.

I vaguely hate undertakers because they intrude on private grief for a living; and because they mess about with human bodies despite having no medical training. I imagine it all began with some Stone Age entrepreneur saying, 'You know when someone dies and his mates just cover him with dirt? I reckon there's money to be made there.'

I am also starting to hate stone masons for using water-soluble rocks and carving only tiny, shallow scratches into them, except for the sturdy, solid ones dedicated to the rich, in which the engraving is deep enough to last a couple of centuries and many coats of rain. I can't find Hilda. Many stones are completely worn. On some of those, although I can't find names, I can just make out dates, some of which are around the time Hilda died. I have rung my daughter while walking along and got her to go into my office and find the death certificate. Hilda died in August 1907.

There is no children's section as such, but there are children's graves, and some graves that are very small but unidentifiable. It's getting hotter. It was nice earlier; one of those summer days that's grey but bright with genuinely fresh air. Now the air is thickening up and has bugs in it. Flies are buzzing around some shit that I hope is a fox's but I suspect is a dog's. A lot people are walking dogs through here.

But I like the sound of the funeral. There is an organ playing hymns that I like but can't remember the name of. It sounds like a proper funeral. I lament the contemporary vogue for uplifting funerals. I don't want a cheerful celebration of my life. I want people's lives torn apart. I'm not letting the humanists get hold of me. And I've determined that I want my remains to be scattered. Not cremated; just scattered. I want to be found in carrier bags in motorway service station lavatories all over the country.

I stop to look at the church notice board. It turns out the rector is a woman. There is also something about solidarity with the Anglican Church in Zimbabwe. And I see this announcement for an upcoming event:

Love for all, Hatred for None. As part of a peace initiative with our neighbours, the Ahmadiyya Muslim Youth Project are doing a series of discussions in village halls to build bridges and clear up misunderstandings. So we would like to invite you to ISLAM, A RELIGION OF PEACE (not of terror). Saturday 20 June, 5–6 p.m.,

Betchworth War Memorial Hall, for an open discussion. Please do pop along, we would be delighted to
have you and explain what concepts like jihad really are
and who the Prophet Muhammad (PBUH) really was,
or answer any questions that may be troubling you.

In case you didn't know, by the way, PBUH stands for
Peace Be Upon Him. I am impressed by this event. Either it's
an extremely bold initiative or this place is a lot more
progressive than I would have imagined it to be. Perhaps we
need to thank the church for reminding Middle England that
there's a whole world out there.

I'd like to meet the rector, but it's a full-length church
funeral service. A crematorium would have done about three
in this amount of time. Finally, people start to filter out, and
I think I could hang around for a chat; but it doesn't really
seem appropriate. I worry that she'll think I'm someone who
hangs around funerals hoping to catch a priest. I decide I'm
going to have to give up on finding Hilda's gravestone. It
might be one of the worn or overgrown ones, and I really
don't want to look at one of the ones that's been moved and
propped up against walls; I wouldn't want to find it's one of
those. So that's it, I tried. I could take a picture of the church,
the place where Hilda's funeral must have taken place, but I
don't really want to. I don't even want to go in it now. I didn't
come here with the intention of feeling sad, but I do.

I start to retrace my steps but much of the road has no
pavement and there's a public footpath that I guess might
lead more directly towards the station. Suddenly I'm walking
alongside a wheatfield. I think it's wheat. I really can't
remember the last time I walked alongside wheat. I feel better

about Surrey because it still has agriculture and now has Muslims. It's actually very beautiful here. And I come to a post office, which is good to see in a rural setting. And then I'm back to the road I walked in on, which encouragingly is called Station Road. I have almost no battery strength in my mobile, so I wait until I get to the station before ringing train inquiries. I just want to discover when is the next train I can definitely get, before the phone dies.

To add some excitement, I don't know whether I need to go through Dorking or Redhill to change, and I find they're in different directions so I don't know which platform I need. If the gates close, I might be stranded on one side of the tracks. I'm ringing from the Redhill side. I get through to Mumbai after a wait for a high volume of calls and he says Dorking. I walk across to the platform I came in on just as the light start to flash and the barriers start to close. In comes my train for Dorking Deep Dene, and I'm gone.

CHAPTER 22

So, Farnham

I n 1972, I was due to leave Mytchett Country Primary
School. There were three possibilities for the next stage of
my education. A new comprehensive had opened in
Camberley. The twins, Joy and Simon, were already there.
The head there was very liberal, but only in his use of the
cane. Susan and Serena were at Camberley Grammar but that
was no longer one of the options. Available to me were
Farnham Grammar, or Robert Haining Secondary Modern.

I heard horror stories about Robert Haining. I'm sure it
wasn't nearly as bad as the stories, but it sounded like the sort
of place from which Sidney Poitier would have run in tears.
Mytchett was quite divided. Our bit was quite solidly middle
class. Only our house and the next-door neighbours', who
were pools winners, displayed Labour posters at election
times. Joan, Grandma and Grandpa lived opposite but they
were Liberals. However, although our road was solidly Tory,
Labour came second in elections, because of the large London
overspill estates that were built in the fifties and sixties. Some
of the kids I was at primary school with were genuinely poor,
and certainly deprived. One of my friends died of diabetes
because his mum thought it was all nonsense.

When Mum and Dad married, they lived at first in a caravan on Coleford Farm in Mytchett. Dad's grandparents, the Hewetts, lived in a bungalow not far away on Coleford Bridge Road, which only had one side. The other side, where we ended up, hadn't been built yet. After the caravan, they had a pre-fab in Farnborough. In case you are young, a pre-fab was a pre-fabricated house, devised in the war to make up for the housing shortage caused by the bombing. After that, they had a council house on Field Road, and then one on Hurst Road, where they were living when I was born. I was the fifth child in eight years and Dad, despite being a boffin, was a civil servant and not well paid at that time.

To buy our three-bedroom bungalow in Mytchett was a stretch. It was a nice bungalow, built in a third of an acre of land, in the 1950s. It was a while before Dad could afford a loft-conversion to provide extra bedrooms and a dark room for himself. We were not deprived, certainly not culturally; the house was full of books and the *Guardian* was delivered. And Dad, being gadget-minded, bought a fridge and a washing machine and a telly in the fifties when such things weren't universal; I think we still had the same ones until the seventies. We must have been the last family in England to get colour telly. It wasn't considered important; in fact, I think it might have been considered vulgar. We didn't watch ITV much either.

In short, we weren't well off at all but it seemed to me that we were middle class, more so than it would have seemed to Susan, the eldest. We became more middle class over time, so I was the poshest. I was a little snobbish, but I didn't associate class with money, because we never seemed to have any.

In any event, I was really scared of Robert Haining, even though most of my contemporaries went there and nothing bad happened to them. And I didn't want to go to the comp because of the head with the cane. So I really wanted to get into Farnham Grammar School. The trouble was, I wasn't all that clever. I was a smart alec, articulate and quite literate, but not that good at those IQ tests that constituted the eleven-plus exam. I've never set much store by 'intelligence' tests; if there is a definition of stupidity it's the belief that life is that simple. But it was the custom in those days to decide when a child was ten or eleven which social class they would be in for the rest of their life. Grammar schools would have been fine if they had been available to everyone. My generation was the last in Surrey to face that test; and in a way I was lucky, because I ended up having quite a good education at quite a liberal grammar school. More than lucky, I was jammy, because I only just got in on the Interview.

The Interview was for borderline cases who didn't do brilliantly on the test but showed potential. We faced a panel of three people; I can't remember if they said who they were. They asked me what I was interested in and I said poetry, meaning *my* poetry. They asked which poets I liked, and I said Wordsworth, because I'd vaguely seen a bit of his stuff in a book. They asked which Wordsworth poems I liked, and I said, 'The one with the rabbit in it.'

It wasn't going terribly well until they asked me what else I liked doing, and I mentioned watching *Monty Python's Flying Circus*. I was normally in bed by eight o'clock, but Mum and Dad made me stay up for *Monty Python*, which I think was very forward-thinking of them for the time. *High*

Chaparral on a Monday evening was a treat, but Mum and Dad thought the Pythons were crucial to my cultural development. Comedy was a big thing in our house. We had records of Flanders and Swann, Peter Sellers and Pete and Dud, and always watched *Steptoe and Son, Till Death us do Part, Morecambe and Wise, Harry Worth* and *Dad's Army*. My dad was a raconteur and Mum had a quick and savage wit; mealtimes always involved at least one of us laughing until we were nearly sick.

Anyway, on my mentioning the Pythons, by which time I had pretty much abandoned any idea that these were people I could impress, one of the panel sat up and said, 'You like *Monty Python's Flying Circus*?' Suddenly, he and I were in our own gang while the other two took a back seat. He must have been the Simon Cowell of the judges because the following day, I had passed the Interview.

So, in September 1972, I went in Joan's car to Ash Vale station to take the train to Farnham for the first time. Joan commuted from there to London every day. In fact, she carried on driving me to the station even after taking early retirement. She was a devoted aunt, taken for granted in the way that devoted aunts always are.

One other boy from my year, Mick Loveridge, also got into Farnham Boys' Grammar, so I wasn't completely alone, although I was daunted. I was small, and surrounded by boys, some of whom were nearly 18. There weren't that many on the train, but once we got off and started to make our way up the hill to school, there were hundreds, almost all of them bigger than me. I had never worn a uniform before, and it felt weird. I had never needed a satchel, nor a geometry set. And I had never used a fountain pen and they were compulsory. They leaked and I lost them. I got through one a day in my first week, emptying the house of them.

I don't know if it was an unusual school but it was a cross between an old-fashioned grammar with public-school pretensions and something more modern and progressive. There was no corporal punishment. There had been pupil unrest in the late sixties and uniform was abolished in the sixth form. In fact, it increasingly disappeared from the fourth year on. Older boys had beards and permed Afro hair. And the head, Mr French, was a liberal, kindly man, amused by the fact that his nickname was Spike, a reference to his long nose.

He did wear a gown, as did all those teachers who liked to be called 'masters', including the deputy head, Mr McLaughlin. Mr McLaughlin was a tall, glowering man, quick to anger and verbally scathing. He was also a marvellous performer, because it was all an act. It took me years to work that out. I finally clocked it when I was hauled before him for an assault on Martin Pratt, who ran the tuck shop. I had lobbed a cup half-filled with cold hot chocolate into the shop one day, just as he was closing up. The last board was going up over the counter, so it was kind of a challenge; there was a second when he could no longer see me but there was still a gap through which a missile could pass.

Martin knew it was me. I didn't dislike him but he ran the tuck shop, which made him some kind of petit-bourgeois falangist, probably because he didn't give the sweets away. So he knew that if anyone would throw cold hot chocolate at him, it was me. And I was duly summoned to see Mr McLaughlin. I think Mr McLaughlin also thought Martin was some kind of petit-bourgeois falangist because he couldn't contain a chuckle while trying to upbraid me. His mask had slipped and I realised that he was a tremendous actor, breaking character for the first time in several years.

Years later, when I first did gigs in Farnham, he started to come along, and I had to call him 'John' for the first time. It still felt wrong, even though secretly he'd been John all the time, and Mr McLaughlin was an invention.

It's a shame he never taught me because I gather he was a very good historian. We had a number of very good teachers, in fact, all the teachers were characters. Each engaged his or her audience by being eccentric or idiosyncratic. Teachers aren't encouraged to be characters anymore, because schools are run like private businesses or Soviet tractor factories. If you think that's a contradiction, I urge you to read up on the theory of state capitalism, which is the best framework for analysing so-called Communism. That sentence caught you unawares, didn't it?

School was all quite relaxed from the start, although I disliked the all-male environment, having been raised in a very female one. I looked forward to the end of the first year, because then we were to merge with the Girls' Grammar and begin the transition into becoming a sixth-form college.

It was strange though, when the first girls arrived on our territory; we'd forgotten what it was like. And they arrived with all their teachers, many of whom were much stricter than ours. The lax regime was tightened up. Uniform was enforced from the fifth form down. And the sixth form became a separate entity because it was now the college. The school was being phased out. There was no new first year; the lower years disappeared as my year moved up. So we were always the youngest, which was a good thing because it probably meant there was less bullying. I could not have stood the humiliation of being bullied by younger boys.

And as we got older, the regime began to relax again, as the school shrank and the college grew, and newer teachers were more modern in their methods. Some even turned their chair round to face the other way, and straddled it like Christine Keeler; or sat on top of the seat back with their feet on the cushion. Probably my favourite teacher from my whole time at Farnham was Mrs Blanks, whose passion for English made me want to please her with my literary skills. I don't care whether you like this book or not, but if she thinks it's shit, I'll be gutted. If you *are* Mrs Blanks reading this, I hope I haven't let you down.

Anyway, as I progressed at Farnham, my love of poetry extended to other people's, including performance poets such as Brian Patten and Roger McGough, whom I went to see at the Redgrave Theatre. The Redgrave was a terrific local resource; a perfect, purpose-built modern theatre opened in 1974 to replace the old Castle Theatre. Today, shamefully, it's mothballed.

My first return to Farnham as a comedian was onstage at the Redgrave. I performed on a Sunday evening in front of the set of the main-house show, which was *Tess of the D'Urbervilles*, so I had Stonehenge behind me. And this was before *Spinal Tap*. I would like to play the Redgrave again, but it seems the prosperous town of Farnham cannot sustain a middle-sized theatre. The Redgrave was where I first started to love theatre, unaware that I was witnessing it every day when Mr McLaughlin walked into assembly. I went to

Saturday matinees on my own, from the age of 13. And I joined a Saturday morning theatre club for teenagers, founded by the director of Theatre-in-Education, Peter Corey. Peter taught us the improvisation games that actors do as part of their training, and from which some people now make a living.

Peter was an inspiration. He is a substantial writer and actor in his own right. He wrote and performed the short play, *Hancock's Last Half Hour.* He is a Brummy, like Hancock himself, and captured him in a way I've never seen anyone else do. And Peter was funny, a funny man who made a living from being funny.

I wrote humorous verse, and I was in school plays, and goofed around at home, but it was Peter and those working with him, Sam Naylor and Nadine Casdagli, who drew out whatever part of me became a comedian. I went every Saturday morning, never missed it. And it was Peter who first put me on a professional stage when our group did a show at the Redgrave one Monday night. I read some of my poems, and we did some improvised sketches which were the best bit of the evening. And people paid. And laughed.

So why don't I love Farnham? I don't know. I should, shouldn't I? Part of the reason I don't love it is that it always felt like a bubble, a bubble of privilege and complacency. When I arrived, I think there was one boy in my first year who could be called working-class. He was also the only Catholic. Only two other boys in my class said their families were Labour, and neither of them was the working-class one; he was a Tory. And there were two boys in the whole school who weren't white and they were cousins.

In fairness, the school's ethnic profile pretty much

reflected middle-class Surrey as it was in 1972. And as the sixth form expanded, Farnham College did start to resemble modern Britain. But Farnham itself seemed to be the poshest and most conservative town in the area, and from the age of 11 I disliked it for that. It wasn't that I had a terrible time. I had plenty of friends. I had a terrible adolescence, as most of us do, and I suppose I associate Farnham with that. But school was fine, and I did lots of writing and lots of drama. I had a lot of good times too, and met some very good people. My friend Julie Ankerson was the funniest person I've ever met.

I expect I needed to rebel against something, kick against something. My parents were kind and reasonable and imposed few strictures on me. The same could be said of school. But I had decided that I was most definitely on the Left. I was confused about what that meant. I'd write the names of anyone I considered also to be on the Left in bubble writing on the covers of my exercise books. This would include trade unionists, Labour politicians and Communist leaders. So you might see Vic Feather alongside Roy Jenkins and Chairman Mao. I think Trotsky and Stalin also shared top billing on one book, and I don't suppose either was very happy about it.

One teacher demanded I cover a book with brown paper, but the rest were benignly amused or admired my spirit. I had very little to rebel against and was hardly ever in trouble. I didn't rebel against schoolwork because I liked most of it, and I was timid because I had been raised to think of the world as quite a dangerous place. I think my view of life was that it's like a stinging nettle: the only way it won't sting you is if you grasp it; and who the hell's going to do that?

So I was a cautious rebel, and my rebellion consisted of despising somewhere that hadn't done me any harm. And that's why I don't love Farnham, although, having said that, I must love it a bit, otherwise I wouldn't go on about it so much, would I?

CHAPTER 23

Hitchin

The first place I got excited about visiting as part of this project was 3 Tilehouse Street, Hitchin, where I found that my grandad, Lionel, lived in 1911. It was the first address I googled and found. And because there's a business there now – the Pentangle Design Company – the likelihood is that they'll let me look around. I also want to try to find Nightingale Road, where he lived when he was a year old, and Hackwood House on Grove Road, where he was born. His mother, Annie Aylott, was born in Hitchin in 1874 and lived with her parents on Brand Street and Ickleford Road. Her parents, Henry and Sarah, had also lived on Brand Street. Lionel's father, Alfred Hardy, came from Basingstoke, and his parents also moved to Hitchin and were living at Dacre Road in 1901.

I'm driving. Hitchin is only half an hour from King's Cross but it would take me an hour to get to King's Cross and I don't want to have to wander on foot as I did in Betchworth. I can use the satnav to find all the roads and just pull up outside houses; impressing locals in the way stars do when they visit the slum where they were born, and giving youngsters a fiver to watch the car.

It's straight up to the A1. The A1 is fiddly in parts but I like it because it's a real road with a history. It was the Great North Road connecting London to Edinburgh, and bits of it follow the Roman Road, Ermine Street. To get to it, I head straight up through Swiss Cottage to the A41. Heading up the Finchley Road, I realise I'm about to pass the turning for the cemetery where my friend Alan Coren is buried. I decide to go and see him. I've been searching for the graves of people I never knew and I suddenly feel like spending some time with someone I did know.

I don't think I've ever done this before, visited a grave to say hello to someone. My grandparents and aunt were all cremated. Paul Foot was cremated. Linda was cremated. Humph was cremated. Rosemary was cremated. Alan had bought a plot in a municipal cemetery he liked, not far from the house in Cricklewood where the family lived for many years. When he was dying, he announced that he wanted a religious Jewish ceremony, which meant the family finding rabbis who would perform in a secular graveyard.

On the day of Alan's funeral, I had to get back from Scunthorpe, getting up at five in the morning in one of those Holiday Inns that's not really a hotel. I stopped off in Golders Green to buy a yarmulke. There's a shop called Jerusalem the Golden that sells religious items. I arrived when it opened.

'I need a kippah.'

'What colour?'

'Black.'

'For a funeral?'

'Yes.'

The old man foraged in a big cardboard box and found one that looked right to him. I tried it on.

'Do you think it's too big?'

'No, it sits well on you.'

I paid him and thanked him and he looked at me in a kindly way.

'Next time for a wedding or a bar mitzvah, I hope.'

I liked the service, though it was hard to hear in the open air with a building site in the background. Someone pointed out that if we were *filming* a funeral scene, one of us would be sent to ask the builders to be quiet. Filming takes precedence over everything.

One of the rabbis was a cantor – a singer, in case you didn't know. I hadn't been to a Jewish funeral before and this was a very unorthodox one even for an unorthodox one, so I don't know what normally happens, but there was singing and a lot of Hebrew.

The reception was in the hall of the Danish church next to Alan's house in Regent's Park. The rabbi and the cantor came and didn't seem uncomfortable to be in a church hall. I was standing with Sandi Toksvig who, being Danish, was very comfortable. Suddenly, the cantor came over, extended his hand and said to her, 'As a gay rabbi, I'd like to thank you for all you've done.' We were a bit stunned; it's not a sentence you hear often. For once, Britain's best-known lesbian wit was lost for words, so I said to him, 'I thought there was a touch of musical theatre about your performance.' He took it in his stride, and told us he'd been an Orthodox rabbi but had had to join a Liberal synagogue because of his romantic persuasion. I thought Alan might be enjoying all this, somewhere.

I find Alan's grave very easily. It's less than two years since we buried him. There's a little wooden plaque; the stone hasn't been set yet. I desperately need to pee so I find a bush, making sure no one's remains are nearby. Then I sit a little while on the grass next to the grave. The building work still isn't finished but they've got the roof on. I know Alan's not here, not in any meaningful way. It's just somewhere to come.

I press on. Hitchin is easy to find, but because of using satnav, the journey's a blur. As I reach the outskirts of town, I see a petrol station with a Marks and Spencer attached. I decide to get a sandwich to eat in the car to save time. I might get more of a sense of the town by finding a local independent café to have lunch, but this book isn't about lunch and I need petrol anyway.

I find myself in Tilehouse Street even before I finish the sandwich. It's a nice street of what look to be sixteenth- and seventeenth-century houses. What it was like in 1911, it's impossible to tell, but I'm sure there wasn't a pair of yellow lines painted on each side of the road.

I head down to Bucklersbury Street which leads to the old market square. I'm looking for somewhere to park. I've already seen a warden shooing people away, but there are all these bays with big blue P signs next to them. I pull up outside Allingham's butcher's shop, being careful not to stop in the bits that seem to be loading bays, but rather in one of the bits to which arrows point with the words 'Parking at all other times'. To my simple mind, that means I can park here at any time, but hardly anyone is parked here and it's the town square, so I suspect it's more complicated than that. I ask the butcher, who says, 'They'll nick you if you park there.' I don't know if he just doesn't want me spoiling his shop frontage or whether he's telling the truth, but I suspect the latter because it all rather looks as though Hitchin has its own peculiar parking system and language, just as Hull has white phone boxes and Cambridge has foot-deep gutters to damage the cars of outsiders trying to park.

The butcher directs me to a car park and I drive out of the one-way system and round to the left to a car park that belongs to Netto. This can't be the car park he meant, as it's £1 for an hour and £10 thereafter, meaning I'm expected to run in, buy two hundred rolls of rough toilet paper and leave as quickly as I can; so I head back around the one-way system onto Sun Street and pull up outside another shop to ask a man selling furniture where the public car park is. It's past Netto. I also go into the newsagent's which, I notice, seems to specialise in maps. They even have one of Hitchin and provide me with a lot of pound coins for the parking machine.

This is back-arsewards. The whole reason I brought the car was so that I could find everywhere by satnav and not have to walk miles. But, having parked, I find all the streets in which I know my ancestors lived on the map, mark them with a pencil and then set off on foot. None of them is that far apart and none is far from the station.

I start by taking a short-cut through the Swan pub car park back onto Sun Street. I see a young woman going from shop to shop with an A4 folder. I saw her five minutes ago going into the newsagent's after me. I recognise the scenario: she's handing out CVs as my daughter does when I nag her to go out and find a job. I want to say, 'You're handing out CVs, my daughter does that,' but I can't see why she would be interested.

But I am full of purpose as I stride up to Tilehouse Street, once my grandad's residence, now a design company.

Number 3 has been knocked through into next door but it's still a very small place. I ring the bell. When a lady comes to the door I go straight into my spiel.

'This might be an odd request but I'm doing my family tree and my grandfather lived here in 1911, and I wondered if I could look around.'

She lets me in but she doesn't know anything about the building's history, except the fact that the bit that's clearly an extension is an extension. The bit of number 3 that's not an extension is just one room with an enormous fireplace. The stairs are on the next-door side. She rings ahead to tell the people working upstairs to expect me. She could shout or take me up there; it's only a few steps. But perhaps that's how the company does things. It's such a short flight of stairs that I have to climb slowly so I don't reach the top before she's finished telling them I'm on my way.

The designers indulge me politely but unenthusiastically. I'm getting used to the look that says, 'We really are very busy.' But one of them knows the history of the building and reels it off rapidly. I catch '...originally a public house...post office...derelict...' I am cheered by the fact that it was a post office. The telephone exchange would most likely have been in the post office and Lionel's mum, Annie, ran it.

So that makes sense. But I can't for the life of me see how they lived here. Unless this was the shop and next door was the house. Ruby Saunders, named as their servant on the census, cannot have lived in. I did search for more information about her, by the way, but drew a blank. It does seem very strange to have a servant in a place so tiny. You couldn't dust or sweep in here; blowing once would do it.

I can see that there were two rooms up here at number 3,

but if downstairs was the post office, there would have been no living space. Unless the extension replaced part of the building that was demolished. Or maybe it was just a house at that time and the post office was somewhere else.

The main thing is that my grandad, whom I knew, lived here and I've found it and I can go now.

I head back up Sun Street to the market square which today is a pleasant piazza with a little coffee truck and seats put out. People are sitting there relaxing in a continental way. Disappointingly, there is also a large Starbucks to accompany Toni and Guy, HSBC, Waterstone's, Millets and Pizza Express. And the Corn Exchange has been turned into a restaurant instead of an arts centre. But there's a nice-looking little deli and café over to the right. I go in and buy a little bottle of locally produced apple juice. While paying, I eye up the meats. They sell haslet! I haven't seen haslet for years. We had it when we were kids and I still don't know what it is.

Past the deli is the church. This is where Lionel's parents married, but I'm getting bored with churches. Most of them are old and they're obviously easy to find. They are such permanent fixtures that it's hard to get misty-eyed about the fact that my ancestors' christenings, weddings and funerals took place in them.

But I think I might have a look for gravestones. As usual, I'm not prepared. I haven't tried to find out where people might be buried. I decide to have a look inside for anyone who might help and, the second I walk in the door, a man in a sweatshirt sitting behind the information table looks up worriedly, as though the last person who came in was sick in the font. He asks if he can help me and I say I'm looking for the graves of Hardys and Aylotts. He says the cemetery was closed to new applicants in 1850 and that anyone who died after that is in the municipal cemetery. But he goes to get a booklet to see if there are any older Aylotts here.

'No. No Aylotts,' he says, seemingly slightly irritated to have helped me.

'Well, thanks anyway,' say I.

I see that his sweatshirt was supplied by the Guild of Vergers. I think he should wear something more ecclesiastical, like the verger in *Dad's Army*. Sweatshirts are always a replacement for something: school blazers, prison uniforms, clothes.

I figure the map of the municipal cemetery will be at the town hall and the verger says that's on Brand Street, where Annie's parents lived in 1871. It's just shops now, although some of the buildings look old. Here's the town hall, but you can't just walk in. I ring a buzzer and explain my query. A lady comes down to talk to me. She tells me it's not really a town hall any more, just a hall for events. I've played in town halls like that. My gigs are usually in places that used to be something else. She says I'll have to ring North Herts District Council, which I do.

I leave a message for someone called Carol who can help me. Then I set off for Ickleford Road, where the Aylotts lived later on. I don't have an address for 1881 but Annie, her parents and various siblings lived there at number 25 in 1891. By 1901, Annie's married, her mother has died and her father has moved into number 23 with some of her siblings and some of his grandchildren. Before I get there, Carol rings back. I ask her about the graves of Henry and Sarah Aylott, and Charles and Jane Hardy, Alfred's parents who seem to have followed him from Basingstoke to Hitchin. Carol finds

Henry and Sarah in one grave. She died in 1901, he in 1911. She says it will be very hard to find the grave but gives me a rough explanation of where it is. There are also separate graves for a Jane and a Charles Hardy, but their graves will be even harder to find. However, she can tell me Jane died in 1904 and Charles not until 1930, aged 80.

That would tally with my Charles Hardy born in 1849. It seems strange to think of him still alive in 1930, when my Dad was four. I remember now that I looked him up in the 1911 census late the other night. I found a Charles Hardy aged 69, which is too old. However, he was born in Hurstbourne Priors, the tiny place in Hampshire where my Charles Hardy was born. I wasn't able to print off the page and forgot about it until now, thinking it wasn't him and that he just came from the same place. Now I remember that the Charles on the census was married to someone called Marria aged 70. Carol's telling me that my great-great-grandmother Jane Hardy, if it's the grave of the right Jane Hardy, died in 1904. So Charles might have remarried an older woman and given a false age. Or perhaps the census taker misheard or wrote it down wrongly.

I don't really like this, the idea that my great-great-grand-father, the one with no father, the earliest Hardy to be found, remarried after his wife's death. And my Dad knows nothing about him so he obviously wasn't spoken about by Lionel, Alfred or Annie. And did he lie about his age? I'm obviously being judgemental; who am I to say he shouldn't find happiness after being widowed? I'm just not getting a good feeling about him.

I carry on to Ickleford Road, and find that 23 and 25 are separated by 24. Number 25 is a much bigger house, perhaps to accommodate the grandchildren. I take a couple of pictures and feel I've done my duty. I'm not going to knock and ask to go in. I've done enough of that, and I'm starting to annoy people.

Instead I move on to Nightingale Road, where I discover that the house where one-year-old Lionel lived no longer exists. I overtake the young woman with the CVs. This is about the fourth time I've seen her. Up until now, it's been as though, if I looked away and looked towards her again, she'd disappear, a figment of my imagination, the spectre of one of my ancestors, who happened to be a 19-year old Asian girl. But I'm close enough to see she's real and I can't resist asking if she's giving out CVs because my daughter does that.

She's Australian, which surprises me though it shouldn't. I always think Asian people should be British or from the subcontinent itself. She is indeed handing out CVs and having no luck. I tell her my daughter just got a job by posting her CV online.

'In Hitchin?' she asks hopefully.

'No, London,' I reply.

Then I feel I've offered false hope. So I say, 'Don't give up,' as though I'm wise as well as old. As though *I'm* the apparition and will disappear when she turns round, leaving only my voice saying, 'Remember the Force.'

Embarrassingly, she turns onto Grove Road, where I'm going, so I say 'Good luck,' and walk really fast to get away. She didn't ask what I'm doing in Hitchin walking around clutching a map. That's because she's a kid. It's no surprise I'm doing something old and weird because I'm a weird, old person.

On Grove Road, I try to find Hackwood House where

Lionel was born. I find a lot of new houses, then some old ones, then a load more new ones and no more old ones at all. There's not much of the old Grove Road left, so I decide to move on.

Next up is Dacre Road, where the now disreputable Charles lived with Jane before she died. I find number 39 and photograph it but, then, as I walk along, I find new council homes, which means the numbers might have changed and quite probably that wasn't the house. I have no note of the address where he lived with the whore Marria in 1911, but I'm not interested.

It's time to get to the cemetery. I ring Carol and ask if you can park there. I might as well get some use out of the car. She says you can if the commuters haven't taken all the spaces. They sound like bad people, the commuters. It's not even very near the station so they must be desperate or live in weird, far-flung places.

Walking down the hill from Dacre Road to the car park, I pass the Queen Mother Theatre. That rings a bell. I've played there; I'm sure I have. And yet I obviously didn't think then to find out about Lionel and the Aylotts. It must have been years ago and things weren't online then. 1911's only just online now. And I wouldn't have known about ringing councils to find out about graves. I've only known that for a little while.

And it was probably just a gig to me. I'd have arrived in the dark and gone straight backstage. Afterwards, I'd have got into a car or legged-it to the station. I'd have told the punters my grandad was from Hitchin because I've always known that. But they wouldn't have cared and back then neither did I. Maybe it wasn't even this Queen Mother

Theatre. I think I don't respect people's towns enough. Note to self.

There's plenty of space to park on Cemetery Road. I manage to follow Carol's directions as far as the toilets and then get confused, so I ring again. She's amused rather than irritated. She talks me to the right bit but again says I'll be very lucky to find Henry and Sarah's grave. I find it almost straight away but I've already let her go.

I'm quite pleased to find Lionel's grandparents, but quite sad too. I picture Lionel here as a boy, in January 1901 and February 1911. He'd only have been 18 months at his grandmother's funeral, and wrapped up very warm. He'd have been ten-and-a-half years old at his grandfather's. I see him clutching a cap in his hands, wearing a scarf, old enough to understand death, already having lost a baby brother, and another baby sibling that I noticed from the printout of the 1911 census.

Then I register the fact that I've been to Loddon where Sarah was born, and now I've found her final resting place. That means I've accomplished something, doesn't it? It's a journey completed.

I start looking around for the Hardys but I can't get through to the council at all now. I'm on hold at the switchboard. I don't want to do this now. Maybe I'll find Charles and Jane in the future some day, and never bother you about it. Time to go home.

CHAPTER 24

The Hardys

Today I'm going to Hampshire, to the area from where the Hardys came. I've just driven past it twice, once on the way down to the Glastonbury Festival and once on the way back. On the way there, I didn't want to stop because I wanted to get a good pitch for the tent. On the way back, I was knackered and just wanted to get home.

I nearly cancelled Glastonbury in order to concentrate on this. To do Glastonbury properly, you have to arrive on Thursday and come back Monday. I could have just driven down on Saturday, done my thirty minutes, turned round and come home, but I didn't want to miss stuff. On Friday, we saw the Specials. I first saw them 30 years ago and I loved them. Seeing them again made me feel that the past isn't lost, which is good when there are good bits of the past. We tried to watch Springsteen, whom I liked as a teenager until punk came along. I really wanted to like him again because he's a good chap, but I couldn't get into it. He's a great showman, but in that American way. After an hour, we slipped off to watch Jarvis Cocker, who is a great showman in an English way; he understands that energy is about focus and glee and mischief. You can have a relaxed intensity. You don't have to stomp up and down the stage trying to make the audience clap along. You don't have to shout, 'Glastonbury, I can't hear you!' which is frankly unwise when you're pushing sixty. It's close to yelling, 'Glastonbury, what did I come up here for?'

It wasn't my favourite-ever Glastonbury but it was only my fourth one. I went in 1985 and hated it so much I didn't go again until 2007. Performers are much better provided for now, although it's still camping. I don't quite approve of camping. There's something morally repugnant about white home-owners posing as Burmese flood victims.

Last year, we hired a camper van at enormous expense. I have to say it was glorious. It had an onboard toilet: satlav. Although what happens is that all the horror of five days of camping toilets is concentrated into the 45 seconds when you have to shake the shit out of the box. It's like a smelly exorcism.

This year we reverted to tent life, but bought every available kind of wipe with us, and the MRSA-preventing spray which you can now buy everywhere, which makes soap and water a thing of the past and sterilised ground-in filth a thing for all eternity. You can't get much sleep and if you're not off your head, it does all feel a bit like a giant village fete gone wrong, but I enjoy it. Performing is weird, especially at my age, standing in a big tent in a field in daylight; I feel like I should be judging leeks. But it's good practice, I suppose. My usual gigs are probably far more comfortable than is healthy.

I'm home now and I'm trying to get back into the swing of things and sort myself out to get down to the Hampshire Records Office in Winchester. I have difficulty leaving the house because I want to make sure I'm fully prepared. I go through all the census returns I've printed off to find addresses, because when I get done in Winchester, I'm going in search of where Hardys lived. Alfred Hardy, my great-grandfather, was born in Sherborne St John, near Basingstoke. His mother, Jane, was born either in Sherborne St John, or Pamber, which isn't far away from there. And his father, Charles, was born in Hurstbourne Priors, near Andover. Charles, you might remember, is alleged to have been the illegitimate son of a servant girl who worked on a large estate. The only estate in Hurstborne Priors was that of the Wallop family, the earls of Portsmouth.

There is added significance to Andover because the Bridles were from there, but I can't make out the addresses and the main thing I'm trying to find out today is who Charles Hardy was. Can there really have been two Charles Hardys born in Hurstbourne Priors who were boilermakers in the mid-nineteenth century and ended up in Hitchin? I rang my dad's sister Muriel to see if she knows anything, but she had always understood that Alfred was the illegitimate one. She didn't know there was a Charles. Dad didn't know Charles's name but understood him to be the illegitimate one. I haven't found a registered birth or christening for either of them on the Internet. Neither can I find the marriage of Charles and Jane.

I found Charles Hardy marrying in 1869 in Basingstoke and again in Hitchin in 1906 and sent off for the certificates, which arrived. This, at least, is one man, I'm sure; a boilermaker with a father called William. In 1906, he marries the Maria or 'Marria' I found in the 1911 census. I thought the marriage in 1869 might be to Jane, Alfred's mum, but it's not; it's to someone called Elizabeth Cook. Moreover, the ages this Charles gives are all over the place, so it's no surprise that they don't fit in with the ages given by my Charles.

I might have found parents for him: the aforementioned William and an Elizabeth, who are on the 1861 census, living in Abbotts Ann near Andover. It says he was born in Andover, which is only a few miles from Hurstbourne Priors. He has a brother, James, who's 11. I've also got people who appear to be the same William and Elizabeth in 1851 with a one-year old son called James, but no Charles. So was he late coming back from a sleepover, or had he been adopted? There's a five-year-old Charles Hardy at another address in Abbots Ann staying with an old lady and her 30-year-old daughter as a 'Visitor'. Perhaps he was with them because the baby was poorly, but, in any case, is this my great-great-grandfather, later to lie up a storm about his age and marry lots of women?

Here's Charles and Elizabeth in 1871 in Basingstoke. He's 28, five years older than he was two years ago when they married. I look at the ages given by the Charles who is definitely (well, supposedly) Alfred's dad. They suggest he was born between 1848 and 1850 and isn't lying but isn't sure either. The margin of error is quite small. The other Charles gives ages that suggest he was born in 1842 or 1846.

For them to be the same person, he's got to have been a fast worker, because he's with Elizabeth in 1871 and Alfred was born that year or the year after. Does Elizabeth die in childbirth and then he hooks up with Jane? Does he get Jane pregnant and leave Elizabeth? I haven't found a registered birth for Alfred, or Charles's marriage to Jane. It's just possible for Elizabeth to have died or for the couple to have divorced just after the 1871 census was taken, leaving Charles time legitimately to marry and impregnate Jane, but it's looking quite likely Alfred was the illegitimate one after all. Unless there really are two boilermaking Charles Hardys from Hurstbourne Priors. Or three. Or four.

Let's see what we can find out. I'm on the road. On my journey to Winchester, I'm trying to figure out what Hampshire means to me. Last night I went to a book launch, which seems an appropriate diversion for someone writing a book. My friend Shappi Khorsandi has written a book about the experience of being an immigrant child. The thing that struck me the most was when she was asked whether she feels English or Iranian, and she spoke about being integrated here but feeling the pull of a place she hadn't been to since childhood. She said that, although it's against all her beliefs to hold an allegiance to a geographical entity, it's hard to explain the feeling as she flies through Iranian airspace.

I'm not trying to equate our experience. Shappi is a refugee unable to return to her homeland because of her father's subversive satire. So thoughts of her origins are bound to involve complex and painful emotions. I, on the other hand, am just going to Winchester for a few hours. In fact, since Shappi went to college there, she has more of a connection to it than I do. I suppose I'm trying to say that the place of one's birth can have an irrational but potent hold, and I was born in Hampshire. I'm still not making much of a case, am I?

I think the main reason I so assertively say I was born in Hampshire is that I was brought up in Surrey. But my mum was born in Hampshire, and I think Dad wishes he was born in Hampshire. I feel that trying to find where Dad was born in Burgess Hill might be something I'll do quietly in the future when I happen to be passing. It might be rubbing his nose in the fact that he's not a native Hampshireman to do it publicly. He was only born in Burgess Hill because his nan's uncle Ted got Grandad that job in the coal office. Nan and Grandad met in Farnborough and moved back there when Dad was quite young. Lionel's dad, Alfred, was from Hampshire as were his parents, if indeed they were his parents. Audrey's father, Henry Hewett, was from Crondall as were all the other Hewetts as far back as anyone knows. That's a lot of Hampshire.

As for Mum, she was born in Portsmouth, as was her mother, and her dad's mother. All in all, I'd say I'm fairly Hampshire. Of the eight dynasties from which my great-grandparents came, we've established that three are from Hampshire, two from Surrey, one from Kent, one from Sussex and one from Hertfordshire. That's not a clear majority, but under the first-past-the-post system, I'm a Hampshireman. And my parents and two of my five siblings live in Hampshire. And I went to university in Hampshire. And I'm going to be in Hampshire all day, so I'm trying to connect with it.

I'm trying to work out whether genealogy is the most introspective hobby you could have or whether it's about finding connections to other people; or finding a reason for the connections we already feel. I'm not a great one for sticking with my own kind. I've been lucky to meet all sorts of people with whom I have nothing obvious in common, often feeling more of a connection with them than I might feel with someone of 'my' culture. There are human bonds that transcend age, race, religion, experience and even language.

Now, that's perhaps easier to say when your culture is the prevailing one. If I were in Basra and I met someone from Hampshire – bearing in mind all the ones from Aldershot are supposed to have left now – I might chat with them about Fleet Services or the Clockhouse roundabout. And there would be a little Hampshire thing going on. Even in London, I can get drawn into conversation with someone who knows where Hook is. I suppose there is some sort of connection because some of our experiences are the same. But I think that, in part, we just open up more if we find links to people. Excuses to talk. We use connections because we crave human contact. Someone might just have the same mobile phone as us, but it's a start.

Our ancestors link us to the past, giving us a place in the world historically as well as geographically. The world was here before us and, hopefully, will still be here after us, and we are part of that process of transition. I don't know how important any of this is. If I were a foundling with no idea who my ancestors were or where they were from, I would be no less of a person and might be even more engaged with my world. Perhaps rootedness makes us lazy in our thinking, complacent in our assurance of what we are like.

There are all sorts of connections between people. I suppose I'm talking about the oneness of humankind. The broadest idea of unity. Not the reactionary idea of unity, whereby you cleave to people of your own race or location. If I'd found out my ancestors were Ulster Unionists or slave owners, I wouldn't feel a new sympathy for such things.

Being British doesn't make me feel proud of the British Empire. But do I feel pride that Britain 'stood alone' against the fascists in 1940? Yes, I suppose I do; it leavens the shame of the fact that we've elected two of them to the European Parliament in 2009. Am I ashamed of all the bad things Britain has done and continues to do? Yes, but clearly not enough to campaign more passionately against them. Is my conscience blunted by a subconscious loyalty?

I do have a love for this land, and I like living in it, and maybe sometimes that means I feel too much at home here. Maybe I don't hate my government as much as I would do if they weren't a bit like me, a bit familiar. No, that can't be the case. That would be pathetically weedy; to be soft on a minister who's turned a blind eye to torture just because we both liked *The Two Ronnies* when we were kids. I loathed the Tories when they were in power. If I'm not hard enough on this Labour government, it's probably because I can't completely shake my youthful attachment to the Labour Party. And because, when I was young, politicians were like aliens; now they are a bit like me. They've taken on human form. That's how they get you.

Before I know it I've arrived in Winchester. I've found my way into the one-way system without even using satnav. I reckon council premises will be in the centre and signposted. This is all very familiar. I've played in Winchester loads of times, once in an old water tower, called, I think, The Old Water Tower. Subsequently I've played many times at the Theatre Royal and still do.

I find the main council building, pull into the car park and find I'm in the wrong place, so I ring the records office and get directions. They'd booked me a place in their little car park, which annoyingly is right opposite the station so now I'm thinking I could have got the train, but I remember that I do need to drive all over North Hampshire when I'm done here.

The records office is like a mini version of Kew but you don't have to provide ID. I can have a pencil and papers in a clear plastic bag, which they provide. Everything else goes in a locker. The lady who helps me is courteous but looks at me as though quite disturbed by my appearance. I look myself up and down to see if I'm inadvertently wearing a badge promoting bestiality.

I get my reader's ticket, which is yellow and lasts for a day, and I go into the library bit. Everyone looks at me as the first lady did, so maybe it's a Winchester thing, or maybe I committed a terrible faux pas last time I did a gig here. But another lady shows me where to find the catalogues for the documents of the Wallop family, the earls of Portsmouth who owned the estate at Hurstbourne Priors, where both Charles Hardys were born. She also explains the microfiche. Blimey, I haven't seen microfiche since university. Next thing she'll show me a banding machine for running off copies.

I like the microfiche. I like the way it magnifies and illuminates; it's a bit like doing Biology at school. Only trouble is, I can't find anything at all. I'm looking for the christenings of any Charles Hardys, but find nothing. I find quite a few Hardys and some Hardings, and some who have been changed from one to the other. I wonder whether the two names sounded any different in a strong Hampshire accent, spoken by people who probably didn't know how their name was spelt. I might be a Harding. Fuck that.

No Charles Hardy anywhere, except on the marriage certificate in 1869, the copy of which I already have. I can't find any other marriage certificate for him, and I go right through the 1860s and 1870s, in Basingstoke, Hurstbourne Priors, Andover and Sherborne St John. Neither can I find a christening of Alfred in any of those places. But why would I? Alfred doesn't appear to have been born, so how could he have been baptised?

I use the computers to go online and check the ancestry site again. There is definitely no birth registered for Alfred or Charles Hardy. I go through my print-outs again. I search for the baptism of William Hardy, who was born in about 1824, and I find a boy of that name in Hurstbourne Priors, son of Charles and Sarah. In all likelihood, this is the William Hardy who was the father of the Charles Hardy who married Elizabeth Cook and Maria Moore, but I still don't know if that's the Charles Hardy who was Alfred's dad.

The only interesting thing I find is that, according to the microfiche, Isaac Newton lived in Hurstbourne, had a bunch of kids there and that he was a member of the Wallop family. You remember Sir Isaac Newton: he discovered gravity when George Washington chopped down the oak tree in which Charles II was burning the cakes. Hang on, that's not right. He wasn't in the nineteenth century. No, this bloke is called Isaac Newton Wallop. His dad must just have been a fan. That's brilliant. You're the Earl of Portsmouth and you're such a fan of physics you call your son Isaac Newton. That's like giving him the names of all the Man Utd players. I suppose if your name is already Wallop, you might as well muck about with it.

I'm at a loss now. I can't even order birth certificates because I need file and volume numbers. I thought parish records were as down and dirty as you could get. I thought everything was here; that this was raw research. I'm getting really fed-up. It's four thirty now. I ask one of my enemies what time I need to get my car out of the car park and she says, 'Just before we close at seven.' They're open for another two and a half hours! I wanted an excuse to leave. I've had a break and eaten my lunch by the lockers. I've had some fresh air on the 'terrace'. I've been to the tea room but found the tea comes out of a vending machine, so just had water. God, visiting someone in prison is better than this.

I just want to say goodbye to this place. With great reluctance, I start looking at the catalogues for the Wallop estate. But there are four volumes here, and it's not fun like it was in Arundel. No jolly archivists are around to help me. No one's flagged up pages. I've already had an insight into how a large estate was run and how servants lived so thirst for that particular knowledge has been quenched. I don't even know if Charles's mother actually did work on the estate or what her surname was, and someone's told me the collection is incomplete anyway.

I have a look at various tenancies but my brain is starting to seize up. And if there was something irregular about Charles's mother getting a cottage, wouldn't it all have been under the counter? I suppose I could ask to see the bundles of private correspondence listed here, and read every line in the hope that somewhere is a mention of an unwed pregnant servant girl being given a cottage but I'm paralysed by the suspicion that I'll find nothing. I feel my ancestors are playing a trick on me. I really do feel like burning all my papers so that no son of mine wastes his life in pursuit of the lost ancestor, but I only have a daughter and she's mainly interested in my record collection.

It's a beautiful, sunny day and I'm stuck among the dead and I can't even find the right ones. I could justify such a tedious and depressing activity if I were doing something vital, like research for a war crimes tribunal. Something essential, no matter how miserable. But I just can't feel anything for Charles Hardy at the moment. He can't get his age right or even decide if he's more than one person. And my life's nearly over, and it's time I drew a line under this.

Still, I mustn't be too despondent. Maybe one day when I have a show here, I could come early and do this by way of whiling away an hour or two. Then, when asked how I warm up before a gig, I can say, 'Reading estate records of the Wallop family from the 1840s and '50s.' But that's for the future. This is the present and I'm not enjoying it, so I'm going to leave and drive around the county of my birth on a lovely summer's evening, listening to the Polish folk CD we bought at Glastonbury.

So, I get in the car and set the satnav for the 'City Centre' of Hurstbourne Priors, since there isn't a 'What's Left of the Village' setting. It takes half an hour and is a pleasant drive, but the Polish band were better live. What's left of the village is not very much. There's a pub, a church and a village hall. There's a cricket pitch and some lovely old cottages and houses, and less lovely new ones. There's an equestrian centre, which I suppose is nice, but you can only ride a horse so much, no matter how dull your village is. There's a house called 'The Old Post Office'. I think it's a mistake to advertise the fact that your home used to be one of the few facilities that was available to the local people. Why not call it, 'The Old Heart of the Community'? Better to deny ever having had a post office. Couldn't locals say, 'Well, everyone here's illiterate, so we never felt the need of one'? But I suppose everyone here is privately educated.

And there really is no centre. It's a crossroads, so at least there's a chance drivers might slow down, something rural motorists rarely do. Or perhaps there are horrendous crashes here, and the locals live by scavenging car stereos and eating travel sweets, like the Cornish used to survive by plundering shipwrecks.

Let's have a look at the church. Very nice but locked. I have a look around the headstones but know I'll find nothing. Nevertheless, it really is a lovely evening. I like it here in the Hampshire countryside, and I've sort of found my roots. Well, not really, but I can say I have.

I'm not far from Andover, so I might as well have a drive round it. It turns out, that's all you can do: drive round it. A town is not a person; you give it a triple bypass, it dies. There are signs to the town centre but I don't find it. The main feature of Andover seems to be its enormous versions of the same retail outlets everywhere else has. Christ, not even Birmingham needs an Aldi that big; how can they need one in North Hampshire? I check to see if the place is populated by a race of giants, but they seem to be normal size.

I did a gig here last year. It was quite a nice walk from station to theatre but that's all I saw. Mark Steel always gets to gigs early and works out some material about the place. He's just done a whole radio series, going to people's towns, finding out about them, interviewing them and performing stand-up entirely about the place, in front of a local audience.

It was a great series but I'm never sure about the wisdom of telling people what they already know about their own town. If Richard Pryor had come to the Fairfield Halls and said, 'What is it with you motherfuckers and your one-way systems?' I'd have felt cheated.

But we're not Richard Pryor, and what came out so strongly from Mark's show was that people loved the respect he showed them, the interest he'd taken in them and his way of involving them, because he valued them. Any comic can say, 'Anyone here got kids? Great aren't they?' to convince the audience he's engaged with them. And sadly, all too many audiences think, 'That's remarkable: I do have kids. This chap's done his homework.' But to find out what a place is for and who lives there, and care about it, shows you're connected. So Mark's right and I'm wrong.

But this place is horrible. At least, the bit they show to outsiders is, and if they don't want me to find the Medieval Quarter, I won't. So many places have quarters now, and many of them have more than four. Forget this, I'm going to find the village of Sherborne St John, where Alfred Hardy and his mother were born. I'm thinking it'll be a pleasant drive but the satnav takes me to the M3. I don't know whether satnav technology is still at the stage at which the little man inside prefers to stick to the main roads. I think the voice should at least say, 'After 800 yards, go straight on. The B road might look inviting, but if you get behind a combine harvester, you'll be here all night.'

We go round the edge of Basingstoke. I'm coming back later to try and find Wendover Street and May Street, and then I'm done. Sherborne is to the north of town off the main road, and it's really very nice. It's got a functioning post office and a red phone box, as well as a church, village hall and pub. I'll bet the post office will sell your surfeit of home-grown onions for you, and also stocks hummus.

Right, so my great-great-grandmother or great-great-stepgrandmother, or someone called Jane, maybe lived in one of these very houses blah blah let's go somewhere else. I drive to Pamber because one census has her born there. Oh, we're here – and it's gone again. If a tiny village can have a tinier suburb, I suppose that was one.

Here's a sign for Aldermaston. Blimey, the Atomic Weapons Establishment; the end point of all those CND marches. In about 1982, I came here with a bunch of friends to be part of a human chain surrounding and linking Aldermaston and some other nuclear weapons places; Burghfield, I think, and maybe Greenham Common. Here's the AWE now. I drive round its whole perimeter. It's vast. I slow down to look at the main gate, and some of the many armed police take an interest so I move on. I'm not paranoid but it's probably illegal to look at armed police outside a site of Outstanding Natural Weapons Capability.

Eventually, I come to the village of Aldersmaston. It's beautiful but how can people live here? I expect they would deny any knowledge of their neighbour: 'Weapons of mass destruction? I don't think so. You could try Reading.'

Right, the time has come: I'm going to Basingstoke. I pull over to put Wendover Street in the satnav. It's half seven now and I doubt I'll find a shop that sells maps. No Wendover Street in the satnav. I was sure I found it online. Let's try May Street. No May Street. So much for the day's grand finale. Bollocks. What do I do now? Well, I'll just drive into town and see what I can find.

Basingstoke has been ruined. I can't think of another town outside the Midlands that has been so heartlessly planned. All right, Swindon. Ironically, when we came to Basingstoke as kids, we thought it was marvellous. We had a small pedestrianised bit in Camberley and there was a bigger one in Reading, but, in Basingstoke, they had all the concrete you could walk on. This was the future. It was before the fashion for pedestrianising existing town centres, which makes you feel you're in a Disneyworld version of an old English high street. These were new, brutal, post-war, Stalinist concrete structures that gave you bins you could sit by. Like drip-dry shirts and plastic shoes, they seemed like a good idea at the time.

But the bit of Basingstoke where we shopped in the sixties and seventies was just a pilot scheme. The new Basingstoke has grown like a cancer from that beginning. I couldn't even tell you where that bit was. It's probably been demolished and replaced by another precinct that's also been demolished. If you build something of no value, it can be endlessly replaced.

This place looks like *Metropolis* recreated by a play-group. It's worse than Croydon. It's almost impossible not to drive into a multi-storey car park. I drive into one and it has a whole bit where you can easily turn round without having to go through the ticket barrier, which means they knew people would drive in by mistake when they built it. The bloke behind me's turning round as well.

Oh hello, I'm suddenly somewhere that looks a bit like a town. There are houses and children playing. How did that happen? There's a human bit of Basingstoke. Right, I need to go and find shops or something. I head back in the direction whence I came, and just keep going, because there's only ever one way you can go here. Oh, here's the pedestrianised old English high street, and a small car park. Let's have a wander about.

There's a cab office and lots of guys standing around. They ought to know if there's a May Street or Wendover Street. But I always feel guilty asking a cab-driver how to get somewhere and then driving there myself. So I just wander. I do quite like the high street. It's got nice buildings, and a museum. Ah, that would have been a reason to get here earlier; I could have looked at old pictures of men in smocks with mutton-chop whiskers holding scythes, but never mind. Oh, there's the Haymarket. That's the nicer, smaller theatre. I've also done the Anvil, which is vast. I can't sell that one out. But we did it on the *Clue* tour and it was good. My sister Sue came. Tim reminded her of Dad. Tim reminds all my siblings of Dad. I should introduce Dad to him one day. That might be spooky.

Here's May Place. Could it have been May Street? Not much left here anyway. Something draws me to a street I was curious about as I drove by. I don't know what it is, but here's a large police station with a map outside. I've left my glasses in the car but I can just make out the street names on the index and see that there's no Wendover. But there is a May! The grid reference seems to be D4, but I can't find it on the map. I get up really close and slide back and forth like a trombone, trying to focus. No good. I could go into the station and shout, 'Quick, there's an incident on May Street, let's run there now!' But the desk sergeant will probably play a recorded message telling me to visit their website. Or shoot me.

I walk back along London Road, which feels homely because it's called London, and leads back to the car park. Ooh, lovely old almshouses on the left. Blimey, they are old. An Asian grocer is open, so I go in. He has a map. I offer to buy it but it's just for helping annoying customers who need directions. I tell him he'll have to do the looking for me because I have no glasses. He's so obliging that I buy some cashews out of gratitude. He finds May Street. It doesn't look very big and I know the satnav doesn't recognise it so I note the bigger street that leads to it is Queens Road.

Back in the car, the satnav does acknowledge Queens Road and says it's five minutes away. But of course, it's all one-way here. I know if I could go left out of the car park, I could then take the first right and be on my way, but I can't go left. So I go right and then the satnav wants me to turn left where it's now blocked off. Fucking satnav. It's the most advanced computer technology and can tell me exactly where I am anywhere in Europe, but it's using street maps from the 1950s.

Oh no, now I'm on a big road out of town. I hope I can get round to May Street the other way but it's telling me to go all the way back, so I go round the roundabout. Maybe I can go back the way I came, past the little car park to the turning I wanted. No, I can't; and now it wants me to drive over the concrete bollards like it did before. I pull up in a weird lay-by and start to make it on foot. I don't like leaving the car here. The houses nearby look like the inhabitants get annoyed if anyone looks the wrong way at the Cortina with no wheels out front. But I think May Street can't be far and my walk takes me past a pub where the Beat are being played loudly. I love the Beat even more than the Specials.

I start to think this is going to be a long walk and I ask someone and they say it is, so I go back to the car. Now the pub's playing the Clash so it's a good pub. I've worked out in my head that I could drive all the way back past the accidental multi-storey car park, round the back of the pedestrian bit and turn where I hoped to. Without wanting it, I've acquired a thorough knowledge of the whole of Basingstoke's road system. Here we go, I'm ignoring the satnav because the bloke inside it is getting hysterical. He thinks his creator will terminate him if I don't do as he asks.

Right, I've found Queens Road. In a second, I'll be at May Street. Ominously, right ahead of me, across my path is one of the big roads I just had to drive along. I think most of May Street was lost to the dual carriageway. Yes, there is just one remaining house, the ground floor of which is a closed-down takeaway.

Now I can go home. I've done Basingstoke. At least I found the bits that actually constitute a place. Sadly, no one any longer speaks with the beautiful accent of John Arlott, Basingstoke's most famous son, and the only thing that made watching cricket bearable. And he was a passionate anti-racist and all-round good chap.

It's getting dark, but still a lovely evening. That's me done with the origins of the Hardys, whoever they were. The lessons for today are that it's never good to be inside on a beautiful day, and that archives are lonely places, that they're dusty and everything is dead. You need people to bring them alive. You need people to have lunch with. People to share things with. I had a great time in Arundel and a shit time in Winchester and Kew. I understand now why the stalwarts at the National Archives huddle in newly formed friendships in the cafeteria. The happiest part of today was when the Asian grocer showed me his map. I always think of myself as a hermetic character who doesn't need people around, and I'm realising it's not true.

CHAPTER 25

Portsmouth

I'm going to see the house where Mum was born on 15 July 1924. I don't know why I've never seen it. It's not as though I haven't been to Portsmouth loads of times. I play at the Wedgwood Rooms every few years, although I tend to arrive by car at night, and can never really remember the way. Once I crashed driving down there. I was doing 80mph and was changing lanes. I don't know if I just lost control or whether I had a blow-out. The front inside tyre was all ripped up, but I'd hit the barrier on the hard shoulder, which would have done that. It was the barrier that stopped me; otherwise, I'd have gone over the bank and down into a river.

This was the early nineties and I didn't have a mobile then. I had to walk over some fields to a house and ask to use the phone. They were quite nice and said it happened all the time. I rang the AA and then the gig. The gig said they could hold the start and send someone out to get me. I said I thought I'd used up my luck that day and just wanted to go home.

I've always been wary of the A3 since then, and usually drive a bit more slowly than I might do otherwise when I get to that section. It would be a very rock 'n' roll death but I'll settle for passing peacefully in my sleep. A car crash would be a bit Eddie Cochrane for Radio 4. I don't want a dramatic death. Although, I'd quite like to die causing maximum inconvenience to other people, on an escalator, or having my blood pressure taken.

I've set the satnav for 74 Gladys Avenue, where Mum was born. That's my main reason for coming. I'm also looking for Arundel Street, where her mum, Rebecca, was born, although the house was bombed in the war; Cottage View where Rebecca lived in 1901; Francis Avenue where she went to school; 125 Penhale Road where she was living in 1911 and until she married, and where I think the family stayed with her sister Esther when they got back from Malta. Also, I'm looking for Landport Street where her parents, Thomas and Eliza, lived before she was born. And I want to find 12 All Saints Road where Charlotte Watson from Borough lived when she married William Bridle from Andover; and 40 St George's Square, where they lived above a pub with their daughter Harriet and her son, my grandfather, Herbert Stagg, after his dad died. There are other streets in Portsmouth where Thomas Monk lived but I've mislaid bits of paperwork and I've got a load of places to go today.

I also want to go to some of the places I went as a kid, when my mum would bring us for day trips in the school holidays. There's a picture of us all at the seafront. The photographer kept squirrel monkeys dressed in little woollen jackets and customers would pose with one on their shoulder. He only had four so my brother said I could have his. I'm wearing my yellow raincoat. The picture is black and white but I remember the coat because it came with a matching sou'wester and they called me the Yellow Submarine at school when the film came out.

I think there was a model village that we used to visit. My family always went to see model villages. And I would take pictures with my Instamatic camera. Damn, I should have looked in the loft for my old photos before I left. I took loads of pictures and we did loads of day trips. We never had foreign holidays but we went to nice places in this country and had a lot of days out, either with Dad driving on the weekend or Mum taking us by train in the holidays. I think most of Mum's day trips were to Portsmouth, but we liked it so we didn't mind. Sea, squirrel monkeys and a model village – what more could you ask for? Oh and HMS *Victory*; I'm definitely going to see that today. I loved HMS *Victory*. I can't remember why. Maybe that was normal for a boy at that time, but I suspect not.

Gladys Ave is in North End which, as you might guess, is in the north of the town, really in the suburbs. It's easy to find and seems quite intact. The houses are large and I know the family didn't live in a whole one. Here it is: number 74. It has a name: Southwold. I shall be going very near Southwold next week when I play at the Latitude festival. I like Southwold and have been there many times. There isn't much significance to that, I know, but I'm trying to build the drama around this event. Mum won't remember this place; they left for Malta when she was two. But I can show her a picture of it.

I'm sure that, soon, someone is going to complain that I'm photographing their house. A passer-by asks me if I'm selling it. Surely I don't look like an estate agent in these shorts and sandals. I must look like a bloody idiot – it's

freezing despite being early July. I've got trousers and a
jacket and shoes and socks in the boot – for eventualities –
but I don't know where or when I'm going to get a chance
to change.

It's a nice building with the original front door and glass
and tiling in the porch. The windows all look new. The brick-
work is white, with that sort of tiling finish. All the blinds are
shut. I don't want to knock. I don't even know which floor
they lived on. Joan, Mum's sister would have remembered. I
wish I'd done all this years ago.

I've seen it and photographed it and maybe some of my
siblings will be interested. Next stop is Penhale Road. I'm in
need of a pee so I pull up outside a pub on the main road. A
man with a dog on a string approaches me and says, 'I'm not
going to bullshit you; I'm an alcoholic and I'm desperate for
a drink.' I give him a pound and go into the pub to use the
toilet. When I come out, I find the alcoholic wasn't so
desperate as to be looking out for unlocked cars with satnavs
on display. I count myself quite lucky.

I look for a newsagent to buy a map but the lady says she
can't get hold of any because everyone now has satnavs. She
tells me to try the garage at the end of Arundel Street, the
next turning on the right. I therefore abandon the Penhale
Road search temporarily and head to the garage, along the
road where my grandma was born. Map bought, I locate all
the streets I'm looking for, none of which are far away.
Cottage View is round the corner. Sue's already told me the
old houses aren't there but I have a look anyway. There is an
old-looking pub but it's called the George V. As I recall,
Queen Victoria was on the throne until Grandma was six,
and Edward VII after that.

I then try to find 40 St George's Square. I googled it and such a place exists. Cruelly, it's now a block of flats. Why completely demolish something and replace it with something of the same name? I'm already suspecting the same is true of 12 All Saints Road. And when I get there I see that of course it is. Either Portsmouth was bombed to fuck in the war or its council has never had a feel for history. Either way, it seems that, according to a signpost on the new All Saints Road, Charles Dickens' birthplace survived. It's in a pretty little half-street tucked behind this new-build estate. And it is actually an old house, rather than an office building that's kept the name Charles Dickens' Birthplace. I could look round it but he's not one of my ancestors. So instead I decide to have a look round All Saints Church, where George Bridle married Charlotte Watson and Thomas Monk married Eliza Jones. I quite like it. It's very light. The walls look like they're Natural Calico, which came up quite grubby-looking in our dark hallway but is quite warm in a well-lit space. The ceiling is a nice light blue. It's late Georgian and has something classical about it. That's as architectural as I get.

Next on my list is Landport Street. Bloody hell, the Luftwaffe must have had some fun here. I'm thinking it's a good job Mum's family were driven out by unemployment; otherwise they'd probably have died in the Blitz. There's only one old and empty building on Landport Street. Let's revert to our original plan and find Penhale Road, the other side of Fratton Road from Arundel Street.

This whole bit of town seems quite intact. The bombers didn't seem to cross Fratton Road. It's further from the docks. And blimey, here's number 125. It's tiny. I suppose there were only three girls including Rebecca living there in

1911, and their father was in hospital, and brother Harry was in the navy. But still, it's hard to imagine my grandmother Rebecca Frances in a two-up-two-down. She never admitted to being so ordinary.

Let's find where she went to school. Francis Avenue is near the football ground. Grandpa supported Portsmouth. I doubt the ground bears much resemblance to the one he went to. Here we are, Francis Avenue. And here's the school. It's a classic late-Victorian primary school of the kind that you see in London, except that in London, most of them were turned into luxury flats in the 1990s on the grounds that they were failing schools – failing to be loft apartments. This looks pretty much as it would have been then, except the infants and juniors seem to be two separate schools. I don't want to take pictures. It would be okay if I were dressed like an estate agent with a loft-apartment agenda, but a middle-aged man in shorts taking pictures of a primary school is asking to be denounced as a paedophile. I figure I could ask if I can look around, though. It's worth a try.

'And you literally just want to look around?' the receptionist in the junior school asks.

'Yes,' say I.

'When would suit you?' she asks, reaching for a large desk diary. I already know this is going nowhere.

'Well, now if possible.'

It's about three, it'll be home time soon, so I can't see why it will be a problem, but I know it will. 'Could you come back tomorrow?' she asks. In fact, I could, but I'm not that desperate.

'No, I live in London,' I say, trying to sound as though that's a really long way away and an impressive place to have a home. But I know nothing's going to budge her and I don't want to appear too keen, so I say, 'It's okay, I just thought I'd try on the off chance' and beat a hasty retreat. I wonder whether, if I'd said that tomorrow was fine, she'd have taken my name and run a police check on me overnight.

I try the infants' reception but there you have to press a buzzer and there's no way I'm repeating my request to an intercom; it sounded feeble enough when I said it to a real person. So I return to the car, perhaps a little too quickly. Now it does feel like I've done something wrong. Why do I always feel like I've done something I shouldn't have? When I was at primary school myself, I used to blush in assembly when the head read out the unattributed transgressions of the previous day, and I was never the culprit. Well, seldom.

Time for HMS *Victory*. I imagine it must be in the Historic Dockyard, for which I keep seeing signposts. For some reason, the entrance to the Historic Dockyard is guarded by two policemen armed with sub-machine guns. What do they think is going to happen? If al-Qaeda wanted to kill lots of people, any ASDA on a Saturday would be a better bet than this. Is there a fear that they would want to strike at the heart of Britain's maritime history? If they did, I should have thought they'd set off a bomb. What will armed police do about that? Shoot a Brazilian tourist two weeks later? Or is there a fear that the *Victory* will be hijacked and crashed into the Isle of Wight? I suspect it's all for show; a way of making visitors feel more unsafe.

In any event, there are a range of ticket prices, because what's left of the *Mary Rose* is here now, along with some other significant ships. It's much more of an adventure park than it was when I was a lad. There are even actors in period costume whom I carefully avoid, because today I can't be doing with people who don't break character. I don't want to ask where the gents is and be told, 'Verily, a man that would make water or dirt might traverse yonder gift shop and cut through the Georgian Bistro.'

The ticket prices depend on how much you want to see. Secretly, I'd quite like to see everything but that's 18 quid and just the *Victory* is £12.50. So I save £5.50 and then spend it in Costa Coffee on a drink and a 'panini'. Every time, that gets me: signs that advertise 'paninis'. I'm not a great traveller or linguist but I do know that you can't have *paninis* because *panini* is already plural, the plural of *panino*. It's like a café in Italy having a sign that says 'Rollsi'.

But I'm getting weak and it's freezing so the panino is welcome, though a bit light on cheese. It's now about four and they shut at five, so I don't even have much time to see HMS *Victory*, but I want to connect with my inner child so I limp over to it. It looks duller than I remember it, probably because the gold colour on my Airfix model was much shinier. I never finished the model. When I was about eleven, Sue met Richard, and at some point he took the model over from me and finished it. I think they've still got it at their house. I was never very practical.

I look around the ship much like I look around all antiquities: without reading any of the information. I like looking at old things, and feel I ought to understand what I'm looking at. But, when I start to read, my brain becomes resistant. I panic, feeling aware of my mortality. I feel myself lying on my deathbed, regretting hours of needless reading and the surfeit of knowledge about anchors and masts filling my head, mourning the fact that I made no time for joy.

But I think I should ask a question to show willing and one does spring to mind. 'How many people were on this ship?' I say, unable to formulate a sentence with words like 'crew' in it. The attendant gives me an enormous smile, a warm and genuine smile from someone who seems to like people and her job. 'It had capacity for eight hundred and fifty but the crew at the Battle of Trafalgar was eight hundred and twenty one.'

This is all about Trafalgar, and Nelson. There is fascinating social and naval history here – although, rather annoyingly, the few things I do read end in 'The original is in the National Maritime Museum in Greenwich.' But, more than anything else, it seems to be a shrine to Admiral Lord Nelson and a bygone age when Britain ruled the seas. I don't know why I was so inspired by such things as a boy; I was progressive in most of my attitudes. But I think I was captivated by the idea that this island has been resisting attack since the Romans. It's a seductive thing, the siege mentality. I've witnessed it among Israeli people. It's not a healthy way to be.

I was quite left-wing at an early age. I can't remember what I made of the class distinctions manifested in the treatment of the ranks, the way sleeping quarters represented every single difference in status as you move down the hierarchy from admiral to toe-rag. And discipline is much in evidence. A recorded voice says, 'Punishments were hard but fair,' and its owner doesn't appear to be practising irony. He goes on to describe how flogged men were brought to the sick bay to have their wounds tended with vinegar and brown paper. I had no idea they really did that. I know vinegar and brown paper was applied to the broken crown of

Jack when he fell down going up the hill to fetch a pail of water, but I thought that was just a satirical allegory for something, not medically accurate.

And I contemplate the wisdom of hospitalising seamen on a warship; going into battle with an injured crew and no space for casualties. I wonder whether the navy suffered from a paranoid addiction to order or whether there was a justified fear of mutiny. Since large numbers of crew were pressed into service, the latter seems likely. On Friday, I'm meeting up with my cousin Brian at Kew and finding out what he knows about our shared great-great-grandfather, Thomas Monk senior, and the navy career that brought him here from Sheerness. I wonder if he was ever flogged.

I find myself momentarily interested in the history of grenades. Two hundred landed on the *Victory*'s deck during the battle of Trafalgar. They can't have been very effective. And then my attention turns to Captain Thomas Masterman Hardy, the one who had to kiss the dying Nelson. I've already looked up his descendants; he had three daughters. The eldest, Louisa, didn't marry, but I think that, if she had given birth to Charles Hardy out of wedlock while working as a servant and at a time when her father was a rear admiral, it would have caused something of a stir. In any case, it seems that her father could seldom stand upright below decks on account of being six feet four inches tall, which probably rules him out as one of mine.

It's too dark in here, and they're closing soon. I'm heading off. My ticket also gets me into the *Victory* Museum, but with crack naval precision, it closes on the dot of five, just as I approach. Perhaps it's just as well. I'm not really remembering being here as a child and I want to head for the front at Southsea. The car park is quiet, so I climb into the back seat and get changed, with the awkwardness of a man removing swimming trunks under a towel. Did I do that here? Did we go in the sea at Portsmouth? I expect we did. I remember that I always came back home from day trips with tar stuck to my bottom. I thought it was a natural marine phenomenon. It was years before I learnt about the ship-wrecked tankers in the Channel. God, I wore home-made knitted trunks, as well. Every dip resulted in the wattle-and-daub effect of crude oil and seaweed woven into what my mother called my 'bathing costume'.

I park in 'Old Portsmouth' and walk along the front to Clarence Pier. I'm sure I remember this. I think this is where the monkey picture was taken. It's a strange sort of a pier, since it doesn't stick out very far into the sea, but it feels familiar, or maybe something I can see is in the picture. There's a 1950s sort of tower thing with 'Clarence Pier' in red lettering. That would have been here. And there's a monument in the distance. I remember the park on the left, but I can't see the model village. It's probably gone. I walk as far as the monument and then turn around. It's really windy and everything's closing. And I'm suddenly feeling very melancholy.

Somebody stops me and says his brother's a big fan – and he is too, he adds quickly – and he asks if he can take a picture, but his camera doesn't work. He asks if I'm on at the theatre and I say no, I'm doing family history. But that's not what I'm doing. I'm trying to find the little boy in the photo-graph and I realise I can't. And it shouldn't matter because it was forty years ago and my memory's rubbish these days. But somehow it does matter. This whole process has subtly depressed me, because most of the people in the story are dead, and some of them, I knew. And many of the homes they lived in have been destroyed, and my parents are old and my youth is gone. And I don't have a son. I have a daughter and I love her with all my heart, but I wonder if the little boy I'm searching for is my son.

This is ridiculous. How would my 19-year-old daughter feel about me mourning the son I've never had? I hate people who feel sorry for themselves because they only have daughters or only have sons or only have one child. Be grateful you've got a child at all and shut up, you self-pitying milksops. I'm not bothered about the continuation of the Hardy name and, anyway, Betty might keep it. And it's not like I've got a ranch someone needs to take over.

Maybe it is Jeremy James Martin Hardy I'm looking for. Did I mention the Martin? It's not on my birth certificate and I don't use it. It was added as an afterthought in tribute to my great-grandfather Albert Martin Hewett who died a few months before I was born. That seems a bit tenuous; a third name that was somebody's second name. I suppose Albert was considered an archaic name in 1961. It's the height of fashion now. I could have used it as a stage name if I'd been quick about it; but I always lose respect for someone when I find out their real name is much posher than their assumed one. Norman Cook is Quentin. Vinnie Jones is Hugo. I made that one up.

Anyway, the point is that Jeremy James *Martin* Hardy is the Yellow Submarine, the boy of seven or so who walked along here with his mum. Blimey, now I'm remembering that they called me 'Jerry' at primary school. Grandad called me that too. I'm not a Jerry; I don't think I ever felt like a Jerry.

But I can't remember how I felt, that's the point. Sometimes I do; I get short flashes of being a child again, but it's more a question of me as I am now looking through those eyes, like Robocop trying to remember his real identity, only not as exciting, obviously. The only feelings I can really remember are the visceral embarrassment and humiliation that occurred on a few occasions. Why have they stayed when the positive feelings haven't? It's not as though I had an unhappy childhood. Nothing bad happened. Everyone was nice. Maybe it's just that negative emotions are so physical in their manifestation: nausea, sweating, flushed cheeks – or is that swine flu?

This wasn't meant to happen. I came here thinking that memories of jolly family days out with ice cream and chips would flood back to me. I even buy some chips. The vinegar is in a spray bottle, like you use for plants or ironing. Maybe that's to ration its use, or so it can be squirted into a wound caused by severe flogging. The chips are quite nice, actually.

I'm feeling a bit better now, and I'm looking forward to going home. The past is another country; it's nice to visit, but I'm not looking to invest in property. I am going to pop into Guildford on the way back, not because I feel a great urge to but because it's on the way and I'm not sure it's worth a separate trip. I'm slightly excited that I found two ancestors the other day; the parents of James Hammond, the bricklayer who was the father of Clara, my nan's mother, the beauty who had her photo taken for free in the 1890s. I still haven't found out whether the photographer was well known at the time. One day I'll go to the museum in Guildford, since local history is almost all sepia photos and pill bottles. One day, I'll go. One day.

Anyway, James's parents were Caroline and Richard. Richard Hammond – same name as one of Clarkson's pathetic sidekicks. Hey ho. The main thing is I've got addresses. Richard and Caroline are somewhere on North Street in 1851. In 1861, they're in Lockwood's Passage, which I think is no longer there but is worth a try. In 1871, James is lodging on Swan Lane, which is still there. In 1891, he's married to Clara and they're living on Swan Lane with their daughter Clara and a lot of other kids, although James has been misnamed Joseph. Apparently, Nan didn't like her grandfather much. He was a domestic tyrant and lumbered her grandmother with an awful lot of children. Anyway, in 1901, Clara's married to Albert Martin Hewett and moved to Crondall but her parents are at 42 Eagle Road and that's where I'm heading first.

On the way, I listen to one of the *Clue*s we recorded in Southampton. I can't get used to Humph's voice not being there. I suppose I will. Jack Dee did a great job in the chair. We're touring the theatre show again soon and Jack's doing all the dates, which will be good. I'm distracted by all this thinking and I miss the turning off the A3 and drive miles before I can turn back. I almost keep going now that 'popping in on somewhere that's on the way' is not how I'd describe what's happening, but the weather's brightening up and I've never crashed on this bit of the A3.

I turn off the A3 again in the area that's called Stoke-Next-Guildford despite being only a few hundred yards from the town centre. I go past the church where Clara and her parents married. And soon I am at Eagle Road. There is an old house at number 42 but the road's been so knocked about that I can't imagine the numbering is the same. I'm speeding up now, giving houses a cursory look, trying to get to all the addresses I've identified without even pausing to reflect. I head to North Street, most of which has been rebuilt, but Swan Lane is still there. There don't seem to be any numbers, but the buildings are mostly quite old, although you have to look at the floors above the shops to tell. It's a narrow lane, too narrow to drive down, and it does feel Victorian, even if there is a Costa Coffee. I mean, there was one in the Historic Dockyard in Portsmouth and that's Tudor.

Anyway, this is where the Hammonds lived, at the time when John Springfield, the cobbler from Zanzibar came to live in Guildford, on Chertsey Street, just around the corner. In fact, Clara, my great-grandmother, was born one year after the Springfields' daughter, and more than likely went to school with her.

I walk through to the High Street. I haven't been here for bloody years. I want to see the clock that sticks out from the Guildhall. My parents had a large photo of it on the wall in the hall when we were kids. I don't know why, but it's certainly a nice clock, dating from 1653, it says. Somewhere above one of the shops was the Corona restaurant. It was the only restaurant we ever came to when I was a kid. I had fish and chips; breaded fish, mind.

I find myself quite liking Guildford. I like the fact that Jim Hammond was a bricklayer, which means he built some of it. I've never done a gig here, except for one at the university in 1984 with Dave Cohen and Pete Sinclair, who now writes with Jack, but was a poet then. We did a package for a while. Our name was *Holocaust on Ice*. It wasn't a reference to The Holocaust, but the feared *nuclear* holocaust. It's strange to think that Ronald Reagan was such a dangerous fool that, during his presidency, a word now synonymous with Nazi death camps was being used more commonly to describe the potential result of his policies. But I think Three Line Whip was an improvement as a name.

I don't know why I've never done another gig here. There's a theatre. There's even the Civic Hall, but that's grim. I saw a couple of bands there. I've just remembered now how I used to go to gigs in Portsmouth when I was at university. So few bands came to Southampton that my friend Simon Pannell started this thing called Rock Trips, booking coaches to take us to Bournemouth and Portsmouth. I can't remember who I saw where, except that the Ramones were definitely in Bournemouth and I danced so much that I actually had to lie down on the floor at the back. And the Beat and the Undertones were in Portsmouth and both were fantastic. The Undertones were so good that I sprained my ankle really badly and then carried on dancing on it. There are some very good things about being 18.

I feel a bit more in touch with my youth now; and it's a nice evening and I'm going to have a quick look for graves, knowing I won't find any and trying not to get morbid. I park up round the corner from St John's where the graves are on both sides of the road. I'm looking at the more recent ones on the opposite side from the church, when it starts to rain. I turn around to leave and a perfect, beautiful rainbow fills the view behind the church. It keeps me company for a long while on the way home. It seems as though I'm going to drive under it, then the road bends and I'm heading towards the end of it. Then it dissolves, but soon I will be home with the woman I love, and I'm okay.

*

At home, I google the model village. The bloody thing *is* still there. I could have gone. I check to see if I have a gig in Portsmouth this autumn and find we're doing *Clue* there. I might buy Barry a pint and force him to walk round it with me so that people think that's how we psych-up before a show. I have a look in the loft and find the first album into which I put pictures taken on my new colour Instamatic in 1972. I labelled everything with my new Dymo printer. I remember the nice clunking noise it made and the satisfaction as it cut off the finished label. On the very first page is a sticker that reads, 'Portsmouth Model Village 1972'. I was eleven then, it must have seen some changes

The village clearly made a big impression on me. I snapped the blacksmiths, the Gypsy caravan, the water mill, the oast house and took a couple of long shots. I'll bring these with me in the autumn and see if everything's the same or if model villages have undergone gentrification or unsympathetic development. The oast house is probably a conversion now, the watermill a brasserie.

I like my pictures. I'm not embarrassed that I was such a nerd. Well, I am a bit, because I'm still a nerd. And then I realise that part of me is still the boy with the camera and the Dymo printer. I think I've found Jeremy James Martin Hardy again.

CHAPTER 26

My Long Lost Cousin

Brian is actually the son of my mother's cousin, so I think that makes him my third cousin, and he was never lost, but his parents took him to America when he was young. His grandmother, Esther Monk, was the sister of my grandmother, Rebecca Monk; and he knows a great deal about the Monks and the Joneses. He sent me the CD with loads of information on it and I still haven't worked my way through all of it, but I'm meeting him today. He's making one of his occasional visits to England, when he fits in as much family history as he can. I am a charlatan by comparison. It's not that I don't care about who our ancestors were; I'm just not in the same league as him and I can't fake it. I realise I would be very bad at being one of those doe-eyed documentary presenters who feigns an interest in people's passions in order to lure them into being subjects of his cynical freak-fest.

That said, I have no reason to believe that Brian is anything other than a sane and reasonable man who happens to be very interested in family history. Moreover, he is an emigrant. He left these shores as a boy and this is a home-coming for him. You're bound to have more of an interest in your roots when you don't take them for granted.

We're meeting at Kew. I'm glad he's given me the incentive to go back because I've been putting it off, to be honest. We've arranged to meet in the café and I don't know how we pick each other out when neither of us has any idea what the other looks like, except that Brian has his 13-year-old daughter Caitlyn with him, and I remember what a 13-year-old daughter looks like.

We've only spoken once on the phone and exchanged emails, but somehow it's all very easy. The fact that we are family counts for something, if only as a point of connection between two strangers. And he is an extremely nice and knowledgeable man. I am, however, embarrassed handing over my paltry findings: copies of the charitable donations made by Duchess Minna to Widow Elizabeth Jones. He already has details of Matthew's wages. He got Heather at Arundel to send them to him. Plus he trumps me because he's found the mother of Harriet Coombs, who was Matthew Jones's wife, and her parents. They are called Hills. And they're from Sussex, which confirms the appalling lack of mobility among my progenitors.

But today I'm going to help Brian find one of his other ancestors who's not on my side of the family at all, so I feel slightly useful. Then we're going to try and find some stuff about our great-great-grandfather, Thomas Monk, who was in the Royal Navy, and his son who was, we think, the policeman, but whom I failed to find last time I was here.

Initially, I tried to ignore some of what Brian sent me because I hoped I could find things out myself, but clearly I'm not very good at it. And before we even start researching, he has new information for me. Firstly, Thomas, our great-grandfather, spent the end of his life in the workhouse. That is why he does not appear at home in 1911. The likely reason for his going into the workhouse was that it was the only way of getting hospital treatment. Brian's established that he spent time in hospital, came home for a bit but ended up back in the workhouse. He died in 1914. When, Esther, his youngest, Brian's grandmother, married in 1920, she gave his occupation as 'Policeman', even though, in 1911, he gives 'Engineer's Labourer' as his profession, and he hadn't been a policeman for 30-odd years. Clearly, Esther thought 'Policeman' was more respectable than anything else he did.

Our grandmothers came from very humble stock indeed, and clearly Becky's fantasies about her noble ancestry were wishful thinking. Brian has also ascertained the meaning of 'Nurse child'. You might remember that there was a baby called Frederick Hill staying with the Monks in 1911. Well, the expression refers to an unwanted child, or a child a single mother simply couldn't look after; she would work to pay others to raise them. Someday I'll find out what happened to Frederick.

Brian has also found all the ships on which Thomas Monk senior served while in the navy and has established that he was in Coraddino Prison on Malta for six weeks in 1861. So I'm descended from a jailbird. And Grandma was so proud of her colonial lifestyle on the same island where her own grandfather had been in prison. Brian says that the explanation for his incarceration that was passed down through the family goes as follows: on shore leave, Thomas saw a lady drop her handkerchief and he picked it up to return it to her. Her husband was jealous and accused him of theft. It was common for loose women to use this ruse to lure young men to whom they took a fancy. I think a sailor would have known that; so, if he was innocent of theft, he was probably on the pull. I'm also struck by the fact that the family didn't hush up the shameful episode and that Esther, at least, was happy to relate it. Rebecca certainly wasn't.

Brian also points out that Thomas only fathered three children, which was very rare at that time and probably the result of his being constantly at sea. This begs the question of how many children he fathered in ports around the world. That's my speculation, not Brian's. He is mainly concerned to find the records of HMS *Hannibal*, on which Thomas was serving when he was arrested. I'm just excited that Thomas was some sort of wrong'un.

Caitlyn, with tremendous patience, waits in the café while we set about our research. We order up a bunch of things, some of which relate to one of Brian's ancestors who came back from Bermuda an orphan. We have a parcel of papers from the Royal Dockyards. After half an hour, we find the child's father working at the dockyard, and mention of his death. Brian found it but I helped by going through half the papers. I cling to the fact of having been this much use.

We are also going up to the Map Room to try and find Thomas aboard the HMS *Hannibal*. We find a complete list of the crew but he's not on it. In fact, we draw a blank on everything we order that might mention him. However, we hope to have more luck with the police career of his son. I am aware that I was getting light-headed when I was last here, so I've ordered the attestation ledger again.

Since I last tussled with my attitude to the police, they have become officially, though probably temporarily, the most hated institution in Britain. While we were in Arundel, the G20 met in London and Plod battered merry fuck out of all sorts of inoffensive people. One man, who was hit and shoved to the ground, died of internal bleeding. Thankfully, protestors have taken to turning their camera phones onto the police to such an extent that the government has been seeking in recent months to criminalise the act of photographing a police officer. Perhaps it's a cultural thing; the police believe they lose part of their soul when their picture is taken.

Police seem to have a particular hatred of climate change activists. The Climate Camp at Kingsnorth power station was subjected to severe violence and disruption. Almost more worrying than the physical brutality was the use of loud music to deprive protestors of sleep. The police are now making up their own powers with reference to no one. Then, a few weeks ago, Nottinghamshire police arrested 114 people in one day on the grounds that they might have been thinking of making an illegal protest. One could get paranoid, but it does raise questions when the people seeking to stop the single biggest threat to our world are being so aggressively targeted. Do the police see climate change as subversives' vehicle of choice? Is it just useful to inflate threats to civil order? Or are they genuinely fearful that the clamour to save the planet will spread far beyond the usual suspects and that the momentum towards a massive political shift might become unstoppable? Climate change means that to save our world we must change the whole way that we live, which is why so many people don't even want to believe it's really happening.

Brian and I work from the back of the ledger, scanning a page each at a time. Not only is it faster, but I'm suddenly a lot less lonely than I was last time. And, here is Thomas

Monk, joining B division of the Metropolitan Police on 22 June 1874. And it's me that finds him. Had it been Brian, I would have felt especially useless. Brian kindly insists that he's not surprised I missed it the first time, even though I know there's no way he would have missed it himself. Anyway, it's a result, the first proof that Thomas really was a policeman. B division was Westminster, which includes Parliament, Downing Street and Trafalgar Square, so I dare say he had to police demonstrations. Oh well.

We've ordered up some police service order books and we order a couple more, but we find nothing and Brian has promised to take Caitlyn to the London Dungeon as a reward for her patience, so I take charge of the books and say goodbye to them. I genuinely look forward to seeing them again.

I'm now in possession of four books and I'm only allowed three at a time, so I leave one in the cubbyhole thing. I know that if I were seen to be in breach of regulations here, it would start something. People would get all self-righteous, like those wankers who tell you to be quiet in the quiet coach on a train. You know that they're not annoyed by your quiet and calm phone conversation; they just like rules.

Once, Brian and Caitlyn have gone, I find I revert to hating it here. I realise that the nice part of the day was sharing something with other human beings. I last about half an hour, and I leave too. There is a pattern emerging. I really enjoyed Brian and Caitlyn's company. That they are family helped to oil the wheels, but the fact that they're nice people to be around had more to do with it. I can be a solitary and unfriendly man, but being alone so much in unfriendly environments recently has definitely made me appreciate people.

Back at home, I think I should have another thorough look at all the stuff Brian had already given me. I'm still excited about the prison career of Thomas Monk the elder. I'm less impressed with the revelation that a Thomas Monk from Portsmouth served in the Confederate States Navy in 1863 and 1864. I'm hoping this is another Thomas Monk. I don't want mine being on the wrong side in the American Civil War, thank you very much. Here's me counting my lucky stars that none of my forebears was a slave owner, and now it seems one of them might have fought a war in defence of slavery.

It seems rather bizarre that a bloke in Portsmouth gets recruited by the rebel states of the old South so I start to research. The Confederates had virtually no navy at the start of the war and cobbled one together quickly. One way of acquiring ships was to buy them in Britain, and pick up experienced seamen wherever they could. Britain's public policy was neutrality between the North and the South, although officially, at least, we respected the Union's claim that the Confederates were insurgents and their attacks on Northern supply ships piracy. British working-class public opinion was hostile to the Confederates, but it seems that, behind the scenes, while eager not to provoke the United States, the government was waiting to see who was most likely to win. Early on in the war, the British seemed to be preparing to recognise the Confederate secession.

I'm going to tell you the story of two ships. CSS *Georgia* was built in 1862 as the merchant ship *Japan*. The Confederate States Government bought it in Dumbarton in March 1863. On 1 April, it left Greenock, ostensibly bound for the East Indies and carrying a crew of 50 who had shipped for a voyage to Singapore. It rendezvoused with the steamer *Alar* off Ushant, France, and took on munitions and other supplies. On 9 April 1863 the Confederate flag was hoisted and it was placed in commission as CSS *Georgia*. Its orders read to attack United States shipping wherever found. After calling at Bahia, Brazil and at Trinidad, *Georgia* recrossed the Atlantic to Cape Colony in Africa, where it arrived on 16 August. It sailed next to Tenerife, from there up to Cherbourg, arriving on 28 October. During this short cruise it took nine United States ships.

While it was undergoing repair at Cherbourg in late January 1864, it was decided to shift its armaments to CSS *Rappahannock*. The *Rappahannock* had begun life as a British sloop-of-war named the *Victor*. Various defects led to its sale in 1863. Confederate agents purchased it ostensibly for the China trade, but the authorities realised the intention to use it as a commerce raider and detained it at Sheerness. The token crew escaped detention, sailing into the Channel with workmen still aboard. A Confederate naval officer boarded, but its bearings had burned out and it was taken to Calais for repairs. The French detained it and it never made it to sea until after the war when it was handed to the US government.

The reason I mention these ships is that Brian found this on a website listing Confederate naval personnel:

Thomas Monk, resident of Portsmouth, Hampshire, England; married; shipped, as quartermaster and boatswain's mate, aboard the CSS *Georgia* off the coast of France, about April 1863; paid 5 pounds, 10 shillings for the first six months, and then 6 pounds; after a cruise of several months in this vessel, returned to France, going into Cherbourg for repairs; sent to the CSS *Rappahannock*, at Calais, then sent home for a week's leave; returned to the CSS *Rappahannock* about the beginning of February, 1864, and promoted to boatswain, at the rate of 18 pounds per month; discharged March 7, 1864.

We don't know if this is our Thomas, but it does say he lived in Portsmouth. My head is spinning slightly. How did I not notice this among the stuff Brian sent me? Somehow I just didn't register it. To be fair, initially he only had it down as an 'interesting possibility'. I must have thought it couldn't possibly be our Thomas because nothing so interesting would ever happen in our family; but Brian is now convinced that it's him.

The British mariners who joined up with the confederates were privateers – mercenaries. Today there is a well-worn route from the services into private security firms, which is the modern way of recruiting mercenaries. Arguably *all* service personnel are mercenaries. They are paid to kill or abet killing without asking questions. But there also seems to have been quite a lot of political sympathy for the Confederacy among the Royal Navy, perhaps because of lingering hostility to the United States. Whatever their motivation, these British naval personnel were opting for a new career championing slavery. There was not widespread ignorance of the issues. There were large meetings and demonstrations in Britain against the Confederacy, largely because of slavery. We can't say that slavery was just accepted as normal in those days. It wasn't. I'm not imposing modern morality and political analysis. People in this country were not conditioned to think it was acceptable, quite the reverse. So what's worse, joining the Confederates for money or joining them to save slavery? Was Thomas down on his luck, having been thrown out of the Royal Navy? Was he lied to? Was he manipulated? Or was he plain ruthless and/or sympathetic to the cause?

Over the next few days, Brian finds more and more information about this Thomas. There are a number of mentions of him, and more evidence that it is our Thomas. It seems he crops up in a book written by the paymaster of the *Rappahannock*, published as *Odyssey in Gray, A Diary of Confederate Service 1863–1865*, in which he is described as a large man with red whiskers. Royal Navy records of our Thomas describe him as being five foot ten with red hair and whiskers.

And, shortly after his discharge, Thomas swore an affidavit that was used later in a public inquiry into the Confederates' conduct of the war. Various things strike me about this.

Firstly, this Thomas is illiterate, as was our Thomas. In place of his signature are the words, 'The mark of Thomas Monk'. Secondly, my grandma spoke of her father going up to London to see London solicitors, something his father had actually done. Thirdly, public inquiries into wars have a history. This one might have been an example of victor's justice, but the very fact that it was considered an appropriate mechanism so long ago is noteworthy, especially when our own government has so dragged its heels over holding an inquiry into the circumstances of the Iraq war.

The Prime Minister has even tried to have part of the inquiry held in secret. Perhaps it's his love of public-private partnerships; but how can you have a private public inquiry? It's like lying to your therapist; you're not going to learn anything and you're not going to grow as a person.

Fourthly, Thomas expresses dissatisfaction with his new job in the following statement:

> I, Thomas Monk, of Portsmouth, Hampshire, England, do truly and solemnly swear, that about eleven months ago I was engaged by a stranger, at Portsmouth, to go to New Haven, and from thence by steamer to the French coast, and ran alongside the confederate steamer *Georgia*, and on arriving on board I joined her as quartermaster. There were three other men taken from New Haven at the same time, and the steamer had guns and ammunition for the *Georgia*. They were taken on board as we lay off the coast. The *Georgia* went to sea as soon as we had received the guns, and cruised towards the Cape of Good Hope. On the passage she took eight American ships, burned three of them, and bonded the other five. After we arrived at the Cape, we returned to France, and went into Cherbourg for repairs. No ships were burnt on the return passage, but one was bonded. After we had been at Cherbourg some time, I was sent to the *Rappahannock*, at Calais, and then I returned home. While I was on the *Georgia* I received for the first six months £5 10s. per month, and afterwards £6 per month; my wife receiving the half pay at Portsmouth, by post office order from Mr Jones, of Liverpool. That

was received regularly while I remained on the ship. I remained at Portsmouth, on leave, for a week, and then joined the confederate steamer *Rappahannock*, at Calais, as boatswain, at £18 per month. Half was to have been paid to my wife by the same Mr Jones, Liverpool; but she did not draw any. I joined her about five weeks back and staid on board until I received my discharge, on the 7th March.

I applied for it, as I found it impossible to remain on a ship that was conducted like the *Rappahannock*—the captain and chief officer always creating some unpleasantness on board; and I did not like to remain on a ship that was intended to burn and destroy merchant ships, unarmed and defenceless.

When I signed articles on board the *Rappahannock*, I made an arrangement with the purser respecting the half pay to be paid to my wife at Portsmouth, which was also to be paid by Mr Jones, of 28 Chapel Street, Liverpool.

his
THOMAS x MONK.
mark.

Sworn at my office, No. 4 Nicholas Lane, Lombard Street, in the city of London, this the 15th day of March, 1864, by the deponent, Thomas Monk.
J. WILKINSON,
A London Commissioner, &c., &c.

The witness to the mark of the deponent being first sworn that he had truly, distinctly, and audibly read

over the contents of the above affidavit to the said
deponent, and that he saw him make his mark thereto,
before me.

J. WILKINSON,

A London Commissioner, &c., &c.

Clearly Thomas felt some degree of discomfort about the
job. Moreover, the reason he made the affidavit seems to be
that didn't receive all his wages. So perhaps herein lies the
grain of truth about our stolen inheritance.

But the thing that's dominating my thinking is the fact that
my ancestor was complicit in a deeply nefarious enterprise. I
feel in some way responsible for the actions of one of my
sixteen great-great-grandparents. I am not ashamed, nor
embarrassed; I'm telling you about it. I know I am not to
blame for something that happened a century before my birth;
but I do feel *responsible*, which is different. Do I feel it means
I have bad genes? No. Nor would I ever curse anyone else for
the behaviour of an ancestor, so why do I feel responsible for
one of mine? I suppose because I am some sort of representative. If the British Government apologises for slavery, it is in
some sense the same British Government that was involved in
slavery, constitutionally at least. I think it entirely right that an
apology for slavery be issued by a President or Prime Minister.
From high street clothes shops it might be more topical, but
the sins of the past are relevant too.

One must be careful. Victimhood is not a healthy
mindset. The Holocaust was undoubtedly the crime of the
century; and I think we must acknowledge that fact before
we criticise the fact that it is also exploited to justify the
abuse of Palestinians. Of course the Holocaust has become

part of Jewish identity. How can anyone not feel its impact, especially those of Jewish descent? And how can people whose recent ancestors were slaves be unaffected by it? I'm not about to tell black or Jewish people to get over it. Black people are often accused of having a chip on their shoulders. I think they are remarkably patient, all things considered. But if you are black or Jewish, and you were to live and breathe the oppression and humiliation of your people through history without channelling your indignation into something positive, it would surely drive you mad.

Victimhood can be seductive, especially so when it's delusional. In America today, there is a widespread complaint that it's now the White Man who is oppressed, despite there being absolutely no evidence of this at all. The South has always had a sense of grievance about the Civil War. In fairness, it wasn't a straightforward fight about slavery and atrocities were committed by both sides. But slavery was a very major issue in the war and clearly the Confederacy was the wrong side to all right-thinking people; and it's a noticeable trait that those who are manifestly in the wrong still feel hard done by when they are defeated.

Furthermore, bigots and supremacists always claim they are being victimised. The BNP whine, 'Imagine if the things that are said about us were said about Muslims and asylum seekers', which is like paedophiles saying, 'How would children feel if they were on the sex offenders register?'

The South's sense of victimhood should be seen in that context. If Southerners are fed-up with being stereotyped, that's understandable, but the stereotype is hardly surprising. We are not to blame for our ancestors' actions, but if we don't appear to have learnt from them, then we will be associated with them. It's taken parts of the South a very long time to change.

And if we feel that our identity is defined by the behaviour of our forebears, there are two possible reactions when that behaviour was wrong: either we feel guilt for something we didn't do or we feel that what was done can't have been all that bad because it was done by our families or our people. Why do revisionist historians seek to say slavery and Empire were not such bad things? Partly because of ideology: ruthless exploitation is consistent with market-driven philosophy. But perhaps also because of misplaced loyalty; an irrational and unhealthy attachment to one's own race, nationality and inheritance.

And surely, feeling guilty for the things our ancestors did is no more sensible than letting them off the hook because they're family. So, what am I saying? I don't bloody know. I'm still getting used to being descended from a Confederate mercenary. And I'll tell you what: it may not make for happy reading but it is bloody interesting.

CHAPTER 27

Sheerness

I 've never been to the Isle of Sheppey. I've always
suspected that it's one of those islands that's only barely
an island, separated from the rest of the country by a
damp patch, but which the natives doggedly refer to as 'The
Island'.

Looking at the map, I see that it is in fact a bobble, joined
to the north Kent coast by one road and separated from it by
a channel called The Swale. One the way there, I want to take
a diversion to Cliffe, where Mary, the mother of George Stagg,
my great-grandfather, comes from. Whatever part of the
family I look at, I keep coming back to the same few counties.

Cliffe is on another sticky-out bit of north Kent at the
mouth of the River Thames. I have brought Katie with me to
take photographs, and because she is curious, never having
explored this bit of Kent either. I try explaining who everyone
in the Monk line was, to while away the hour on the M2, but
I realise I'm now getting so familiar with my subject matter
that I can't explain it very well. Perhaps that's why Dad
couldn't explain Physics to me.

Once we leave the motorway, we're in a very flat bit of
rural Kent. It's farmland and there are actual hops. I tell Katie

the thing about how cockneys picked hops by way of a summer holiday, one of the bits of random knowledge my parents imparted to me. Her parents are from Birmingham and Yorkshire so she would have heard different regional facts about her agricultural heritage. Everything's different up there. I'm not even sure swans can break your arm once you get past Northampton.

We stop at a pub for lunch. I order a ham salad, on the basis that it involves the word salad and the ham is home-cooked. I'm never really sure why that's a good thing. I suppose it depends on your home. The pub is full of people in suits who know each other and the bar staff. One has his own tankard. There's no obvious workplace from which they could be on lunch break. It's all farms for miles. It's Wednesday so maybe rural Kent still has a half-day. Or maybe there's a large hotel specialising in conferences tucked away around the corner, and these chaps have been being motivated all week.

I don't know what a Kent accent was, but I doubt much of it still exists. Most people here sound like Londoners, some in a pronounced way. Just as east Londoners north of the river migrate to Essex, those from south of the river move this way. I've had many conversations with people who have moved down to Kent and who tell me how lovely it is. I always suspect they mean white, but only because they don't seem to be able to specify any lovely things. They'll usually say they moved for the schools, as though that's self-explanatory. They don't say what Kent's schools have, or don't have.

One thing people do say about Kent is that people are friendlier, and it's true that everyone seems very nice in the pub. But it's possible that people are forced to speak to one another because there's nothing else to do. Moreover, living in London is tough, as it is in any big city. We withdraw. We don't want people to speak to us on the Tube. Of course we don't. How can you talk about the weather when you're half a mile underground? We don't say hello to people we meet in the street because they pass at a rate of one per second, so if we greeted everyone we'd turn into an air stewardess. But that doesn't make us bad people. We just quite like being left alone, in the way you do if you come from a large family. We feel crowded. But when you live in the arse end of nowhere, you start talking to the cows.

That said, it is rather beautiful here, and yet people don't look that friendly as we drive on to Cliffe. People seem nervous and hostile, as though we look like big city people who've come to investigate something they know rather too much about. Perhaps they just fear we've come to buy property. I don't think we look physically threatening. We look quite small and nice. The people in the pub were all right, but they sounded like Londoners and one of the bar staff was from the North. Maybe these are the real locals looking up at us now. It starts to feel as though people will be expecting us in each village we reach.

One group of people don't look up. They are bent double in a field picking something. There is a white van parked up and absolutely no question as to whether these people are being exploited. Someone's making money and it's not them. The women are Roma; the men are Sikhs. Why are people in the pub in the middle of the day, when there's crops to be brought in? They're probably discussing the blight of immigration.

We arrive in Cliffe. It's a lovely little village with a pretty church called St Helen's. But behind it in the distance, ships seem to be sailing in the marshes. We realise that they're on the Thames, and that the huge industrial complex behind is even huger than it looks because it's on the other side of the river. It's the petrochemical works on Canvey Island in Essex. That's not even a not-really-an-island; it's just land.

The marshes are home to lots of birds and it is a protected site. The village fought off an attempt to build another London airport here in 2002. No wonder they're nervous. It is quite remarkable to look out at the marshes and think that someone seriously thought it would be a good idea to devastate them so that we can get more planes in the air. Perhaps that's how people feel about every bit of wilderness threatened with development. But the fact is that more and bigger airports are one of the last things the world needs.

We must make haste to the Isle of Sheppey, as the day's half gone already. We head back to the motorway and see the turning for Sheerness. Shortly, we come to an elaborate, sweeping bridge that curls right up into the air, perhaps in an attempt to exaggerate Sheppey's island status.

First stop is Queenborough, where young Thomas Monk senior (now of Confederate Navy fame) lived on the high street with his parents Edward and Harriet. Harriet was a teacher. Given that Thomas was illiterate, I'm thinking he was dyslexic. Or maybe his mum just didn't like to bring her work home with her.

We find the high street easily. There are some old buildings, including the church, which is locked. A lady passing with shopping asks us if we'd like to look around, as she can be back in a moment with the key. We say yes and hope that she literally means a moment, which she does. It's a small church with a very old painted ceiling that was damaged in a fire and needs restoring, so I put two pounds in the restoration fund box.

The lady is very pleasant and says it's a shame it's not a Saturday as there's a heritage place up the road that opens on a Saturday. She tells us the town needs development, especially the Creek, where the harbour is. She also refers to 'the mainland' but we don't take the piss. I want to see the Creek because that's where Edward would have had his dredger, or at least boarded the dredger he worked on. There are still a couple of fishing boats, but the town is very quiet, and all the looks we get are weird ones. Maybe it's because we're driving slowly. People don't usually do that outside of London. We imagine that many of the young people here either leave or descend into drug use. The Continent is a short boat ride away and you could land tons of drugs here without ever being noticed. It's an attractive town but there's probably nothing for young people to do but fix up old minis and drive them as fast as possible to nowhere in particular. Without a major input of public funds, they'll need a celebrity chef to get this place going.

The area ought to do well. They've got the sea and unspoilt landscape; they've got plentiful local farm produce; and it's not that far from London. Metropolitan foodies pay a fortune for salt-marsh lamb, and here they're the bulk of the population. Half an hour away is Whitstable, where we're already thinking we might have dinner. Whitstable's so thriving it's ridiculous. There must be ten marketing executives to each fisherman. It's famous for its oysters and restaurants and beach huts. Queenborough's been a bit wrecked by a ridiculous sea wall but it's got lots of charm. Although I'm not sure I'd fancy the seafood here as it's quite close to industry. Whitstable is washed by the North Sea, which is better for bottom-feeders; hence all the marketing people.

In fact, Kent has a lot going for it but it's pretty much dead in terms of visitors. There was a huge flap about migrants a few years ago, when people started noticing the Roma refugees arriving from Europe. Locals went nuts about hotels in Margate filling up with refugees, ignoring the fact that the last time anyone stayed in any of those hotels, there were bathing machines on the beach and the swimmers looked like the Taliban had dressed them.

We've seen all we can in Queenborough. Now it's time to hit Sheerness, where Edward was born and where Thomas joined the Royal Navy. There is a heritage centre open every day, but only till 3 p.m. so we're too late for that. We're heading straight for Blue Town, where Thomas junior was born on Chapel Street and where the family lived on Sheppey Street in 1851. We find one remaining old building on each street.

We find our way onto the high street, which only has one side. The other is bounded by the huge dock wall, which serves as a view for the residents, There are no longer many shops, only houses, a pub and the Heritage Centre. Oh, and a sex shop sandwiched between people's homes. It seems out-of-place and a sign of decay until Katie points out it was possibly a brothel originally; one of many in a naval port, I should think.

I want to find out what or where the Blue Houses are. That is where Edward was born. The website for the Heritage Centre gave a home phone number for Paul, one of the workers, so I ring it. Paul is very helpful and would have arranged to meet us if he'd known we were coming. He tells me Blue Town was originally just called Blue Houses. The town grew out of the docks. Houses were built from stolen timber and painted blue with stolen paint from the navy. In the nineteenth century, all the blue houses were replaced by brick ones. Before the old wooden houses were built, dock-workers and their families lived in the hulks of old ships. God, even in the eighteenth century people lived in conversions. I can imagine a proud docker's wife showing off to visitors, 'We've preserved some of the features; that ballast is original and the kids all have scurvy. But where the utility room is now, that was just one big cannon.'

It was a man called Coffin who forced them out of the hulks. He also demolished the north side of the high street to build the wall. He was not liked.

Paul asks if my ancestors were Jewish. I get asked that a lot, but he can't see me so I'm puzzled. It turns out Blue Town had a substantial Jewish community and a synagogue. Finally: hope that I'm not as Anglo-Saxon as I've dreaded.

The Gambles lived in Mile Town, which is no distance at all. The Belle and Lion pub where Frances lived is long gone. A Boots stands there now. There are some old buildings on the high street, which now seems to be an extension of Blue Town high street. Mile Town is now the main bit of Sheerness. There are still a number of Victorian terraces but I can't tell if any are old enough to have housed any of my lot.

Frances and Thomas married in Minster a few miles away, and lived on its high street in the 1840s before moving back into Sheerness. We nip up there and find it still has an abbey, but can't work out if that serves as the parish church. No one seems to know. Katie asks a teenage boy. I am immediately embarrassed. It's the sort of thing my mum used to ask. She thought nothing of approaching a group of brawling skinheads to ask, 'Do you know where we can get a cream tea?'

The high street has one remaining old building, parts of which look as though they might be early nineteenth century. And nothing that has been built since was a good idea.

I think we're done exploring the towns of my bloodlines. Yes, I think that's it. I'm taking my girlfriend to Whitstable for our last posh fish dinner before we foreswear the endangered harvest of the sea. I'm having oysters today; it's my heritage. Tomorrow is my final journey; to see my mother's cousin David Haswell and plunder his photos and documents, and that will be that.

CHAPTER 28

The Last Journey

I don't have to be at all descriptive about where I'm going today because none of my ancestors, to my knowledge, lived in Alderholt in the New Forest. But David Haswell does, and he is the son of my great-aunt, Zina Rose Monk, known as Cissy. Zina, like Rebecca and Frances, were names borrowed from the Gamble family on Sheppey. Thomas Monk junior's only siblings were Frances and Zina; his mother was also Frances and her mother Zina. She had a sister called Rebecca. My grandma was Rebecca Frances, known to all as Becky but to herself as Frances.

Before setting out for the New Forest, I do a quick computer search of Sheerness Jews. The main surnames are Jacobs, Abrahams, Levy, Solomon, Alexander, Russell and Moses. And the name Monk comes up on a Jewish heritage website! In 1918, there was a fire originating in the grocery shop of a Mr Monk, and Mrs Jacobs perished in the flames. I am excited. But, hang on, it doesn't say whether Monk himself was Jewish. Oh. It might only be that his negligence was responsible for an old Jewish lady burning to death. I think I should set off for David's.

The last time I met David and Doris was at the family

reunion in 1990. I used to see David's brother Sam quite often when he and his wife Doreen visited my grandparents, but I don't think I ever knew how they were related. Grandma spoke little of her siblings, save for Mattie who was killed in the trenches, and her younger sister, Esther, who died in the 1960s. Esther was the mother of Desmond, Rene, Daphne and Diana (Brian's mother) all of whom we saw when I was a child, although Diana and her family were in California, and Daphne in Holland. Grandma also talked about Eva, her sister. She was the one who was supposed to have been a bootlegger. Eva married a French Canadian called Gallipeau. I met her once at my grandparents' Golden Wedding anniversary, very elegant and severe-looking, and she scared me. Apparently Cissy was there too but I don't remember. Becky had a huge family and I was always fuzzy about who everyone was and how I was related to them.

David and Doris live on a new bungalow estate just the other side of the New Forest. They couldn't be more welcoming. I am quietly pleased and surprised that they have one of my very old publicity photographs on the wall. The fact that anyone is at all proud to be related to me is very flattering.

David also wants to take a picture of me today. I hope he doesn't place it next to the old one. He fiddles with his digital camera and says, 'Give me a box camera and a roll of film.' In his life, he's owned two camera shops, and been a photographer, but also a cinema projectionist and a film extra. He asks if I know of a film called *Churchill's Bodyguard* in which he played the part of some key figure of the Second World War to whom he bears a resemblance. I promise to look out for it. I also make a mental note that at least one other family member is in the performing arts, although, to be honest, I'm more impressed that he was a projectionist, which sounds like a much more exciting job.

It turns out to be a thoroughly pleasant and interesting afternoon, and I am able to tell David lots of things he didn't know about the family. He is even inspired to think of getting the Internet, so impressed is he about the things I've found online. Doris plies me with coffee, tea, ham rolls, sausage rolls and cake, and then apologises for not having made lunch.

And David sheds light on things in a way I hadn't expected. He says his mum was a no-nonsense and successful businesswoman. She owned and rented out houses while his father ran a greengrocer's. She felt others in the family resented her success. She was not close to my grandma but 'Bert and Becky' often came to visit. Becky was fussy and seemed to have delusions of grandeur. I can imagine she took the comedown of the return from Malta very badly. To go from being a colonial to the wife of an unemployed clerk, and to have to move in with Esther in the old house in Penhale Road, must have galled her. Meanwhile, Cissy was doing very well.

David says his mother was not given to flights of fancy, and I know Becky definitely was. I ask if he knows anything about the Christopher Wren story, expecting a thorough dismissal. However, according to Cissy, members of the Monk family worked as labourers for Sir Christopher Wren and never got paid. For generations, the family talked about this grievance and it was suggested that a legal case be launched to get monies from his estate.

This might all have been guff, but suddenly I see Becky's reverie in a new light. There was no lost estate in Kent, neither are we Wrens, but there *was* talk of legal redress against the estate of Sir Christopher Wren. Becky had to make do in the 1930s and seems to have concocted two nourishing myths from the bones of one leftover story. And in the depths of the Depression, and probably in a depression of her own, some aggrieved brickies transform into Wren's family and some Kent landowners. Moreover, when her dad disappeared from the family home to the ignominy of the workhouse, I think it's quite likely she was told, or chose to believe, that he was on business in London.

And there's more. Rebecca always claimed she hated fresh strawberries because she was eating them when news arrived that her brother Mattie had been killed in the Great War. My mum remembers one of Joan's suitors coming to their home during the Second World War and presenting Becky with a punnet of strawberries, which was a rare treat. They went straight into a saucepan. I also remember a family holiday in Somerset that included Grandma. One day my brother and sisters picked bowls and bowls of strawberries from the garden of the cottage we were staying in. While no one was looking, Grandma boiled the lot.

I just thought she was nuts. She insisted that day-old bread was better for her digestion, which was what poor people used to tell themselves when they bought yesterday's bread cheap from the baker. She claimed she couldn't manage anything 'rich', yet when insisting that she didn't want much trifle she'd say; 'I'll just have the cream from the top, dear.' And she made tea with half the cup filled with gold-top milk. I assumed she just had some warped hatred of raw berries. But it turns out the story was true; Cissy felt the same. David hands me the letter they received that day:

15 June 1915

Dear Mrs Monk,

It is with deepest regret that I am writing to tell you
that your son was killed yesterday. He was in his dug
out when a shell hit it and a piece hit him in the head,
and he died almost immediately. We carried him back
and buried him in a quiet spot. I am afraid this will
come as a very great shock to you, and I give you my
deepest sympathy. I have known him ever since I took
over the Battalion Signallers, and can realise what a
loss he will be both to you and to the battalion. He
was one of the best men I have ever had, and it was a
pleasure to work with him. I am afraid words cannot
express what I would like to say, but he died a gallant
death, which we all hope to do.

Yours sincerely,
EF Barker Lieut.
4th Battalion to the Rifles

David says Mattie was a sniper, like Dad's dad, Lionel. Of
course he was, I have his medals and two are for his shooting
prowess. David mentions the medals before I do. He used to
play with them as a boy because his mother had them, until
Becky wrote to her and said that it was written that she must
send them to her. David doesn't know where they are now. I'm
pleased to be able to say that I've got them and will bring them
to show him when I come back with all the things he's lending
me. I've wondered why the ribbons are so tatty compared to
Herbert's, which were pristine. A little boy playing with them

would do that, which is quite likely the reason why Becky claimed that her custody of them was ordained.

He also gives me two letters written by Mattie. The first has no date but is sent on notepaper headed 'The YMCA with HM Troops':

Dear Cissy,

Sorry for making your place a temporary dumping place for my old kit, but knowing that Ma was out nursing, it would have been no good addressing it home.

We leave Winchester tomorrow (Sunday), presumably for Froggyland.

With love to all

Your loving Brother,
Matt

This one is in pencil, dated 7 March 1915.

Dear Sister and Brother,

Many thanks for the P.C. and parcel to hand. I received both the day following my return from the trenches (Saturday). The contents of the parcel were well chosen and very acceptable, and will be thoroughly enjoyed, I assure you.

Things have been very warm around our quarter lately, but good fortune has remained with me and I am still sound and in good health. I suppose you know I am not permitted to mention my whereabouts, or how things are going, so you must excuse the shortness of

my letters and wait for me to tell you a little about it
when I return home.

   Hoping all are in the best of health, and thanking
you again for parc.

Your Loving Brother
Matt

If this were the telly, they'd be expecting me to force tears
now. I just feel humbled and touched. And, despite the fact
that I have no sense of structure at all, I started my journey
with a box of medals and am ending it with the handwritten
word of the man who earned them, my great-uncle Mattie,
whose loss my grandma never stopped speaking of. I doubt
she ever got over it. It must have hung like a cloud over her
wedding two years later. She must have had letters too, but
she was a great one for destroying anything that in any way
distressed her. She was forever ripping herself out of photos
that were not flattering. She once tore the front off the *Radio
Times* because it had a picture of Jimmy Savile poking his
tongue out. I can't imagine she would have kept letters from
her dead brother. She did get hold of the medals and later
promised them to me. But she never once took them out for
me to look at. The first time I ever saw them was when I
started writing this.

   There's one other story David might be able to help me
with: the one about my great-aunt Eva being a bootlegger.
The way he describes her, she sounds like quite a rebel. She
and her French Canadian husband definitely had a car.
Now, if she was living in Canada during the time of
Prohibition in the US, and she had a car, it would have

been quite easy to take some liquor over the border. It wouldn't surprise David at all but he says that the person who would know is Val, Eva's daughter. Val is someone we knew quite well and visited when I was a boy. She lives in Bexhill-on-Sea and I have a number for her. So I'm going to ring her tomorrow.

I say goodbye to David and Doris, who seem to have enjoyed the day as much as I have. I have to bring back everything I've borrowed at some point, so I can take more things to give them and tell them whatever I've found out. I'm feeling positive about the way things are going. I might not have found an identical twin who was lost at sea; but I have expanded the thing I call my family. I knew of people's existence, but I wasn't in touch with them. It's not about blood-ties, but the fact that I am connected to people; and the fact that a connection isn't severed completely by time, distance or even death. I feel confident that I haven't lost touch with all the friends I haven't seen for ages, or those who are dead. They're all still with me.

And so, in the morning, I ring Val, whom I haven't seen since Rene's funeral a few years ago. There is no awkwardness at all; it's very nice to catch up. I don't suppose I've ever had a conversation with her about her mum. When I was a boy, she was just Val, married to Dennis Hillman. They were a slim, attractive couple and I think they seemed quite groovy (as we would have said then) to me in the sixties and early seventies. They had married young and were youthful parents with sons a lot older than me. She is my mum's cousin and they seemed fond of each other. And she has kept up with how we're all doing via the convoluted network of cousins who spring from the Monk sisters.

So, might her mum have been a bootlegger? Well, Val wouldn't put it as dramatically as that, but her father did distil his own whisky, they did have a car and they did drive to New York. So it might have been true. And might is good enough because, in a family, everyone's version of what happened is different, and true for them. I'm not sure you ever really get to the bottom of what happened. So I'm just going to decide it's true. And it was lovely, speaking to Val again.

I have one more call to make. Jenny is the daughter of Rene, who was my mum's cousin and the daughter of Esther Monk, my grandma's younger sister. Jenny has helped Brian in doing a lot of the research. The Tourle family, of which Jenny was the eldest daughter, live around Pevensea in Sussex. And they used to visit us unannounced, save for a call from the phone box at the end of our road to say they were on their way; and then they might stay for a number of days. Jenny admits that it was always she who demanded to visit us if they were anywhere within striking distance, because she loved coming to see us. In particular, she loved my mum.

She says it was she who told Brian the hanky thing about Thomas Monk, and it comes from Esther, her grandmother, who wouldn't have lied. I think it has the ring of truth. Thomas was only jailed for two months and then went back to his ship; so whatever he'd done can't have been very serious. So why wouldn't it be true, or at least partly true?

When it comes to Sir Christopher Wren, Jenny never heard anything about unpaid labourers at St Paul's Cathedral. But Rene had said we were indeed supposed to be descended from him, her take on it being that he was a notorious womaniser and probably had any number of illegitimate offspring. So now, paternity, rather than unpaid wages, seems to me to be the more likely cause of a long-standing claim on Wren's dynasty. I reckon Becky's version now seems closer to the truth than Cissy's. St Paul's was finished in 1710. Surely any story of unpaid wages would have been forgotten, or at least any hope of recouping them forsaken, by the twentieth century. But no one would forget the fact that a bastard sired by him was one of us.

And the money owed to Thomas Monk but unpaid by the Confederacy was owed during the lifetime of Becky's father, Thomas junior, who became a policeman and quite likely did develop an obsession with seeing justice done, having seen his father diddled out of what was rightfully his. Perhaps Cissy, or, more likely her mother, cleaned up the Wren bastard story and transferred the unpaid wages to it.

And maybe Becky wasn't such a fantasist after all. Her grandfather did run away to sea, in as much as he joined the navy, later he was unjustly accused of something, the stolen hanky. He did go to London to make a legal statement, after leaving the *Rappahannock,* and the family was owed something: his wages. And it's entirely possible that we are descendants of Sir Christopher Wren because bastardy counts. And the brilliant thing is, it's impossible to prove, one way or the other.

And more importantly, Jenny speaks so warmly of my mother. She says she remembers her laugh and her smile, and the way she always welcomed Jenny's family, despite two minutes' warning of a family of six arriving late in the evening to stay for an indeterminate period. My dad would have pottered in the background; and now I think how tolerant he was of my mum's large and complicated extended family. Jenny has fond memories of, and a lasting attachment to all of us, the Hardys. And I think, yes, we are the Hardys. And we're not a bad lot. And I feel closer to all my family, without any of them knowing it.

CHAPTER 29

That's It For Now

I was very ambivalent at the start of this process. Without the fact of having a book to write, I doubt I would have done a fraction of this researching or exploring. And I'm glad I've done it. And the fact is that I've got to put this project to rest now to get on with other things. I will continue to find out stuff about my family, but it'll have to be as a hobby.

I will get round to getting my DNA tested one day. If you notice me speaking with a strange accent on the radio in future, it will be because I've found out something remarkable and got carried away. Last time I spoke to the DNA company, the lab they used had gone broke and they were waiting to get a new one sorted out.

And I will somehow investigate the Paul Robeson thing, perhaps when I'm old and can't get gigs anymore. I will go to the Surrey History Centre in Woking, and I've got a gig in Woking as part of the new *Clue* tour, so I might just pop in then. The tour will be strange. We've got Jack Dee in the chair, which is great because he's an old friend and, although I still miss Humph and always will, I like working with Jack. It's a shame I'm so sober these days; he's a good man to get drunk with. If they ever catch Bin Laden, they should sit him down with Jack and a bottle of wine; Osama wouldn't be able to keep up that angry front for long. He'd be laughing like a tickled toddler and as pissed as Patrick in no time. He's probably all right when he loosens up. Unless he's a mean drunk. Hmm, it could go either way.

Speaking of which, you'll like this. I have obtained a copy of *Odyssey in Gray* by Douglas French Forest, CSN, Assistant Paymaster, CSS *Rappahannock*. I've found Thomas:

> Monk our Boatswain (a good name for he is about the same as *nun* at all) a tall, ungainly, red whiskered man of about 40 without education or force – a stupid and a drunken, is away from ship and although of course, such a worthless fellow has not deserted, we have taken it for granted and given him up with out a search. He is, doubtless, drunk, with his hag of a wife. He is to be discharged when he returns.

It seems like Frances went all the way to Calais to be with Thomas. There is another mention two pages later:

> Paid off Monk our drunken Boatswain.

So, perhaps my great-great-grandfather was just too pissed, and not bright enough, to grasp the politics of the American Civil War. Actually, this book is published in America; I'm sure I can sue for injured feelings. Look at this other bit:

> Heard to day the mode of salutation of our late Boatswain, Monk and his *lovely* wife. He would see her

on her way to the ship and remark 'Here comes a sail,' and when she was within hail cry out, 'Ship ahoy.' She would reply, 'Aye, aye mate.' He would rejoin, 'Is that you my Duchess?' and she, 'Aye, Aye chummy. Can't you come ashore and talk with a gel.' Poetic is it not?

This Confederate bastard Forest is really pissing me off now. The Monks might have been drunken dimwits, but they were *my* drunken dimwits. But actually, there is something quite remarkable about this. These seem to be actual words of love spoken by my great-great-grandparents in the 1860s. How many people have something like that?

I'd still like to find out more about the Staggs. I did actually speak to a man at the Surrey History Centre to ask if they have trade records for Croydon in the 1880s (that's how much fun I'm having these days) and he said that, because Croydon's now a London Borough, its own council would have everything there is. He said he doubts whether a watchmaker's records would still be held but I am going to go back to Croydon anyway, because he turned out to be helpful on another matter. I mentioned not being able to find the grave of George Stagg, the watchmaker, in the churchyard and he said that, if George died in 1893, he would have been buried in one of the municipal cemeteries. So I rang the council and got through to a cemetery lady and found out he's in the Queen's Road cemetery, number 25132 in K section, and that they have helpers there who will assist me in finding him.

I was right about one thing. My genealogical research hasn't taken me very far geographically. Norfolk was as far afield as any of my lot came from, as far as I know.

There does seem to be some truth in the family legends.

Someone else in the family might untangle the Hardy dynasty one day. Perhaps with technology it will be much easier for future generations, or perhaps technology will make games so much fun that nobody in their right mind will hunt ancestors as a leisure pursuit. I should leave some research for my nieces and nephews to do. There's a lot of them: Hattie, Laura, Matthew, Joan, Michael, Callum, Ross and Jenny. Perhaps, some day, what I've done will inspire at least one of them to carry on. I have left a trail unexplored when it comes to the Wren thing. I have made various failed attempts at finding descendants of Henrietta and Sarah Wren. You see, I haven't told you everything. You think some of this has been hard work for you but I've actually *protected* you from things more tedious than you can imagine. There are things I've dealt with on my own. So I'm sorry I never resolved the Wren thing, especially now I've opened up this whole new and exciting possibility of bastardy, but, anyway, it was all a very long time ago and I don't want you stressing about it.

Now, you might be asking, 'Won't your daughter want to carry on your research?' Well, the answer is that I'm not sure, since she's not related to me. She loves her cousins and her grandparents, but she's not related to them either. If and when she decides to investigate her own family history, she will have a job on her hands, because she was born in a Romanian Gypsy village. I don't know what kinds of records exist. I know the names of her birth mother and sisters and the name of the village they live in, and when she's ready to find them I will help her.

I don't know what it all means to her, and I don't try to impose an identity on her. I've taken her to see Gypsy bands but she's seen all she wants to see for now. She puts down 'Roma' or ticks 'Other ethnic' on all forms that require – or rather, demand – such information. And she definitely does not look 'White British'. But, in south London a lot of people are a different colour from their parents.

And she has my unconditional love. I could not love her any more than I do. She is my daughter. I wiped her arse and one day she might have to wipe mine. Don't think I haven't threatened her with that. And if I were to become a biological father or, indeed, if I adopt again, it would not change how I feel about Betty. The fact that I might not be able to sit down with her like a Maori elder and tell the story of how the Hardys arrived in Basingstoke on the back of a terrapin, without her asking, 'What does any of this have to do with me?' doesn't really matter. Maybe she'll be interested in my ancestry because I'm her dad, even if my ancestry isn't biologically hers.

So there you go, this part of the story is over. I didn't really get that far but it's the journey that's important. And anyway, don't we want to create a society in which people are not defined by their birth; in which family, clan, tribe, race, dynasty and inheritance are part of what we are but are not *who* we are? And in an ideal world, we would all be brothers and sisters. In Loddon, they probably are.

For me, the worst part of this has been silently staring at official records on my own; the best part of it has been talking to people. In future, I plan to spend more time asking people who might know, and less time trying to answer my own questions. I might even ask for directions as a first resort, instead of being defiantly lost. I realise I risk expulsion from the male sex.

I will see David again when I return the photos. And I plan to pop in on Val when I'm down Bexley way. I'll see Jenny and the other Tourles, probably when I have a gig nearby. I will keep in touch with Brian, and I will maintain an interest in family history. I'm also quite keen to help Katie research hers, now that I have acquired some of the necessary skills. We already know she's a quarter Welsh and probably has Gypsy ancestors; so I'll enjoy her relative exoticism vicariously.

But I won't be jealous, because I've made peace with the fact that there is nothing immediately remarkable about my forebears. If you were to ask me what I've found out about them, I'd have to say that they were just people; and ultimately, aren't we all? And that's what makes us interesting, whoever we are.

Acknowledgements

My thanks to all family members who helped, especially Susan, Richard and Brian; to Heather Warne and Margaret Richards at Arundel Castle Archives; to my partner Katie Barlow; to Nick Ranceford-Hadley; and to Charlotte Cole, Justine Taylor and Andrew Goodfellow and all at Ebury.

About the Author

Jeremy Hardy is one of the UK's best-loved stand-up comedians. His work includes the acclaimed film *Jeremy Hardy versus the Israeli Army*, the BBC Radio 4 show *Jeremy Hardy Speaks to the Nation* as well as numerous live tours. He is also a regular panellist on Radio 4's *I'm Sorry I Haven't a Clue* and *The News Quiz*.